P9-CBP-642

THIRD EDITION

# Negotiating the Special Education Maze

## A Guide for Parents & Teachers

Winifred Anderson
Stephen Chitwood
Deidre Hayden

WOODBINE HOUSE ▪ 1997

© 1997 Winifred Anderson, Stephen Chitwood, Deidre Hayden.

Third Edition

All rights reserved under International and Pan-American copyright conventions. Published in the United States of America by Woodbine House, Inc., 6510 Bells Mill Rd., Bethesda, MD 20817. 800-843-7323.

Cover Illustration by: Lisa Handler

**Library of Congress Cataloging-in-Publication Data**

Anderson, Winifred.
  Negotiating the special education maze : a guide for parents and teachers / Winifred Anderson, Stephen Chitwood, Deidre Hayden. — 3rd ed.
    p.   cm.
  Includes bibliographical references (p.     ) and index.
  ISBN 0-933149-72-7 (pbk.)
  1. Handicapped children—Education—United States.  2. Handicapped children—Civil rights—United States.  3. Home and school—United States.  I. Chitwood, Stephen.  II. Hayden, Deidre.  III. Title.
LC4031.A66   1997
371.91'0973—dc21                                             96-37779
                                      CIP

Manufactured in the United States of America

10 9 8 7 6 5

# To Daniel Reed Chitwood

*whose life inspired us all*

## ATTENTION READER...

Throughout this book, you will note the symbol [★] following passages of text. This symbol indicates information that was changed in 1997 when Congress reauthorized the Individuals with Disabilities Education Act (IDEA 97). In the back of the book you will find a listing of each page that contains text marked with a [★], together with an explanation of the changes in IDEA.

# TABLE OF CONTENTS

# Acknowledgments

From experiences as trainers of parent advocates, as educational and legal advocates, as educators, and as parents, we have endeavored to write a practical guide based on methods proven effective in obtaining appropriate special education services for children. This book represents the results of many people working together—the group brain—as we like to call it. In particular, we express thanks to the entire staff of the Parent Educational Advocacy Training Center for their encouragement, support, and expertise as educational advocates: Cherie Takemoto, Barbara Anselmo, Carolyn Beckett, Silvia Borges, Jean Durgin, Kypee Evans-White, Nona Flynn, Elizabeth Karp, Jo-Ann Lambert, Linda McKelvy Chik, and Theresa Rebhorn. We also want to thank Melinda Goss, Virginia Houston, Nancy Hitz, and Ning Douglas, whose educational advocacy for children gives reality to the case studies included in the book. Special appreciation goes to the many reviewers whose critique of this new edition provided fresh perspectives, accuracy, and clarity: Emily Crandall, Alfretta Gibson, Carol Gonsalves, Bruce Hoover, Thomas Jefferson James, Kathe Klare, Pat McKeil, Catherine McQuilkin, Suzanne Ripley, Mary Ann Toombs, Sharon Walsh, Barbara Willard, and Frances Wang. And finally, thanks to the staff at Woodbine House, in particular Irv Shapell and Susan Stokes, for their vision and perseverance in creating and distributing the *Special Needs Collection* of which this book is a part.

We express admiration and appreciation to those parents and professionals who work as teams to teach the process of educational advocacy to other parents in communities throughout Virginia, West Virginia, Maryland, Illinois, and other states. These team members use this book to inform and guide their work with parent groups and have provided us with valuable comment. To the thousands of parents who have participated in our training courses in educational advocacy we say thank you—for teaching us as you shared common and unique experiences with us.

Winifred Anderson
Stephen Chitwood
Deidre Hayden

# FOREWORD

One might question whether it is still timely to have a book on *Negotiating the Special Education Maze.* After all, it has been twenty-two years since the federal law now called The Individuals with Disabilities Education Act (IDEA) passed Congress. Shouldn't one assume that in twenty-two years school personnel and families have learned to negotiate the special education maze in a collaborative way so that the information contained in this book is "nice to have" but not "necessary to have"?

For the answer to this question, listen to the voices of families and professionals who testified on IDEA reauthorization in late Fall 1994, in hearings sponsored by the National Council on Disability:

> "I was one of those parents who left... IEPs [feeling] like someone who has left a foreign movie without the subtitles. I felt a very small and incidental part of this procedure, and at times I felt that my daughter really wasn't getting her full share or placement of services. It wasn't until I started networking with other parents that I started feeling empowered to all the services you rightfully should have."
> *(Diana Sullivan, Milwaukee, WI)*

> One parent was told by an administrator, "[Your son] can either go to his neighborhood school, where he will be teased and humiliated, or he can continue to go to the segregated school, where he will have the opportunity to be class president and captain of the basketball team."
> *(E.J. Jorgensen, Des Moines, IA)*

"Throughout the due process, we were given notice about meetings practically at the last minute. No one encouraged us to bring an advocate to help us. There were people at the meetings who we did not know and who did not have any involvement with our son, particularly at the school-based level.... The administrator in charge of disabled students here in Charlotte told us that we could be arrested for truancy because we refused to place our son in a class [when we] were not involved in the decision on change of placement."

*(Rachel Friedman, Charlotte, NC)*

These comments are not the exception. In the ten regional hearings conducted by the National Council on Disability, the overwhelming testimony from families and professionals pointed to the need for parents to be as informed and savvy as they can possibly be in order to negotiate a maze that too often is characterized by chaos rather than by reasoned and systematic decision-making.

This is why *Negotiating the Special Education Maze* is so critically important to families as well as professionals. Win Anderson, Steve Chitwood, and Deidre Hayden have done a masterful job in this new third edition. They offer some major expansion and refinement over the second edition, which itself was a very successful contribution.

The third edition adds two new chapters—Chapter 8, Early Intervention: Beginning the Journey, and Chapter 11, Nondiscrimination Protection: Alternative Routes through the Maze. These chapters offer solid and relevant information for starting the journey on a firm foundation and for using all protections, including those of Section 504 of the federal Rehabilitation Act of 1973 and the Americans with Disabilities Act of 1990, to obtain full educational opportunities for students with disabilities. Throughout this book, the clear emphasis is on families as experts on their children. This philosophy is consistent with state-of-the-art principles related to family-centered services. It can be the catalyst for forming collaborative partnerships in which all participants are empowered to take action to ensure that students with disabilities receive a quality education.

I plan to use this new edition as I have the two previous editions—learning from it myself and sharing it with families and professionals who are committed to ensuring that the vision of free appropriate public education is equal to the reality in their local and state school district.

Ann P. Turnbull, Co-Director
Beach Center on Families and Disability
University of Kansas, Lawrence, KS 66045

# INTRODUCTION

Throughout the nation, parents of children with disabilities face a confusing array of information and service systems. Those who have just learned that their infant or toddler has special needs may have heard of new laws that provide for important services to enhance the developmental progress of their babies. Yet they wonder how to begin the process. Whom should they contact? Are services really necessary for a very young child?

Parents whose older children are already in the school system may well be aware of the Individuals with Disabilities Education Act (IDEA), a strong federal law which provides for special education for all children with disabilities. Yet they, too, have many questions. For example, when talking with school professionals, a father might wonder what educational jargon such as "scaled scores," "least restrictive environment," and "projective tests" mean. What have they to do with his lively, lovable child? A mother comments, "For years I have heard school people say, 'If only we could get the parents involved . . .,' yet when I try to speak out for my son, why do I feel they want me to accept only what they think is best for him?"

Parents of young people who are nearing graduation from school and from special education have other concerns. They ask, "Will our daughter have a job when she graduates?" "Are there laws that guarantee her services and benefits as an adult?"

These and many other common concerns of parents of children with disabilities are addressed in the Individuals with Disabilities Education Act (IDEA). The following chapters discuss those parts of the law which are most relevant for you to know as you make your way through the maze of special education rules and procedures. This book gives primary attention to Part B of the law, which covers school-aged children. You may be familiar with the terminology of P.L. 94-142, or the Education for All Handicapped Children Act. Its name was changed to IDEA in 1990, along with some key provisions of the law. Public Law 94-142 laid the foundation for all later federal special education legislation and legitimized parent involvement in the education of children with disabilities. Specifically, IDEA and its predecessor, P.L. 94-142, have mandated the role of parents* as equal partners in making educational decisions for their children.

A major provision of IDEA provides for identifying and serving infants and toddlers who have disabilities. An amendment to the law called Part H of the Individuals with Disabilities Education Act (IDEA) extends many of the legal protections previously available to children three and older to infants and toddlers from birth through two years of age. This amendment recognizes the value of family involvement in their child's growth and development and gives family members a strong role. Chapter 8, new in this edition of *Negotiating the Special Education Maze*, was written for parents who have discovered that their family and very young child might need some special services.

Additionally, this edition includes a new chapter on Section 504 of the Rehabilitation Act of 1973 and the Americans with Disabilities Act (ADA). Both of these laws prohibit discrimination against persons with disabilities. ADA and Section 504 require school districts to provide necessary supportive services to students who have disabilities but do not qualify for special education services under provisions of the Individuals with Disabilities Education Act (IDEA). Chapter 11 provides detailed information about how Section 504 and the Americans with Disabilities Act (ADA) apply to public school programs and the ways in which parents can use these laws to benefit their children.

The mandate for parent involvement is a worthy goal. Yet, you may be wondering how such involvement is brought about. The answer lies in *educational advocacy.* An advocate is one who speaks on behalf of another person or group of persons in order to bring about change. There are consumer advocates, working to influence regulatory agencies to bring about change in the quality of products we purchase. Political advocates seek to bring about social and economic change through state and national legislatures. Legal advocates use the court system to bring about change in the interpretation of laws that affect our lives.

---

\* The term "Parents" in this book means anyone who is in charge of the care and well-being of a child. Included are one or both parents, guardians, grandparents, foster parents, or surrogate parents.

# ■ Your Role as an Educational Advocate ■

The Individuals with Disabilities Education Act empowers parents to become *educational advocates* for their children. An educational advocate is one who speaks knowledgeably for the educational needs of another person. You, the parents, are the ones who know your child best. It is you who can speak most effectively on your child's behalf in order to secure her* educational rights under the law. This book was written to assist you in your role as educational advocate by helping you gain the knowledge required to be an effective educational planner for your child, assisting you in presenting your child in the best possible way, suggesting how to cope with your feelings, and guiding you through the often complex maze of special education.

To be an effective educational advocate for your infant, child, or young adult, you are well advised to understand the major provisions of IDEA. IDEA requires that all school-aged children with disabilities be provided a full educational opportunity. Under IDEA, disabilities covered are autism, mental retardation, hearing impairments, deafness, visual impairments, speech or language impairments, serious emotional disturbances, orthopedic impairments, traumatic brain injury, specific learning disabilities, or other health impairments. Special education is defined in IDEA as specially designed instruction to meet the unique needs of a child with disabilities. This individualized instruction is in contrast to most general education teaching, where children are taught in groups with educational plans made for groups of children. Also in contrast to general education, instruction is provided by special educators, who are trained in the teaching techniques that best meet the learning needs of children with disabilities. These techniques, coupled with the individualization of instruction, promise that each child will be given the opportunity to travel successfully down her developmental pathways.

The following brief explanation of the six major provisions of IDEA will provide a background for you as you read and work your way through this book and through the education system as your child's advocate. Each of these provisions is discussed in detail in later chapters, along with reference to other relevant legislation.

**1. All children will be served.** Congress intended that no child in need of special education will be excluded from receiving services, even those children with the most severe disabilities. Prior to 1975, many parents were told by the school administrators, "We are sorry, we just don't have a program for her.

---

\*\* To avoid sexist use of pronouns, the masculine gender is used in odd-numbered chapters; the feminine gender, in even-numbered chapters.

She is too severely disabled." Then parents had no recourse. Today, all states provide services for children from birth through eighteen, and most states provide them for children from birth through twenty-one. Part H of IDEA*, detailed in Chapter 8, extends entitlement to services to infants and toddlers with disabilities and their families through Early Intervention Programs.

**2. Children will be tested fairly to determine if they will receive special education services.** Before children can be declared eligible for special education or placed in a special education program, they must be evaluated by a team of professionals. Schools and other agencies are required to give tests to children that show both their strengths and their weaknesses. All tests must be given to children in their own language and in such a way that their abilities and their disabilities are accurately displayed. This is called nondiscriminatory testing. Children will be placed in special education based upon several tests, not upon one single test or test score. Nondiscriminatory testing ensures that children who do not need special education will not be placed there, and that children who need special school services will get them.

**3. Schools have a duty to provide individually designed, appropriate programs for every child at no cost to their parents.** IDEA requires public schools to provide a *free, appropriate public education* to all children who have been identified as needing special education. The state and local school systems bear the responsibility to pay for the education even if it is provided in a private or residential school outside of the local public school system. In addition, each child is guaranteed an *appropriate* education. The appropriateness is determined by a group of people, including parents and educators, who work together to design a program that addresses the child's individual educational problems. This program is called an Individualized Education Program (IEP). Your child has a right to a full range of educational services, which may include such related services as special transportation, speech/language therapy, counseling, occupational or physical therapy, or other services necessary to enable her to benefit from special education. A description of the process for determining an appropriate education by writing an IEP is found in this book in Chapters 6 and 7. Schools must also provide individualized transition services for those students enrolled in special education. Chapter 9 describes the components of transition for students leaving high school and moving into the world of work, further education, and life in the community.

If your child is younger than two, you will find that the process for receiving services differs somewhat from that of school-aged children. Services for very young children are covered by Part H of IDEA. You, as a parent, will be working with professionals who are not necessarily employees of the school system, but are specialists in infant development. In some states these professionals will be school employees; but in other states they will be employees of agencies such as the Health Department or the Department of Mental Health and Developmental Disabilities. You will be partners with these infant specialists in writing an Individualized Family Service Plan (IFSP) for your baby. The IFSP is a written plan detailing the early intervention services a family requires to enhance their child's development. Assessment and case management services are to be provided at no cost to families. Other early intervention services, for which there may be a fee, include family training and counseling, as well as direct services to the infant or toddler. The skills and knowledge you will gain from this book are valuable no matter what the age of your child as you work with professionals to write an IEP or an IFSP. The emphasis on these plans is to *individualize*—to write a unique program for the education of your unique child.

**4. Children with disabilities will be educated with children who do not have disabilities.** Before IDEA, our schools almost always segregated children with disabilities from children without disabilities. Now, however, our nation has legal requirements that all students have equal access to education. As a result, increasing numbers of children with disabilities are being integrated into their community's regular schools. Under IDEA, students with disabilities are guaranteed services in the *least restrictive environment.* That is, when the Individualized Education Program (IEP) is written, a determination is made regarding the amount of time each student with disabilities will spend with nondisabled peers both in classroom and all other school activities. Students are to be educated in a separate classroom or school only when the nature and severity of their disabilities makes it impossible to meet their educational needs in a less restrictive environment.

**5. The decisions of the school system can be challenged by parents.** Prior to the passage of the Individuals with Disabilities Education Act and the acts that preceded it, parents had little or no recourse if they disagreed with the decisions made by the school authorities. Under IDEA, parents and students have a right to *due process.* Under these due process rights, there are provisions for settling disputes by an impartial third party. Parents have the right to challenge decisions made about their children in the areas of inclusion or exclusion from special services, testing in a nondiscriminatory manner, the appropriateness of the education as written in the IEP, the placement of their child in the least restrictive educational environment, and other related areas.

In addition to guaranteeing the right to challenge, IDEA provides parents with the right to notice. When any change is to be made with regard to testing, provision of new services, the withdrawal of services, the IEP, or the amount of time the child will be with nondisabled children, the parents must first be notified. In many situations, the consent of parents is also required before school personnel can make changes.

**6. Parents of children with disabilities participate in the planning and decision making for their child's special education.** The basic premise of this book is that parents are their child's first and best advocates. Who else can possibly know your child in the ways that you do? Your love and caring were seen by the Congress of the United States to be a vital contribution to educational planning for your child. Therefore, IDEA mandates the partnership between parents and school personnel. You, as parents, will be working with school and other professionals to see that a free, appropriate public education in the least restrictive environment is provided for your child. That is your child's right. And the school system has a duty to provide it. At each step along the way, the partnership ideally will ensure that your hopes, visions, and expertise will be combined with the caring and the specialized training of professionals to educate your child.

Each of the six major provisions of IDEA involves you, the parents. The continuing importance of your involvement in the special education process has been reflected in numerous Congressional actions and court decisions. Since the passage of the law in 1975, Congress has made several amendments strengthening the rights of parents and their children. Likewise, court decisions have clarified various legal terms such as appropriate education, support services, and parent involvement so parents can now understand more precisely the breadth and limitations of their rights. Still, parents often feel overwhelmed by the complexity of this legislation and the way it is implemented by state and local education agencies.

Because of the law's complexity, many school systems and interest groups have written manuals to assist parents and teachers to understand and to fulfill their roles under IDEA. Most of these books or pamphlets describe the legal requirements for special education, the procedures of the school system, the characteristics of various disabilities, and regulations prescribed by the state and local school systems. They are limited in that they all stress what the school system knows—its rules and regulations—and seem to overlook the parent and the child. *Negotiating the Special Education Maze* is different. It begins with what you know better than anyone—*your own child.* This is a practical step-by-step guide based upon the experience of thousands of families as they have worked to secure special education services for their children. These parents have increased their knowledge of school systems' procedures, learned skills in organizing and presenting observations of their children, and become more assertive and effective in their role as educational advocates for their children. The understanding these parents have gained of the value of active participation in educational planning is shared with you; indeed, their experience is the basis for *Negotiating the Special Education Maze.*

This book alone may provide you sufficient information to become an influential educational advocate. You can also build on this text by joining an advocacy course for parents in your community, or by starting one if there is none. This involves organizing a group of parents and locating someone to be a leader of the course. Parents can then work through the steps outlined in this book with help from others, enabling them not only to communicate about their child more meaningfully but also to learn from others' experiences in working with school systems. This book points the way toward additional sources of assistance—books, resource groups, and other training courses.

Whether you read this alone or with a group, this book was written with you, the parents, in mind. Some of you have already spent many years working to get appropriate school services for your children. Others of you are just embarking on the road through the special education maze. Whatever the stage of your journey, the authors hope this road map will assist you in making a productive journey where your own personal resources are used and appreciated. At the end you should find your child making progress, because you and school personnel are partners in her well-being.

# 1. PEOPLE & PROCEDURES

## CHARTING YOUR COURSE

As you prepare to explore the special education maze, you will need to know how the process of special education works. Your knowledge of the school system's procedures and your skills in communicating information about your child are essential to becoming an effective educational advocate. The introduction to this book explained the basic design and layout of the special education system, including the requirements for services for infants, toddlers, and preschoolers. This chapter will get you started down the corridors of the special education maze. It will help you learn the terminology used, introduce the important people with whom you will be working, and review the various decision points and meetings required as you advocate for your child.

Thinking back on times you have worked with various teachers and other professionals, you may find that you, like many other parents, experienced feelings similar to those listed below:

- inadequate
- fearful
- tentative
- anxious
- angry

- hopeful
- intimidated
- challenged
- overwhelmed
- frustrated

- exhausted
- confused
- worried
- troubled

Although these feelings are shared by many parents, such feelings usually make it difficult to communicate your hopes, plans, and expectations for your child's school life. Why might you be experiencing these feelings?

As parents going into school meetings, you are moving into a situation where the people you meet use a language and a body of knowledge you may not understand completely. They are familiar with routines and regulations you know little or nothing about. Then, too, everyone carries some remnants of their own school experience–good and not so good–into school buildings. Your perceptions of school professionals and your own school experiences may cause you to question your ability to say the right thing at the right time and to convey your cares, hopes, and opinions about your child's best interests and needs.

What helps you overcome your feelings of anxiety and confusion? To begin with, you can learn about the required educational planning process and the people who participate in that process. This will help you be more comfortable in your role as advocate for your child. Since an advocate speaks on behalf of another person–that is, your child–to bring about change, you will need to have as much information possible, both about your child and about the school system, to be effective. As you gain skills in presenting your view of your child to the school officials, your negative feelings will diminish, allowing you to be a more effective partner in the educational planning process. This book will help you gain the knowledge and skills you need.

# ■ THE SPECIAL EDUCATION PLANNING CYCLE ■

Almost as important as understanding *how* schools make decisions about your child is understanding *when* they make those decisions. Often, one of the first sources of conflict between parents and schools is the sequence and timing of the major decisions in the special education process. As the following case study shows, differences in how and when the parents make plans for their child can lead to problems and frustrations on both sides.

## SUSIE MARTIN: A CASE STUDY

During Susie Martin's year in kindergarten, her parents became concerned when they noticed that Susie could not use pencil and paper as well as the other children. Susie's crayon pictures were mainly scribbles, and even toward the end of the school year, she was still unable to copy the letters in her name. Susie was also restless. During group and story time she often jumped up and moved about the room, playing with objects on other children's desks or in the storage cabinets. She didn't listen to the story. When her teacher called her back to the group, she would roll around the floor, twisting her hair, apparently off in her own world.

For the first months of the school year, the teacher said Susie would soon learn what was expected of her in the classroom and that her skills and behavior would improve. Mr. and Mrs. Martin continued to worry, but listened to the teacher's suggestions. Finally, late in the year, the kindergarten teacher recommended that Susie be tested by the school psychologist. This testing would help to determine whether or not she needed special education during the coming school year. Mr. and Mrs. Martin readily consented to the testing. They felt relieved that something was finally being done to see if Susie had a learning problem.

Since most of the school psychologists were away during the summer, Susie's testing had to be postponed until early in September. Reluctantly, the Martins waited. When September came, the testing began. But in the meantime, Susie was having an even harder time in the first grade. She noticed that other children could easily do many things she couldn't, and her behavior both at school and at home was often unacceptable. The Martins were angry that the school system was not giving Susie the special help they were now sure she needed. The school administrators, on the other hand, defended themselves by citing the regulations they were required to follow before declaring a child eligible for special education. Everyone was frustrated and angry.

What can ease a situation like this? Parents and school systems each have their own planning cycle for children with special needs. Understanding the two cycles and how they should work together can often help to resolve the disagreements. The parents' cycle looks like this:

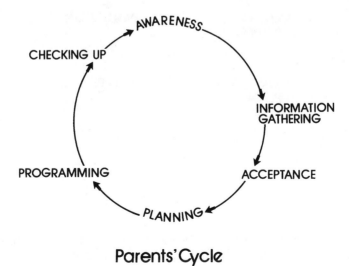

**Parents' Cycle**

## THE PARENTS' CYCLE

The Martins' *awareness* of problems in Susie's school life came early in her kindergarten year. They began to *gather information* that might help them to understand and to help Susie. They talked with their pediatrician, observed other children Susie's age, read books on child development and learning problems, and talked frequently with the kindergarten teacher. On the basis of their observations of Susie and the knowledge they gained through other sources, the Martins gradually came to an *acceptance* of their original hunch that Susie did indeed have some problems needing special education at school. At this point, they talked again with the school principal and kindergarten teacher, hoping that *planning* for Susie's special needs would begin. They were ready early in Susie's kindergarten year for Susie to have special education *programming*.

## THE SCHOOL SYSTEM'S CYCLE

The school system, on the other hand, was reluctant to refer Susie for special services so early in her school life. The kindergarten teacher at first adopted a "wait and see" attitude. Toward the end of the school year, though, the teacher activated the school system's planning cycle. She made a *referral* to the school principal, requesting that Susie be considered for special education testing.

## School System's Cycle

The principal convened the local screening committee, sometimes called the child study committee, to discuss Susie's problems and consider whether her difficulties warranted a full evaluation. This set in motion the *evaluation* process of psychological, educational, and other testing. A teacher, the school psychologist, the school health nurse, and a social worker comprised the multidisciplinary team that worked to understand Susie and her educational problems. This evaluation process, interrupted by summer vacation, was completed in the fall. The results of the series of tests were presented to a committee of school professionals who determined that Susie needed special services; they recommended Susie's *eligibility* for special education. The Martins were invited to participate in this meeting, which summarized the findings of the evaluation and made the determination of her eligibility for special education.

Following the eligibility decision, the Martins and the school personnel, including a special education teacher, met together to plan an *Individualized Education Program* (IEP) for Susie. The IEP included long-range educational goals based on Susie's needs, as well as the special services she would require to help her reach her goals. After the IEP was developed, the *placement* decision was made identifying the appropriate school program which would provide the services needed to meet Susie's educational goals. Only at this time did the parents' planning cycle and the school system's planning cycle come together.

Finally, some of the tension and frustration was alleviated. The Martins had been ready for Susie to receive special education *instruction* several months before the school system had completed the required cycle of referral, evaluation, eligibility, Individualized Education Program, and placement. Once the two cycles meshed, cooperative planning for Susie's well-being became possible. Subsequently, Susie began to have a more successful time in school.

Susie Martin's case illustrates only one type of conflict that can arise when parents' and school systems' planning cycles differ. Not all parents realize as early as the Martins did that their child needs special services. Sometimes school personnel recommend a formal evaluation of a child whose parents feel certain that there is no problem. Often the parents believe that their child will outgrow any difficulties in school, and are therefore unwilling to give the required permission for the school evaluation to proceed. When this happens, the school is ahead of the parents in the cycle. Whereas the parents are barely, if at all, in the first stage of their planning cycle– the awareness phase–the school system is ready for the second step in its cycle– evaluation. This means that before the school and parents can work together as a team, school personnel must first convince the parents of their child's educational needs.

These planning cycles, both for parents and for school systems, repeat themselves. The IEP must be reviewed at least once a year at a meeting in which the parents, teacher, and school administrator discuss the child's progress. During this *checking-up* and *annual review,* a need for change is sometimes apparent. Further, at any time there is a major change in your child's educational or behavioral needs or there is a change proposed in the IEP by parents or school people, the team meets to determine the steps to be taken to revise the special education program. In addition, every three years, there is a new evaluation and eligibility decision, called the *triennial review*, for each child in special education. During this review, a multidisciplinary team determines whether the child's educational placement is still the appropriate one for him, and recommends a new one if it is not.

For you, the parents of a child who may need special education, a better understanding of the school system's cycle can help to clarify your participation as educational advocates. The school system's cycle is described in the rules and regulations published by the school system in your community. These rules and regulations must comply with the minimum requirements set forth in the federal law, the Individuals with Disabilities Education Act (IDEA), P.L. 101-476. A brief description of the major provisions of IDEA is found in the Introduction to this book. The following two activities will help you understand how your school's special education process works. The understanding you gain will help to change any feelings of inadequacy and uncertainty you may have into ones of competency.

# ▪ ACTIVITY #1: RULES OF THE ROAD ▪

Every school system in the country has a set of regulations governing special education. The complexity of these regulations varies, however, from locality to locality. Some large school systems have documents of a hundred or more pages outlining their procedures. Other school systems have no more than a page or two of printed regulations. The first part of Activity #1 is to contact your school superintendent, director of special education, or special education advisory committee and ask for a copy of your local school system's procedures and regulations for special education. These are available to all citizens. Having a copy of your school system's regulations will help you gain confidence in your ability to be an advocate for your child–you, as well as the school people, will know the procedures!

When your local school system wrote its procedural guidelines, it had to follow the regulations of your state division of special education. So a second part of Activity #1 is to write your state director of special education at the address listed in Appendix B and ask for a copy of the state regulations governing special education. This step is especially important if your school system's regulations are not highly structured and developed. Your school system, like many local school systems, may simply follow what the state has written with no elaboration. While you are requesting a copy of your state regulations, ask about the availability of handbooks describing the special education process in your state or locality. Again, because you are a citizen and because special education regulations are public documents, you should have easy access to this information. At the very least, these documents should be available in either your public library or a public school library. If you have trouble locating the regulations, contact the office of your state legislator for assistance.

Once you have the regulations as developed by your local school system and your state department of education, you are ready for Activity #2.

# ▪ ACTIVITY #2: KEY PEOPLE ▪

Key individuals are involved in every phase of the educational planning process. Among others, these include people such as the principal of the school who chairs the committee which decides whether your child should have special testing, the school psychologist who conducts some of the testing, and a teacher who knows your child particularly well. By making your own personal directory of school personnel, including names, addresses, and telephone numbers, you will better understand the roles of certain individuals in the educational planning process, and you will save time in identifying them when you need their assistance. On the next page you will find an example of a Key People Chart.

As you read the parent handbook or regulations from your locality, you may find that terminology and titles of key positions differ from those in the example. Generally, however, titles will be similar. Using your parent handbook and state and local regulations as a guide, you will want to modify the Key People Chart, as found on pages 8–9, to reflect the process in your school system.

In addition, many parents find it very helpful to keep a Phone Call Record in order to keep track of the people with whom they talk and the content of their discussions. A Phone Call Record is found on page 10.

This chapter has introduced you to the cycle of referral, evaluation, eligibility, IEP, and placement that your school system must complete before your child can begin special education. You have also obtained the rules and regulations describing and guiding the special education process in your school system. Along the way, you have identified the key people who can help you secure appropriate services for your child. Now you are ready to begin developing the picture and the understanding of your child you wish to convey in school meetings.

# KEY PEOPLE CHART

School
Jurisdiction _____

Director of
Special Education _____


| Name | Address | Telephone |
| --- | --- | --- |

**I.      Referral/Child Study Committee**

Principal or designee
(chairperson)

Referring person

Teacher(s)/Specialist(s)
(as appropriate)


**II.      Evaluation Team/Multidisciplinary Team**

Evaluation Team Coordinator

Case Manager

Teacher(s)/Specialist(s)
(with knowledge of
suspected disability)

Independent Evaluator
(when appropriate)

Classroom Teacher

# KEY PEOPLE CHART (CONTINUED)

**III.     Eligibility Committee**

Administrator of Special
Education Program or
designee

Evaluation Team Member(s)
(presents evaluation
findings)

Appropriate Special
Education Administrators

Other professional staff

**IV.     Individualized Education Program/Placement Meeting**

School division representative
qualified to provide or supervise
special education services

Teacher

Others, at your or school's request.

**V.     Individualized Education Program Annual Review**

Same team as in the IEP Meeting.

# PHONE CALL RECORD

Who: _____    Date: _____
_____    Phone: _____
_____

Notes:

Need to follow up?    _____ No    Who: _____
_____ Yes    When: _____

Who: _____    Date: _____
_____    Phone: _____
_____

Notes:

Need to follow up?    _____ No    Who: _____
_____ Yes    When: _____

Who: _____    Date: _____
_____    Phone: _____
_____

Notes:

Need to follow up?

_____ No    Who: _____
_____ Yes    When: _____

# 2. YOU & YOUR CHILD

## STRENGTHENING EXERCISES FOR THE JOURNEY

You, as parents, have invaluable information that can be helpful in identifying the special education needs of your child. This chapter will guide you in identifying the unique knowledge you have of your child, understanding the importance of that knowledge for educational planning, and learning ways to develop and provide that critical information to professionals working with your child.

## ■ PREPARING FOR THE JOURNEY THROUGH THE MAZE ■

How do you prepare for your journey through the maze? You begin by carefully looking at the central figure in the whole planning process—your child. This book suggests a number of activities, or "strengthening exercises," to help you observe your child and to clarify and organize what you know about your child. These exercises are useful at any stage of the planning process, whether you are preparing for your baby's first infant assessment, your school-age child's first formal evaluation, or your child's IEP meeting. You can wend your way through the maze without completing the "Strengthening Exercises," but they will make your trip more productive—you will be less likely to go up blind alleys in the maze. The exercises build upon each other; each prepares you for the next.

To help you focus on your child, a Learning Style Questionnaire, Strengthening Exercise #1, follows on page 22. Take some time to write your responses to the five questions. Examples of Strengthening Exercise #1 completed for Sara and Tony by their parents can be found on pages 23-24.

Save this questionnaire. As you will see later in the chapter, your responses will help you to pinpoint specific information about your child and to discover keys that make it easier for her to learn.

# ■ OBSERVING YOUR CHILD IN A SYSTEMATIC WAY ■

Sometimes parents have trouble answering the questions in Strengthening Exercise #1. You know a lot about your child, but your knowledge is often "felt" in a general sense rather than in the specific terms needed to answer the questions. Yet while you are absorbed in the routine of everyday living, you are constantly and automatically gathering information about your child. Perhaps you do not realize how much you do know!

Since planning an appropriate program for your child requires specific, documented facts rather than generalized impressions and concerns, you will need to collect your own facts. To convey personal knowledge of your child to school personnel—people accustomed to dealing with test scores, specific behaviors, goals, and objectives—written, concrete facts will be most influential.

One way to collect these facts is to observe your child in a formal way. "Observe!" you say. "When? How?" You think of the days you barely have enough time and energy to brush your teeth before turning in for the night. But there are many natural, spontaneous opportunities during the day to watch your child. Gathering and organizing information is a vital part of becoming an effective educational advocate for your child.

For example, family uproar occurred almost every morning in Sara's house because she was so slow getting dressed. Sara's mom wondered if the reason was her difficulty in using her hands to fasten buttons and zippers, or if it was her indecision about what to wear. As a result, Sara's mother decided to observe her getting ready for school one morning.

Another family was troubled because their son Tony made such a mess as he ate at the table. Tony's parents decided to observe their son carefully during mealtime. The family hoped that his behavior could be changed so that mealtime would be more pleasant for everyone. The next section offers suggestions to help you develop and sharpen your observation skills.

## BECOMING A SKILLED OBSERVER

**Step Back.** Suspend for a brief time (three to five minutes) your normal role in family life. Step back from your family situation to put some distance between you and your child. By not intervening where you normally would, you may see your child's abilities and problems in a new light. For example, to understand why Sara was so slow getting ready for school, her mother decided not to push and prod her as usual. She asked her husband to prepare breakfast that morning so that she would be free to observe Sara.

**Start Fresh.** Try to be open to new aspects of behavior you may have overlooked before. Observe behaviors occurring in the present. Although reports on the past are important in describing a child's development, school personnel are interested in fresh, up-to-date information on what she can do now. Start fresh, also, in how you view your child. For example, rather than becoming irritated as Tony ate with his fingers, his father decided to watch carefully when Tony tried to use his spoon. In this way he noticed new things about Tony's difficulties in the precise use of his hands.

Be alert and relaxed, yourself, as the observer. A preoccupied observer cannot record what is happening as accurately as one who can concentrate.

**Get Focused.** Decide upon a specific behavior or skill to observe. How, you ask, should you make this decision? The best rule is to look at those areas that trouble you or your child. You may want to examine one of the problem behaviors you have listed in Strengthening Exercise #1, or you may want to ask a doctor or other professional to suggest behaviors to observe. For example, your pediatrician might suggest you watch your baby to see how she rolls from her stomach to her back. Sara's mother wondered if her daughter was late because she had trouble getting into her clothes properly, or if she had difficulty deciding upon and assembling what she wanted to wear.

You can plan your observation to include various factors: *who* will be with your child, as well as *where* and *when* you will observe her. Concentrate on the one skill you have chosen, ignoring as best you can other aspects of behavior.

**Go with the Flow.** As you watch your child's activities, record what you see actually happening, not your interpretations of your child's actions. You should become a "candid camera," waiting until later to reflect upon what you see. For example, Tony's dad observed that Tony held his spoon upside down and that he missed his mouth when he raised the spoon from his bowl. Tony's dad wrote down both of these observations, waiting until later to interpret what seemed to be the cause of these problems.

Write down detailed, factual information. You will find this is easier if a short time is spent observing—perhaps five minutes or less. Short, frequent observations allow you to record facts—exactly what happens. You can go back at another time, review your collection of observations, and then interpret the data.

When parents observe their children carefully and systematically, they are able to offer specific information to teachers and other professionals to assist in educational planning. One mother noticed that her daughter's friends used complete sentences when they talked. She was concerned because her child's language seemed less advanced. She wrote down exact words and phrases her daughter used as she played with a friend. At another time she used a tape recording as the children played. These specific examples were very useful when it came time to talk with her child's teacher.

In another family the pediatrician suggested the parents watch their baby to see if her eyes followed an object as it moved in front of her face. On several occasions during the week they observed their daughter's eye movements. When they met next with an infant specialist, they were able to share their careful, repeated observations and to learn ways to help their baby.

On the next page you will find examples of people, places, and activities you might include as you plan to observe your child.

## ■ GUIDELINES FOR PLANNING AN OBSERVATION ■

Before you begin to observe your child, here are some guidelines to assist you:

**A. WHAT** will you be looking at in the observation? Here is a sample of information you can seek and obtain through observation:
1. How your child solves disagreements or problems.
2. How your child moves her arms and legs when crawling.
3. What distracts your child; what holds her attention.
4. How your child dresses or feeds herself.
5. Which toys or games your child prefers.

**B. WHO,** if anybody, will be interacting with your child?
1. parent
2. relative(s)
3. brothers or sisters
4. unfamiliar person(s)
5. best friend
6. tutor
7. several friends
8. teacher(s)
9. unfamiliar children
10. professionals

**C. WHERE** will you observe your child—in what setting?
1. Home
   a. your child's room
   b. dining room
   c. homework space
   d. TV room
   e. backyard

2. Neighborhood
   a. neighbor's house
   b. playground
   c. friend's house
   d. park

3. Family Events
   a. picnics
   b. birthdays
   c. car trips
   d. visits to relatives

4. Large and Small Groups
   a. eating out
   b. museums
   c. ball games
   d. zoo
   e. shopping
   f. riding the bus
   g. parties

5. School
   a. classroom
   b. field trip
   c. evaluations
   d. therapy session
   e. playground
   f. vocational classroom

**D. WHEN** will you observe your child?
1. at meals
2. at bedtime
3. at work or homework
4. during leisure time
5. under stress
6. when sick

Now! Actually observe your child with a specific behavior or skill in mind. Children behave differently, with different people, in different places, and at different times. In order to understand more fully your child's strengths and problems, you will want to have several examples of behaviors and skills you have observed under various circumstances.

The information you gather by observing will add to the specific data necessary in planning an educational program to meet your child's unique needs. Strengthening Exercise #2, Parents' Observation Record (page 25), provides you with a sample form to assist you in keeping a log of your observations. Examples of the Parents' Observation Record completed for Sara and Tony can be found on pages 26-27.

# ■ ORGANIZING YOUR OBSERVATIONS ■

After you collect several observation records, you can compare and contrast them, looking for trends, consistencies, inconsistencies, or changes in your child's behavior. Organizing your observations is a vital step in preparing yourself to meet with school personnel.

Here are some examples of behaviors parents recorded in their observations in Strengthening Exercises #1 and #2:

- Jason does homework best in a quiet, uncrowded place.
- Fred can recite the alphabet.
- May Lin can put two words together to speak in phrases.
- Virginia has learned to catch herself with her arms as she falls.
- Barbara can roll from her stomach to her back.
- Orin catches and throws a large ball.
- Enrico can write a short paragraph with the ideas in proper sequence.
- Jamie puts on her shoes and socks by herself.
- Henry can pull himself to a standing position in his crib.
- Tyrone shares his toys with Sandra.
- Dee eats with a spoon.
- Carl makes his own lunch to take to school.
- Steve writes capital and lower-case letters in cursive.
- Shantell learns best when she is with one or two good friends.
- Denise can copy a pattern of colored beads strung together.
- Carolyn shows off her school work with pride and excitement.
- Margaret understands thirty-two words in sign language.
- Susie identifies the right bus to ride to her after-school job.
- Sylvia does her homework subjects in the same order each day.
- Alexander can put together a three-piece puzzle.

Organizing your observation records into general areas of child development will help you think about and discuss your child in language similar to that used by educators. To use your observations to your child's best advantage, you can group the bits and pieces of observed behavior into developmental categories like those used by school personnel.

The preceding list of behaviors parents have observed can be organized into six broad developmental areas:

1. Movement
2. Communications

3. Social relationships
4. Self-concept/independence
5. Thinking skills
6. Senses/perception

## DEFINITIONS OF DEVELOPMENTAL AREAS

**Movement.** The ability to use muscles to move the body and to control small and detailed movements such as walking, jumping, writing, holding objects, rolling, chewing, and balancing.

**Communication.** The ability to understand and respond to spoken language, gestures, or written symbols, and to express oneself clearly and with meaning.

**Social Relationships.** The ability to relate to others—for example, to play with other children or to develop attachments to family members and friends.

**Self-Concept/Independence.** The ability to distinguish oneself from others and to care for one's own needs.

**Senses/Perception.** The ability to use eyes, ears, and the senses of touch, smell, and taste to learn about the environment.

**Thinking Skills.** Often called cognitive skills, they include the ability to reason and solve problems, to classify, to make associations, to understand similarities and differences, and to comprehend cause-and-effect relationships. School skills such as reading, arithmetic, and spelling can be placed in this category.

Now, you ask, are these the categories child development specialists or school teachers use? In fact, other common terminology might include such terms as cognition, self-help skills, gross or fine motor skills, expressive language, receptive language, auditory or visual perception—and on and on. There are many classification systems, but basically they accomplish the same purpose. They serve to structure observations about human growth and development. Some people suggest parents should learn the terminology of physicians, educators, therapists, and other specialists. *This guidebook's view is that your language about your child is the best language.* So, for purposes of educational advocacy in this book, very generalized developmental categories are suggested. They should fit with very little squeezing, translation, or interpretation into the categories used by teachers and specialists working with your child.

## ■ YOUR CHILD'S LEARNING STYLE ■

In addition to having different abilities in the various developmental areas, every child has a particular learning style. *A learning style is the combination of unique personal characteristics that determine the way in which a person learns best.* For instance, some people learn best through reading and writing; others, through listening and talking. Often a talent in one area—drawing, music, or athletics, for example—can influence how a person learns. Characteristics such as neatness, sensitivity to noise, accuracy, and distractibility will also affect learning. Think for a minute about the way you learn best, your learning style. For example:

- You may learn best by reading information.
- Perhaps you understand things better when you have participated in group discussions.
- You may need to work in a neat environment, or you may feel more comfortable having a messy desk.
- You might need absolute quiet when you concentrate, or you might prefer music as background to your thinking.
- You may need to draw pictures, diagrams, or charts to help you analyze a problem.
- You may take frequent, short breaks while working, or you may concentrate until the task is finished.

Thinking about your own learning style can help you become aware of your child's special ways of learning. Remember, there are no right or wrong ways, only different ones. In addition, most people learn using different aspects of their learning style in various situations. Sharing information about your child's individual ways of learning with those who are teaching her can help to create the best setting to meet her needs. Good teachers make adaptations to the classroom and to their teaching methods in order to accommodate children's various learning styles.

## ■ ANALYZING YOUR OBSERVATIONS ■

The following section shows how to analyze your observations from Strengthening Exercises #1 and #2 so that you can communicate effectively with school personnel. The recorded observations parents have made of their children, found on pages 28-30, can be placed within these areas of development and learning style:

## MOVEMENT

- Virginia has learned to catch herself when she falls.
- Orin catches and throws a large ball.
- Steve writes capital and lower-case letters in cursive.
- Barbara can roll from her stomach to her back.
- Henry can pull himself to a standing position in his crib.

## COMMUNICATIONS

- May Lin can put two words together to speak in phrases.
- Margaret understands thirty-two words in sign language.

## SOCIAL RELATIONSHIPS

- Tyrone shares his toys with Sandra.

## INDEPENDENCE/SELF-CONCEPT

- Jamie puts on her shoes and socks by herself.
- Dee eats with a spoon.
- Carl makes his own lunch to take to school.
- Carolyn shows off her school work with pride and excitement.

## PERCEPTION/SENSES

- Denise can copy a pattern of colored beads strung together.
- Susie recognizes the right bus to ride to her after-school job.

## THINKING SKILLS

- Fred can recite the alphabet.
- Enrico can write a short paragraph with the ideas in proper sequence.
- Alexander can put together a three-piece puzzle.

## LEARNING STYLE

- Jason does homework best in a quiet, uncrowded place.
- Shantell learns best when she is with one or two good friends.
- Sylvia does her homework subjects in the same order each day.

Perhaps you are puzzled by the way some of these behaviors have been organized into developmental categories. No single behavior falls exclusively into one category or another. For example, you might think that Jamie's ability to put on her shoes and socks independently fits into the areas of *movement* and *thinking skills*, as well as *independence*. Jamie's movement skills are not a problem. Physically she is able to put on her shoes and socks. The emphasis she needs is in developing her independence. Therefore, her parents place "putting on shoes and socks" under *Independence/Self-Concept.*

Think about the developmental areas you believe are particularly important to your child's growth now, and put your observations of her accomplishments into that category. Remember, there need not be only one "right" category.

To organize your observations about your child's development and learning style, transfer your work on the first two Strengthening Exercises into a Developmental Achievement Chart (page 28). Developmental Achievement Charts completed for Sara and Tony are found on pages 29-30.

Notice that Question #1 on the Learning Style Questionnaire provides information for the column *Can Do.* Question #3 on the Learning Style Questionnaire coincides with the second column, *Working On.* Question #5 corresponds with the column *To Accomplish in 6 Months.* Questions #2 and #4 give information about your child's *learning style.* These observations about learning style can be recorded in the bottom row of the chart.

If your observations have not given you a complete picture of your child's development, repeat Strengthening Exercise #2, targeting the specific developmental areas in which you need more information. For example, if you are satisfied with what you know about your child's movement skills, but want to know more about her social skills, you can arrange to observe that area of her development.

# ■ OTHER SOURCES OF INFORMATION ■

Often people outside of your immediate family can offer fresh perceptions of your child and new insights into her growth and development. Bear in mind, too, that when your child participates in activities outside of the home, opportunities may arise to observe skills and behavior she does not demonstrate at home.

Family documents and projects can also provide a wealth of information as you build a complete picture of your child. One family brought pictures of their son to show in a meeting with school officials; another mother made tape recordings of her child's language while they were riding in the car. Your imagination will tell you many ways to use your daily routines to increase your observations of your child.

There are many times, places, and ways that you can collect information about your child's growth and development. Here are some sources other parents have found useful—add your own to the lists:

**PEOPLE**

| | |
|---|---|
| Grandparents | Playmates |
| Brothers, sisters | Bus drivers |
| Scout Leaders | Teachers |
| Coaches | Doctors |
| Neighbor | Employers |

**PLACES**

| | |
|---|---|
| Restaurants | Church |
| Family camping | Grocery store |
| Doctor's office | Scout troop |
| Car pools | Swimming pool |

**FAMILY DOCUMENTS & PROJECTS**

| | |
|---|---|
| Photo albums | Art projects |
| Examples of school work | Tape recordings |
| Preparing for holidays | Gardening |
| Home movies | School and hospital records |

## ▪ CONCLUSION ▪

Throughout your child's infant, preschool, and school years, you will need to make new observations of her growth and development. Collecting fresh observations prior to meetings with teachers and other professionals can help you provide specific recommendations for her special education program. By completing the first two Strengthening Exercises, you gain a better understanding of your child's unique strengths and needs. By having this valuable information at your fingertips, you will feel confident as you participate in the special education planning process.

## STRENGTHENING EXERCISE #1

### Learning Style Questionnaire

1.  List three things your child has recently learned or accomplished.
    1.

    2.

    3.

2.  Choose one of the items in question#1. What about your child helped him/her learn this?

3.  Think of three things your child is working to learn now.
    1.

    2.

    3.

4.  Choose one of the items in question #3 that your child is having trouble learning. What is causing him/her trouble?

5.  What one thing would you like your child to learn within the next six months?

## STRENGTHENING EXERCISE #1 —EXAMPLE 1

### Learning Style Questionnaire

1. List three things your child has recently learned or accomplished.
   1. *Sara can ride her bike without the training wheels.*

   2. *She can make her bed and takes her dishes to the kitchen.*

   3. *She answers the telephone correctly.*

2. Choose one of the items in question#1. What about your child helped him/her learn this?

   *Sara marked a chart of home chores each day which pictured the different activities she was learning to do. She received a reward if she completed her chores at least five times during the week. Sara could see (and count) how she was doing. Sara also likes to have her room neat.*

3. Think of three things your child is working to learn now.
   1. *Sara is learning to write her name and address.*

   2. *She is learning to set the table.*

   3. *She is working on getting ready for school without constant reminders from Mom.*

4. Choose one of the items in question #3 that your child is having trouble learning. What is causing him/her trouble?

   *Sara has difficulty choosing what to wear and trouble remembering all needed items to go in her school bag. Sara dresses very slowly.*

5. What one thing would you like your child to learn within the next six months?

   *I would like Sara to be ready for school—dressed appropriately, school bag packed—in time for the bus, without Mom's help or reminding.*

## STRENGTHENING EXERCISE #1—EXAMPLE 2

### Learning Style Questionnaire

1. List three things your child has recently learned or accomplished.

   1. *Tony hangs his coat on the hook by the back door.*

   2. *He can sit for a few minutes and listen to a story.*

   3. *He pats Gretchen (the dog) gently instead of hitting her.*

2. Choose one of the items in question #1. What about your child helped him/her learn this?

   *The classroom aide sat next to Tony with her arm around him when he became restless during story time—he responds well to people.*

3. Think of three things your child is working to learn now.

   1. *To wipe his face with handkerchief when he drools.*

   2. *To learn the sign for "thank you."*

   3. *To climb stairs without help.*

4. Choose one of the items in question #3 that your child is having trouble learning. What is causing him/her trouble?

   *Lack of fine motor control.*

5. What one thing would you like your child to learn within the next six months?

   *To eat a meal without smearing food on his face, in his hair and on his clothes.*

## DEVELOPMENTAL ACHIEVEMENT CHART— EXAMPLE 1

| Sara | Can Do | Working On | Accomplish within 6 Months |
|---|---|---|---|
| MOVEMENT | Rides a bike, walks a balance beam. Writes in print (not cursive). Throws a ball. | Pedalling faster and pumping up hills on her bike. Smaller and neater printing. Catching a large ball. | To keep up with a group when bike riding. Printing on wide-ruled paper. Catch and throw with more accuracy. |
| COMMUNICATIONS | Responds to simple directions. Answers the telephone clearly; can respond appropriately to caller. | Following directions without getting mixed up. | Understand and follow through on more complex directions. |
| SOCIAL RELATIONSHIPS | Goes to Brownie Troop meetings. Sits with a small group of girls on the bus. Plays with younger neighborhood children. | Learning to make her way into a group of girls without her Mom's help. Establishing close friendship with girl her own age. | Participate in small group activity without adult hovering over. Have a friend come over to play and have dinner regularly. |
| SELF–CONCEPT/ INDEPENDENCE | Gets dressed in the morning if clothes are laid out and if Mom helps. Walks from bus stop alone; expects Mom to be waiting at home. | Getting dressed and ready for school in the morning without Mom's help. Learning what to do if Mom is late coming home. | Dress completely without help or reminders. Know what to do if Mom is not home. |
| SENSES/PERCEPTION | Takes care of matching clothing, coordinating colors. Sings along with songs on radio. | Learning names of shades of colors. Learning words to songs in music class at school. | Name one or two shades of each primary color (i.e., "peach," "turquoise"). Be able to sing two songs from memory. |
| THINKING SKILLS | Knows name, address and phone number. Counts to 20 by ones. Knows upper case alphabet letters. | Learning to count to 100 by ones. Learning to recognize lower case alphabet letters. | Know how to count accurately to 100 by ones. Recognize at least half of the lower case alphabet letters. |
| LEARNING STYLE | Very neat and orderly. Needs visual aids to see progress. | Works for rewards (prizes, candy, praise from adults). Daydreams and is easily distracted. | |

## DEVELOPMENTAL ACHIEVEMENT CHART— EXAMPLE 2

| Tony | Can Do | Working On | Accomplish within 6 Months |
|---|---|---|---|
| MOVEMENT | Holds spoon in either hand. Climbs stairs while holding someone's hand. | Using his right hand to hold the spoon. Climbing stairs without help. | Use a spoon to eat his meal. Climb the 4 front porch stairs by himself holding the rail. |
| COMMUNICATIONS | Understands signs for hungry, thirsty, thank you. Can say yes and "no" in a way that family understands. | Signing "hungry," "thirsty," "thank you." so he can be understood. Saying "yes-no" more clearly. | Will be able to sign "hungry," "thirsty," "thank you" clearly. To say "yes-no" so most people understand him. |
| SOCIAL RELATIONSHIPS | Watches a group of friends playing a game. Says "no" to classmate who pushes him, then pushes him back. | Playing the game with his friends. Ignoring pushy classmate rather than pushing him back. | Be able to play a game with a group of friends. Say "no" to pushy classmate; ask someone for help. |
| SELF–CONCEPT/ INDEPENDENCE | Can turn bathroom faucets on and off. Hangs up coat on hook by the back door. | Identifying hot and cold. Unzipping coat by himself. | Wash hands with little or no supervision. Take off coat with some help. |
| SENSES/PERCEPTION | Looks at person calling his name. | Keeping eye contact when spoken to. | Always look at familiar people when being spoken to. |
| THINKING SKILLS | Can follow a simple one-step direction with help: for example, "pick up the spoon." | Following a simple two-step direction with help. | Follow a one-step direction without help. |
| LEARNING STYLE | Tony is cautious about trying new things, and learns best by watching an activity before trying it. He is persistent when allowed to try tasks on his own. | | |

# 3. Referral & Evaluation
## Ready? Go!

**Y**ou have collected important information describing your child's educational and developmental achievements and learning style. By systematically observing your child in a variety of situations, you have developed a picture of his present strengths and needs and have also begun to set goals for his future accomplishments. But where does all this fit within the school system's special education planning process? How, and at what point, can you get school personnel to discuss with you your concerns and findings regarding your child's educational needs? How do you obtain a thorough evaluation from the school system? What information is contained in these evaluations and other school records which may be used to obtain appropriate educational programs and services?

Chapter 1 briefly described the phases of the planning cycle used by school systems to provide educational services for children with disabilities. This chapter examines in detail two of these phases: *referral* and *evaluation*. Each phase is described in terms of its purposes, activities, and participants. More important, suggestions are made as to how you, as parents, can actively participate in these phases.

## ■ IDENTIFYING CHILDREN WITH DISABILITIES: ■ THE REFERRAL PHASE

Every school system is required by IDEA to conduct a public awareness campaign, often called "Child Find," to inform the public of the rights of children with disabilities to an education that meets the child's individual needs and is provided at no cost to the parents. School systems must also tell parents in the community about the availability of special education programs. Additionally, each school division, as part of the Child Find process, must identify, locate, and evaluate everyone from birth through twenty-one in need of special education services.

Efforts to identify and to provide services for very young children with disabilities increased greatly in 1986 when Congress amended IDEA to include programs for pre-schoolers and infants and toddlers with disabilities. This new law brought about significant changes for young children with disabilities. One part benefits preschoolers who have developmental delays. The law extends the rights and protections of IDEA to all children with disabilities ages three through five. Schools were required to provide educational services to these preschool children by school year 1990-1991 in order to continue receiving federal funds for preschool programs.

A second part, often referred to as Part H*, benefits developmentally delayed infants and toddlers ages birth through two and their families. This law authorizes federal grants to the states to develop and provide comprehensive services to these very young children and their families. Chapter 8 discusses Part H and early intervention services at length.

Once a school-aged child has been identified as possibly having disabilities, the rules and regulations of both your local school system and your state division of special education specify how to make a referral for special education services. Generally, however, the first action is a written referral to the principal of the school the child is attending or would attend if he were in a public school. If a child is just beginning school and parents or others believe that special education is needed, they may request that the child be considered for such assistance immediately. If you think your child needs special services, you can obtain a referral form from the principal, or you can write a letter to the principal requesting your child be referred for special education. Or if teachers and counselors notice your child is having problems in school, they, too, may make a referral.

No matter who makes a special education referral, the next step is for the principal to convene a committee to consider the referral. Committee members most often include: (1) the principal or someone designated by the principal; (2) the person who referred the child, if that person is from the school system; and (3) teachers or other specialists who have particular knowledge of the problems the child seems to be experiencing.

In many school jurisdictions this initial committee is called the "local school screening committee." Other terms for the same committee might be the "child study committee," the "school-based committee," or the "educational management team." The committee's major purpose is to determine whether a child's learning and developmental problems are severe enough to require a formal evaluation by the school psychologist and other specialists. To reach a decision, the committee discusses the child's problems, considers adaptations to the current school program to address those problems, and suggests strategies to the classroom teacher that might help the child. If the committee members believe a full evaluation is required, they send the necessary recommendation to the school's special education administrator. The committee's decision must be made in writing and include the information leading to the committee's conclusions. The number of days in which the committee must act should be set forth in your school's rules and regulations.

In some instances parents may be unaware that their child has even been referred to the local school screening committee, unless they themselves have made the referral. School systems treat the initial stages of the referral process in a variety of ways. Some are very careful to notify parents of any meetings held to consider or to make decisions about a child's needs for special education. Others are more informal about their approach and will notify you of the meeting only if they want to obtain your consent for a formal evaluation.

When you have referred your child for initial screening, or are otherwise aware of the screening, you should request that the chairperson of the local screening committee notify you as to when they will meet and allow you to participate in that meeting. The regulations of some school systems require parents to participate in this stage of the process; others do not.[*] In any case, schools usually are agreeable to parent participation when asked. In preparation for this meeting, you should observe your child as described in Chapter 2 and develop a presentation of information you believe would help the local screening committee reach its decision.

As previously discussed, the purpose of this screening committee meeting is both to review your child's records and other relevant material and to decide whether to recommend further evaluation. If you attend the screening meeting, you should ask to take part in the discussion leading to that decision. Once again, the regulations will probably not require the committee to allow your participation in their final discussion and decision-making. At your request, however, they often will let you remain for the discussion and decision. So go ahead and ask.

If the screening committee does not recommend that your child be referred to the special education director for formal evaluation, you can dispute the decision through a formal procedure called a *due process hearing*. Chapter 10 describes the due process procedures you may follow in appealing this and other decisions made by school officials.

If you have not been part of the screening committee's activities, you may first learn that your child is being considered for special educational services upon receipt of a letter from the school requesting permission to evaluate your child. Under federal and state laws, the school system must notify you of its wish to evaluate your child for purposes of receiving special education services. It must explain to you what tests will be done and the reasons your child is being evaluated. Further, in the instance of a first-time evaluation, your consent must be granted before the testing begins.* If you refuse to give consent, the school system cannot proceed with the evaluation unless it initiates a due process hearing or court action and a hearing officer or judge rules in the school's favor. Again, see Chapter 10 for a full explanation of due process.

# ■ *Taking a Look: The Evaluation Process* ■

Forms requesting parental permission for evaluation are frequently overwhelming. Their technical language and bureaucratic style can generate great anxiety in parents. Most parents know very little about educational assessments, psychological evaluations, and audiological, speech, and language testing. For these reasons, some school personnel telephone parents ahead of time or set up conferences to talk with parents about the need for a complete evaluation of their child. They discuss the tests and procedures to be used in order to help parents gain confidence in the evaluation process. Nonetheless, if you have not been aware of your child's learning problems, the letter and form requesting your permission for evaluation may still be intimidating. And, even if you have suspected your child may need special education services, the formal language and the "fine print" can be confusing. A sample letter requesting parents' permission to evaluate their child is on the next pages 35-36.

What should you do when faced with the school's request to evaluate your child's learning needs? Maybe, you think, the school knows best. So you sign the form, grant permission for your child's evaluation, and then wonder if you did the right thing. You may be relieved the school is finally going to do something. Or maybe you refuse to grant permission for evaluation and again wonder if you made the right decision.

Neither of these responses may be the most helpful to you or your child. What you need is a greater understanding of the evaluation process and a knowledge of specific actions you may take in response to the request to evaluate your son or daughter. You need some information about the rights and responsibilities of the people involved in your child's evaluation. Knowing what to do will reduce your feeling of helplessness and begin to let you

Mr. & Mrs. Austin          RE      Evaluation
1519 S. West Street        SCHOOL  Westview Elementary
Alexandria Va. 22355       ID NO.  10094

Dear   Mr. & Mrs. Austin:

As we have discussed, the following individual evaluations are
essential in understanding your child's particular needs.

| | |
|---|---|
| Audiological | X |
| Educational | X |
| Psychological | X |
| Sociocultural | X |
| Speech and language | |
| Vision | X |
| Medical | X |

The evaluations may include conferring with your child, testing of
general ability and educational achievement, and/or an evaluation of
feelings.

If you have any questions about the evaluations or why they are
necessary, please call   Ms. Pilerton   at   624-5525 . When the
evaluations are completed, an opportunity will be provided for you
to discuss the results. You also may have access to these and any
other educational records pertaining to your child.

We are not able to proceed with these evaluations until we have your
permission to do so. Please return the attached form to me, at the
above address, within ten working days after receipt of this letter.
You do have the right to refuse to give your permission. Should you
refuse to give permission, the _____ County Public Schools has the
right to appeal your decision.

If a recent medical examination is required, the examination may be
scheduled through a private physician—at your own expense—or through
the _____ County Department of Health Services—free of charge. If
you wish to schedule a free medical examination for your child, please
contact  County Health Dept. at   524-6660 .

If you would like to be informed of the time, date, and place of
subsequent meetings held to discuss your child's educational needs,
contact   Ms. Pilerton   at   624-5525  who will inform you of
the local screening and eligibility committee meetings.

Sincerely,

Marcia J. Pilerton
Principal
/ct

Attachment

cc: Cumulative File

## PARENTAL PERMISSION FOR EVALUATION

I GIVE PERMISSION for the _____ County Public Schools
to proceed with the following evaluations for my child,

_____ Sara Austin _____ :
    *Name of child*

| | |
|---|---|
| Audiological | X |
| Educational | X |
| Psychological | X |
| Sociocultural | X |
| Speech and language | |
| Vision | X |
| Medical | X |
| | |

I understand that I have the right to review my child's school
records and to be informed of the results of these evaluations.
I understand that no change will be made in my child's educational program as a result of these evaluations without my
knowledge. I understand that I have the right to refuse to give
permission for these evaluations.

I have arranged to have a medical examination for my child through:
*(Please check if*
*a recent medical* ☐ A private physician ☐ County Department of Health Services
*examination is*
*required)*

_____    _____
    *Date*                           *Signature of Parent*

- - - - - - - - - - - - - - - - - - - - - - - - - - - - - - - - - - - - - - - - -

I DO NOT GIVE PERMISSION for the _____ County Public Schools
to proceed with the evaluation of my child, _____.

I understand that I have the right to review my child's school
records. I understand that the _____ County Public Schools
may use established procedures to obtain authorization to
proceed with the evaluation and that if the _____ County
Public Schools appeals my decision, I will be notified of my
due process rights.

_____    _____
    *Date*                           *Signature of Parent*

cc: Cumulative File

and your child "do" something about evaluation, as opposed to being "done in" by evaluation.

# ■ THE EVALUATION PROCESS: PURPOSES, ■ ACTIVITIES, AND PROFESSIONALS

There may be many reasons why a child's physical, social, or intellectual development is slower than others his age. Some children merely mature more slowly than their peers; time will find them "catching up." In some instances, a child's home environment and family or cultural background may cause learning to proceed at a slower-than-average rate. Other children may have physical impairments that interfere with their development. Perhaps they have a visual or hearing problem. Still other children may have mental retardation, learning disabilities, or emotional problems. Any and all of these conditions could interfere with a child's general educational and developmental progress.

The purpose of the school's evaluation process is to identify your child's learning difficulties. While attempting to determine the source of the learning problems, information is also obtained concerning your child's present developmental and academic abilities. This information is helpful in understanding the nature of your child's problems and in planning his future educational programs.

School systems use many different tests and materials to evaluate children. In fact, IDEA requires that the evaluation be conducted by a "multidisciplinary team," a group of professionals with expertise in different areas. In some states the types of tests used in evaluation are specified by state regulations and vary according to the child's suspected disability. Generally, all tests and materials may be grouped into five categories, or as schools sometimes call them, *assessment components.* Not all states require that specific components be completed for every child. Therefore, it is important that you check your state and local procedures to see which components are required. The five categories that are often used and the professionals who gather information for each category are:

**1. The Educational Component.** An analysis based on selected tests that identifies your child's current educational performance and specific instructional needs in such academic areas as reading, math, spelling, and language performance. Specific tests may be given by the classroom teacher, when qualified, and by educational diagnosticians trained in using these tests.

**2. The Medical Component.** An assessment from a physician indicating general medical history and any medical/health problems that might impede your child's learning. Although many parents obtain this assessment at their own expense, each school system maintains a list of physicians and clinics where free medical examinations are available.

**3. The Social History Component.** A report developed from interviews with parents, teachers, and others describing your child's background and behavior at home and in school. The report is usually prepared by a school social worker who interviews the parents at home. If parents wish, however, they may request that the interview take place elsewhere—for example, at school.

**4. The Psychological Component.** A report usually written by a school psychologist and based upon numerous tests and the psychologist's observations and interpretations. The psychological testing assesses your child's general intelligence, social skills, emotional development, other thinking skills, and his ability to coordinate eye and hand movements. If your child's learning or behavioral needs are complex, this component may also include an evaluation by a clinical psychologist or a psychiatrist.

**5. Others.★** Assessments in other areas which may be necessary to complete the picture of your child. Areas of development that may be assessed include your child's communication skills, such as imitating sounds, cooing, responding to language, or talking; his social skills, such as separating from parents and getting along with others; and his movement skills, such as rolling, raising his head, walking, and using his hands. In addition, your child's brain and central nervous system functioning may be assessed through a neurological examination, and his senses and perception may be evaluated through hearing, vision, and other tests. For very young children and infants, the purpose of the evaluation is the same as for older children: to identify their strengths and weaknesses as a basis for planning the services they need. Your pediatrician can give you guidance regarding specific tests necessary to provide a comprehensive understanding of your child's strengths and needs.

# ■ FORMAL EVALUATION REQUIREMENTS ■

All school systems are required by IDEA and by state laws to follow certain procedures when evaluating a child.

**First, the administrator of special education must inform you in your native language and primary means of communication—vocal, sign language, or Braille—of:**

1. the school's intent to evaluate your child;
2. your rights as parents pertaining to special education for your child;
3. a list of anticipated tests to be used—in the instance of initial evaluation; and

4. the need for your consent prior to the initial evaluation and your right to notification of any subsequent evaluations.

**Second, the school system must ensure its evaluation procedures provide for the following:**★

1. your written consent prior to the initial evaluation;
2. the assignment of surrogate parents if you are not available to protect the interests of your child;
3. confidentiality of all evaluation results;
4. an opportunity for you to obtain an independent evaluation of your child if you believe the school's evaluation is biased or invalid;
5. an opportunity for you to have a hearing to question evaluation results with which you disagree;
6. an opportunity for you to examine your child's official school records; and
7. testing that does not discriminate against your child because of racial or cultural bias or because the tests are inappropriate for a person with your child's disabilities.

**Third, the school system must make sure its testing procedures meet these requirements:**

1. The tests and evaluation materials are administered in your child's native language and primary means of communication.
2. The tests must be professionally approved for the specific purposes for which they are used.
3. The tests must be given by trained professionals according to the instructions of the publishers of the tests and materials.
4. Tests and evaluation materials that assess a wide range of educational and developmental needs and capabilities should be used in addition to tests designed to provide a single general intelligence quotient.
5. Tests should be selected and administered so as to ensure that they accurately assess the child's aptitude, achievement level, or other factors they are designed to measure, rather than reflecting the child's disabilities.
6. The evaluation should be undertaken by a team or group of persons from several professional backgrounds, including at least one teacher or other specialist with knowledge in the area of your child's suspected disability. Your child should be assessed in all areas related to the suspected disability, including, where

> appropriate, health, vision, hearing, social and emotional
> status, general intelligence, academic performance,
> communication skills, and motor abilities.

These are the minimum requirements school officials must meet when evaluating your child's need for special education services. The regulations of your state and local school district may include additional procedures. For example, your school may provide for a conference between you and the evaluation team members to discuss the results of your child's testing. Before proceeding with the evaluation for your child, review your school's rules and regulations carefully. Remember, if you believe your school system has not fulfilled the evaluation requirements as stated above and in your school's procedures, you can take various steps to protect your child's right to a thorough, accurate evaluation. Chapter 10 outlines these due process and complaint procedures in detail.

# ■ PARENT ACTION-STEPS FOR EVALUATION ■

Now you know, generally, the purposes, the activities, and the professionals involved in the evaluation of a child, as well as the general requirements that school systems must satisfy. But your interest is not a general one. Your interest is in the particular evaluation being proposed for your child. With this specific concern in mind, "Parent Action-Steps for Evaluation" were developed for you to follow in each of the four phases of the evaluation process:

1. giving or refusing permission to evaluate;
2. activities before evaluation;
3. activities during evaluation; and
4. activities after evaluation.

For each phase of the process, you will find a series of actions and accompanying steps you may take to participate in your child's evaluation. This list of action-steps suggests activities other parents have found helpful when entering the evaluation phase of the special education process. Some of the actions and steps are applicable to testing conducted by private or public agencies outside the school system rather than in a school setting. Other steps are appropriate for young children rather than older students. You will want to undertake only those actions and steps that:

1. make sense to you;
2. are appropriate to the age and developmental level of your child;
3. will help you make a confident decision; and

4. will give you a feeling of managing, rather than being managed by, the evaluation process.

You need not, and should not, take all the actions and all the steps outlined. Look over the list and choose the actions and steps to follow that will be most helpful to you and to your child in assuring that the evaluation is fair and thorough. In making your selection, you will want to keep in mind your family's needs, and your child's age, disability, and past experience with evaluations.

## PHASE I: GIVING OR REFUSING PERMISSION TO EVALUATE

After the school system has notified you in writing of its intent to evaluate your child, you must decide whether to give or refuse permission for this evaluation. School system regulations prescribe the amount of time you have to respond, usually within ten days of notice. To help you decide, you may wish to:

**ACTION A:** Explore your feelings about this evaluation by:
1. talking to your spouse, a friend, or a helping professional such as a teacher, counselor, or advocate;
2. recalling what was difficult and what was helpful in previous evaluations, unless, of course, this is the first one.

**ACTION B:** Learn more about your local evaluation process by:
1. asking the director of special education or your school principal to identify the person in the school system most responsible for your child's evaluation;
2. obtaining all relevant written policies and procedures from the person responsible for the evaluation, the school's public information officer, or the department of special education;
3. obtaining parent handbooks and pamphlets on evaluation;
4. making a list of all your questions;
5. meeting with a knowledgeable person such as an experienced parent, a school representative, an advocate to discuss evaluation.

**ACTION C:** Learn more about the evaluation planned for your child by:
1. requesting in writing from school officials the reasons for this evaluation;
2. requesting a detailed plan for evaluation, to include:
   a. areas to be evaluated;
   b. tests or portions of tests to be used;
   c. reasons for selecting tests;

    d. qualifications of persons giving tests;

    e. statement as to how the evaluation will be adapted to compensate for your child's suspected disability.

### ACTION D: Assess the appropriateness of the tests by:

1. consulting a knowledgeable person such as another parent, an independent professional, or a school psychologist;

2. reviewing literature on evaluation. (See annotated bibliography in Appendix D.)

### ACTION E: Explore the independent evaluation alternative by:

1. learning about your right to an independent evaluation, as described in Chapter 4;

2. learning your school's procedures for providing independent evaluations;

3. talking with parents whose children have had independent evaluations;

4. consulting a psychologist, diagnostician, or other professional in private practice.

### ACTION F: Explore the consequences of refusing evaluation by:

1. talking to the principal and teachers about alternatives to special education at the school;

2. discussing your concerns with the person in charge of the evaluation;

3. learning your school's procedures when parents refuse evaluation;

4. talking with knowledgeable professionals about your child's learning needs and the reasons you are considering refusing the school's evaluation.

## PHASE II: BEFORE EVALUATION

If, after completing the action steps just described, you decide to give permission for your child to be evaluated, you can take several steps to prepare for the evaluation. You may wish to:

### ACTION A: Anticipate your child's needs in this evaluation by:

1. talking with your spouse, your child's therapist or teacher, or an earlier evaluator about how your child handles evaluations, specifically his:

    a. reaction to strangers

    b. tolerance for testing demands

    c. ability to sit still for long periods

    d. response to doctors and other professionals

    e. fatigue threshold - how long until he gets too tired to work at his best

    f. need for an interpreter if non-English speaking or a user of sign language

    g. high and low points in the day;

2. reading pamphlets or articles on children and evaluations;

3. talking with your child about prior evaluation experiences and his thoughts about the new evaluation.

**Action B: Prepare yourself for this evaluation by:**

1. talking to other parents about their experiences;

2. seeking tips on rough spots and how to work around them from an organization for parents of children with disabilities;

3. listing your practical concerns about the evaluation, such as:

    a. schedules

    b. costs

    c. child care

    d. transportation

    e. obtaining an interpreter

4. learning the evaluation facility's expectation for your involvement;

5. choosing among various roles you may take, such as:

    a. observer of your child

    b. supporter of your child

    c. information source about your child.

**Action C: Plan for your child's evaluation with a representative of the evaluation facility or school's psychological services by:**

1. arranging for a meeting or a phone conference;

2. preparing for this meeting by listing your questions and concerns in priority order;

3. requesting information on, or clarification of, the evaluation process;

4. sharing your plans for your involvement;

5. raising concerns you might have over keeping the experience a positive one for your child.

**ACTION D: Prepare your child for the evaluation by:**
1. talking together about the reasons for, and process of, this new evaluation;
2. giving your child opportunities to express his feelings and ask questions;
3. visiting the place where the evaluation will be conducted so your child will be familiar with the people and the surroundings;
4. planning together for a special activity when the evaluation is completed.

## PHASE III: DURING EVALUATION

During the evaluation process itself, the actions and steps you select will be strongly influenced by your child's age and his past experience with evaluations. In many instances your child will be tested in school, during school hours, making it difficult or inappropriate for you to be present during the evaluation. When it is appropriate for you to be present, especially with an infant or preschooler, you may want to consider some of the following actions and steps. Keeping in mind your child's age, personality, and disability, you may wish to:

**ACTION A: Ease your child into the situation by:**
1. allowing him to become familiar with the areas in which he will be tested;
2. introducing him to the people who will be giving the tests;
3. reviewing the day's plan with him;
4. reassuring him that you will be available to him at all times;
5. encouraging him to ask questions and share worries.

**ACTION B: Monitor the evaluation process by:**
1. requesting that the evaluation start on time;
2. inquiring as to any changes in personnel or tests to be used;
3. observing testing of your child whenever appropriate;
4. recording your impressions of your child's performance;
5. recording your impressions of each evaluator's interactions with your child.

**ACTION C: Monitor your child's performance by:**
1. keeping an eye on his fatigue and stress levels;
2. staying with him during medical procedures - shots, blood tests, EEG;
3. asking for explanations of unexpected procedures.

## PHASE IV: AFTER EVALUATION

Parents and children usually have a need to feel that the evaluation is truly completed. There are a number of ways you and your family can wrap up the evaluation experience and begin to use the information gained from the evaluation for educational planning. You may wish to:

**ACTION A: Help your child round out the experience on a positive note by:**

1. encouraging him to review the experience through storytelling, drawing pictures, or dramatic play;
2. discussing with him the people and activities he liked and disliked;
3. sharing your own feelings and perceptions of the experience;
4. informing him of the evaluation results—what was learned about his strengths and needs;
5. throwing an end-of-evaluation party!

**ACTION B: Help yourself complete the experience by:**

1. recounting the experience to a friend or parent support group;
2. checking the actual evaluation experience against what you had planned or anticipated;
3. writing a letter to the evaluation facility describing your sense of the strengths and needs of the process;
4. giving yourself a graduation-from-evaluation gift!

**ACTION C: Prepare for your parent conference with the evaluation team by:**

1. reading through your child's previous evaluation records, if he has been tested previously;
2. reviewing your information and notes on this evaluation;
3. asking the head of the evaluation team for the record of this evaluation, including individual reports;
4. analyzing the records by using the Four-Step Record Decoder described in Chapter 4;
5. noting your concerns in the form of questions to be asked at the parent conference;
6. asking someone to go with you to the parent conference.

To help you systematically negotiate the evaluation phase of the special education maze, a Parent Action-Steps for Evaluation Chart follows on pages

47-48. The chart has space for writing each action and step you will take in the evaluation phase. At the end of the chart is a section for names, phone numbers, and dates related to those actions and steps. The chart allows you to plan steps you choose to take in your child's evaluation, to monitor the progress of the evaluation, and to maintain a record of how and when the evaluation was conducted and completed—all useful information.

## ■ THE EVALUATION CONFERENCE ■

Once the formal evaluation of your child has been completed, many school procedures call for a meeting or conference with you to explain the results of the testing. If the person in charge of your child's evaluation does not suggest such a meeting, you should request one. Unless you fully understand the results and conclusions drawn from the evaluation, you may have no idea whether your child needs or is eligible for special education services.

Your participation in all the remaining phases of the special education process depends in large part on how well you understand your child's learning problems. In order to work confidently with professionals during the upcoming meetings required to plan your child's special education program, you need to know the evaluation team's perspective of your child's current abilities and problems. Therefore, before attending any meetings following the completion of your child's evaluation, make certain a person knowledgeable of the evaluation process has explained to your satisfaction the results and conclusions of the evaluation process and that you have requested and received a copy of the reports in writing.

## ■ RE-EVALUATION ■

At least every three years, each child in special education must be evaluated through a process known as the *triennial evaluation*. Under federal regulations, parents do not have to give permission for the re-evaluation,[*] but must be notified that it is going to take place. Some states, however, require school districts to obtain parents' permission each time an evaluation is conducted. In addition, parents or teachers may request a re-evaluation of a child at any point they believe one is necessary. Evaluations must be conducted when there is a request or recommendation for any significant change in placement, such as a change from the number of hours per week spent in general education versus special education, or a change in eligibility category of, for example, specific learning disabilities to mental retardation.

# Parent Action–Steps
# for Evaluation Chart
## (Worksheet)

**Phase I: Giving/Refusing Permission to Evaluate**

Action: _____

    Step: _____

    Step: _____

Action: _____

    Step: _____

    Step: _____

Action: _____

    Step: _____

    Step: _____

**Phase II: Before Evaluation**

Action: _____

    Step: _____

    Step: _____

Action: _____

    Step: _____

    Step: _____

Action: _____

    Step: _____

    Step: _____

(CONTINUED NEXT PAGE)

**Phase III: During Evaluation**

Action: _____

    Step: _____

    Step: _____

Action: _____

    Step: _____

    Step: _____

Action: _____

    Step: _____

    Step: _____

**Phase IV: After Evaluation**

Action: _____

    Step: _____

    Step: _____

Action: _____

    Step: _____

    Step: _____

Action: _____

    Step: _____

    Step: _____

| Important Telephone Numbers | Important Dates |
| --- | --- |
| _____ | _____ |
| _____ | _____ |
| _____ | _____ |
| _____ | _____ |
| _____ | _____ |

# 4. SCHOOL RECORDS & REPORTS

## JOURNALS OF THE JOURNEY

To this point, you have collected information about your child's educational needs from two primary sources: from your own and others' observations of your child, and from observations made in the formal evaluation process. Chapter 2 helped you organize your personal observations into a clearly understandable framework, but what do you do with new information produced by your child's evaluation? Even when the results of the evaluation have been interpreted for you by school personnel or other specialists, you still may worry about remembering all that was said. Luckily, the school system does not depend solely upon the memory of its professional staff to recall specific children, their progress, and their needs. The memory of the school system is contained within its official records.

As a parent of a child with disabilities, you have special interest in knowing what is contained in your child's school records. This is true because of the significant information these records offer you about your child and also because of the emphasis schools place on these records when making educational decisions. If any information in your child's records is inaccurate, biased, incomplete, inconsistent, or just plain wrong, this material may well result in inaccurate decisions regarding your child's right to special education services. For these reasons you must know how to obtain, interpret, and correct these records and how to use them effectively in school meetings. This chapter will guide you through the corridor in the special education maze pertaining to school records.

# ■ OBTAINING YOUR CHILD'S RECORDS ■ FROM THE LOCAL SCHOOL

Schools are required by federal and state laws to maintain certain records and to make these records available to you upon request. The federal *Family Educational Rights and Privacy Act*, also known as the Buckley Amendment, and IDEA establish the minimum requirements school systems must meet in maintaining, protecting, and providing access to students' school records. These requirements are described in the remaining pages of this chapter. State laws will sometimes go beyond these minimum requirements and provide parents with additional rights to review, modify, or seek other changes in these records. For this reason, you should obtain a copy of your own state's school records law by contacting your local director of special education.

The Family Educational Rights and Privacy Act and IDEA require that every school district have a written policy governing the management and confidentiality of records. Further, the policy must include a procedure for parents to gain access to confidential records. The term "parent," as used in these Acts, is broadly defined. It includes natural parents, guardians, anyone acting as a parent in the absence of the natural parent, and foster parents. Divorced or noncustodial parents have the same rights as custodial parents with respect to their child's school records unless a state law, court order, or binding custody agreement declares otherwise.

Getting copies of your child's school records should be virtually automatic. While federal law does not specifically require school systems to provide parents with copies of these records, in practice most school systems do so upon request. Begin by asking the school principal about the location of your child's various files or records. These will include a cumulative file, a confidential file, and, sometimes, a compliance file. The principal will have the local school's *cumulative file,* which you will want to see and copy. Often the cumulative file contains little more than a profile card with personal identification data and perhaps academic achievement levels, some teacher reports, and report cards.

Also accessible to parents, the *confidential file* may be kept at your child's school, or in a central administrative office where the special education program offices are located. The file is called confidential because access to the information is limited to certain individuals. Your child's confidential record includes all of the reports written as a result of the school's evaluation; reports of independent evaluators, if any; medical records that you have had released; summary reports of evaluation team and eligibility committee meetings; your child's Individualized Education Program (IEP); and, often, correspondence between you and school officials.

Some school systems keep the report of eligibility meetings, correspondence between the parents and school officials, and other similar documents in a separate *compliance file.* The contents of the compliance file demonstrate that the school system has complied with timelines, notification, and consent regulations under IDEA. In addition, schools may also maintain a separate file regarding discipline issues involving long-term suspension or expulsion. A good bit of detective work is sometimes required to understand your school system's individual filing system!

Once you know the location of the records, how do you best proceed to obtain copies of these files? If you want to get a copy of your child's records through the mail, you will most likely be required to sign a release-of-information form. This can be obtained by calling or writing your school principal or special education director. Other school systems will send records upon receiving a written request for release of information from parents. For this service, a school system can charge you only for the cost of reproducing and mailing the records, not for personnel time or other costs incurred by the school system.

Another way to obtain a copy of your child's records is by appointment. A telephone call to the appropriate office requesting a mutually convenient time for you to review and to make copies of the records often results in a school professional being on hand to guide you through them and to answer any questions. Again, your only expense will be the reproduction costs.

You might ask, "Wouldn't it be better if I go into the office unannounced to see the records?" In fact, there are several reasons why a surprise visit may not be the best strategy:

**1. Perhaps you are concerned that if you give the school system prior notice, someone might remove parts of the record and then replace them following the appointment.** Although isolated cases of schools removing material from files have indeed been reported, the good faith of both parents and school systems is needed in this area. Should problems develop, several procedures enable you to challenge and request removal of records of questionable value to your child. These procedures are described later in this chapter.

**2. Even if you do visit the office unannounced, school personnel are not required to show parents their children's records on demand.** Often, however, they will accommodate you in an emergency. School systems are required by the Buckley Amendment to make records available within forty-five days. Most systems respond to a parent's request within two to five days.

**3. A school office, like any office, is run most efficiently when the needs of the people working there are taken into consideration.** If you arrive unannounced and ask for services that involve the time of office staff, you can interrupt important routines and schedules. By asking for an appointment you continue to build the bridge of mutual respect and consideration needed in effective educational advocacy.

# ▪ RECORDS OPEN TO PARENTS ▪

Once you have gained access to your child's records, does this mean you can see any and all records pertaining to your child? Just what records is the school system legally required to show you?

Under the Buckley Amendment, schools must show parents all records, files, documents, and other materials that are maintained by the school system and contain information relating to their children. This includes all records referring to your child in any personally identifiable manner—that is, records containing your child's name, social security number, student ID number, or other data making them traceable to her. Excluded from the records schools must show you, however, are the following: (1) notes of teachers, counselors, and/or school administrators made for their personal use and shown to nobody else (except a substitute teacher); and (2) personnel records of school employees.

These exclusions often cause parents concern. Frequently, parents whose children are evaluated by school psychologists want to see their children's test papers. Psychologists sometimes refuse to show parents these papers, claiming the tests fall within the personal-notes exemption or that the tests are copyrighted and cannot be disclosed to nonprofessionals. According to the Office of the General Counsel, U.S. Department of Education, test papers (protocols) completed in psychological evaluations and maintained in personally identifiable form are educational records under the Buckley Amendment. Therefore, upon your request, psychologists must show you the test papers and other materials completed by your child during her evaluation. To protect the future validity of the tests, however, psychologists cannot give you copies of these materials. Similarly, parents often feel they should be able to examine the personnel records of their child's teacher to assess the teacher's academic qualifications and experience. But these records are exempt from such review under the Buckley Amendment and are not open to parental examination. (Note: If either the raw scores from your child's evaluations or the qualifications of your child's teachers become issues in due process hearings, you may obtain this information either from the files or from direct examination of witnesses during the hearing. More about this in Chapter 10.)

# ▪ EXAMINING AND CORRECTING ▪ YOUR CHILD'S RECORDS

Even when you have your child's records in your hands, you may wonder what you've got. The language of the educators, psychologists, educational diagnosticians, and other school professionals often appears unintelligible at best and nonsense at worst. If this is the case for you, all you need to do is ask someone to help you. The law requires school personnel to explain the records to you when you do not understand them. Or you may take a friend or a knowledgeable professional with you to help review the records and explain confusing parts. When you do this, however, you will be asked to sign a form giving that person permission to see your child's records.

As you review the records, you may find places where information given about your child or family conflicts with your own assessments. If left unchallenged, this material could lead to decisions about your child's educational program that are not in her best interest. To prevent this from happening, you can follow two paths. First, you can informally ask the principal or the director of special education to delete the material, giving your reasons for the request. Often school officials will honor the request and no problem arises. If difficulties do develop and they refuse to remove the requested material, your second approach to correcting the records is the formal hearing.

When you ask for a formal hearing, you should do so in writing, with a letter addressed to the school principal or the school official designated in your school's written procedures. Be certain to keep a copy of the letter for your files in the same way you will want to keep track of all correspondence with the school. The hearing you request will involve a meeting between you and school professionals, presided over by a hearing officer. The hearing officer in this case is usually an official of the school system who does not have a direct interest in the outcome of the hearing. The purpose of the hearing is to allow you and the school system to present evidence about the school record in dispute and to let the hearing officer determine who is right.

Under the Buckley Amendment, the school must schedule a hearing on any disputed records within a reasonable time, and you must be notified of the time and place of the hearing reasonably in advance. What is reasonable in your school system will be spelled out in your local school or state board of education regulations. These same regulations will also explain: (1) your right to have someone, even an attorney, assist or represent you at the hearing; (2) the length of time the school system has to make its decision after the hearing; and (3) the requirement that the hearing officer include in the decision a discussion of the evidence and the justification and rationale for the decision reached.

Since the hearing officer at a records hearing can be a school official, parents might feel that the proceedings are not fair. Although unfair decisions have been rendered, more often than not the hearing officer will act impartially in deciding the issue. Even if parents are denied their request to have a record removed, further actions may be taken to reduce the negative impact of the disputed report.

The most effective way to handle this problem is to amend the record by attaching a written explanation of your objections, detailing why you believe the material is inaccurate, biased, incomplete, or otherwise inappropriate. Because the school must, by law, keep your statement with the record, everyone who sees the record will be informed of your objection to its contents.

Besides amending the disputed record, you can take several other steps when you believe your requests to correct the records have been improperly refused. First, you can file a complaint with your state education agency following the procedures described in your state's school records law. Second, as soon as possible after the incident, you could also send a letter of complaint to:

Family Educational Rights and Privacy Act (FERPA) Office,
Family Policy Compliance Office
U.S. Department of Education
600 Independence Avenue, SW,
Washington, DC 20202-4605
Phone: (202) 260-3887

This office is responsible for enforcing the Buckley Amendment and will look into your complaint.

A final action you can take in some areas is to sue in court. Since most recent court decisions deny individuals the right to private suit under the Buckley Amendment, you should consult an attorney to see if such action is possible where you live. All three of these options require significant time before action occurs. Therefore, if you use them, you should also amend the record in anticipation of having it removed later.

Finally, you should examine your own state laws regarding your rights to review, to control access to, and to correct your child's school records. State laws may provide parents with more rights in this area than does the Buckley Amendment. To determine if this is the case, you must first obtain and examine copies of the laws and policies regarding records in your state. Again, these laws and policies should be obtainable from your superintendent of schools or other designated officials.

## ■ CONTROLLING WHO SEES YOUR ■ CHILD'S RECORDS

The Buckley Amendment prohibits schools from disclosing your child's records to anyone without your written consent. The only exceptions are:

1. school officials, including teachers, in the same district with a legitimate educational interest as defined in the school procedures;
2. school officials in the school district to which your child intends to transfer (before the records are sent, however, you will want to review them and challenge their content, if necessary);
3. certain state and national education agencies, if necessary, for enforcing federal laws;
4. anyone to whom a state statute requires the school to report information;
5. accrediting and research organizations helping the school, provided they guarantee confidentiality;
6. student financial aid officials;
7. people who have court orders, provided the school makes reasonable efforts to notify the parent or student before releasing the records;
8. appropriate people in health and safety emergencies such as doctors, nurses, and fire marshals.

With the preceding exceptions, schools must have your permission to release material from your child's records to anyone other than yourself. When requesting release of the records, the school must tell you which records are involved, why they have been requested, and who will receive them. Likewise, if you want someone outside the school system to see your child's records, you will be asked to sign a release granting such permission. All these precautions have been instituted to protect your privacy and that of your child.

## ■ WHEN YOUR CHILD REACHES EIGHTEEN ■ OR GOES TO POST-SECONDARY SCHOOL

When your child reaches the age of eighteen or enters a post-secondary educational institution such as a vocational-technical school, a college, a university, or trade school, most rights to records previously available to you are transferred to your child. The only parts of her record your child will not have the right to see are your financial records and any statements or confidential recommendations your child has waived the right to see. This means if you wish to see the school records of a son or daughter who is eighteen or who is attending post-secondary school, he or she must first sign a waiver permitting this action.

IDEA gives parents of children with disabilities special consideration when transferring record rights. The law grants states the authority to develop individual policies which take into account the type and severity of the child's disability and the child's age when transferring record rights from parents to their children. Thus, if your child with disabilities has reached age eighteen or is about to reach eighteen and is in secondary school, you should ask the director of special education if your state has a policy that allows you continued access to your child's records. If not, you and school personnel may want to develop a waiver form which your child can sign allowing you continued rights to review, to control access to, and to seek changes in those records.

# ▪ WHEN YOU MOVE ▪

In today's society, people are always on the move. Your child's school records, of course, will move with you. To be certain your child's new school receives only relevant and current records, you should examine the records and identify specifically the material you want forwarded. Most school systems will honor your request and send only the information you want released. Should the school wish to send material you want withheld, you can initiate the hearing procedure described earlier to prohibit its action. In any case, before you move, always review your child's school folder. You will want to eliminate the irrelevant, inaccurate, and dated material or attach your critique to those records you believe should have been removed but were not.

Because of the importance of your child's records in determining special education eligibility, you should review and correct them annually, whether or not you move. You should also be certain you have a duplicate copy of all the material in the official files. Then, if the records are lost, as they easily can be in a large school system, you will have copies to replace them.

# ▪ A FINAL NOTE: THICK RECORDS ▪

Classroom teachers have been heard to comment, "When I see a thick set of records of a child new to my class, I know trouble is coming." This is another reason for your diligence in reviewing your child's records annually. Many reports, especially those written several years previously, give little if any information that will be useful in current decisions about your child. A careful weeding out of irrelevant documents can help to avoid the thick record syndrome.

# ▪ THE FOUR-STEP RECORD DECODER ▪

When you have obtained the school's records, often a stack of documents an inch or more thick, what will you do with them? How can you begin to make sense of all this material written about your child? You have already organized your home observations of your child into the framework of the Developmental Achievement Chart; now you will organize the school's observations of your child by employing the Four-Step Record Decoder. The decoder helps you organize, read, analyze, and evaluate your child's school records.

## ORGANIZE

1. After obtaining the complete set of records from the school system, separate the documents describing your child (teacher reports, psychological evaluations, social history, IEPs, etc.) from other documents or correspondence of an administrative nature (the minutes of an eligibility committee meeting, consent forms, etc.). The other documents and correspondence help you keep track of your contacts with the school system.
2. Make an extra copy of the records. This way you will have an original and a copy you can mark, cut, paste, and use however it will help you.
3. Arrange each set—descriptive reports and other documents— in chronological order.
4. Secure the pages in a folder with a clip or in a loose-leaf notebook so that if you drop them you won't have to back up three steps.
5. Number each report and make a chronological list that can be added on to as new records are generated. The list might look like the chart on the next page.

EDUCATIONAL REPORTS OF SUSAN MARTIN

| REPORT | DATE | REPORTING PERSON |
| --- | --- | --- |
| 1. Psychoeducational evaluation | 5/3/97 | Katherine Connor |
| 2. Teacher's report | 5/97 | Cathy Porterman |
| 3. Social history reports | 5/12/97 | Patricia Roberts |
| 4. Psychiatric evaluation summary | 6/8/97 | Dr. Gerald Brown |
| 5. IEP | 6/14/97 | Katherine Connor |
| 6. Psychological evaluation summary | 8/23/97 | Dr. Ronald McPherson |
| 7. Teacher's report | 9/14/97 | Dru Dunn |
| 8. Psychologist's memorandum | 9/14/97 | Barbara Hager |

# READ

1. Read through the entire record to get overall impressions and tones of the school's view of your child.
2. In the margins of your working copy, put a question mark beside the statements or areas of the reports you do not understand or with which you disagree.

# ANALYZE

1. Now reread the reports and underline the phrases or sentences you feel best describe your child's strengths and those that describe your child's problems. Put an "S" in the margin opposite a description of your child's learning strengths; a "P" opposite the problems. When you come to a phrase or sentence reporting your child's learning style, write "LS" in the margin.
2. Using a worksheet similar to the one on pages 63-64 place these phrases or sentences about your child's strengths and problems within the developmental categories of movement, communications, social relationships, self-concept/independence, perception/senses, thinking skills, and learning style.
3. After each piece of data, put the source and date. Often you will find trends beginning to emerge. The same observation, said in similar language, may occur in several reports over a period of time.

4. List recommendations made by each evaluator or teacher in the last section of the analysis sheet. Recommendations might include services needed, classroom environment, class size, type of school setting, recommendation for further testing, specific teaching materials, or equipment.

## EVALUATE

Using the question-mark notations you have made in the margins and your overall sense of the records from your analytical work with them, evaluate them against the following criteria:

**Accurate.** Do the reports and portions of the records correspond with your own feelings, perceptions, observations, and assessments of your child?

**Complete.** Are all the documents required by the school system for the eligibility, Individualized Education Program (IEP), and placement decisions available in the file? For example, medical report, social history, psychological examination, educational report, and others as may be required by your local or state guidelines.

**Bias Free.** Are the reports free from cultural or racial bias? Do they take into consideration the effect your child's disability might have had upon the outcome of the results of the tests?

**Nonjudgmental.** Do the reports reflect a respect for your child and your family? Do they avoid the use of language that judges rather than describes? Examples of judgmental statements include: "She is fickle." "He is incorrigible." Examples of descriptive statements include: "She is inconsistent in stating what she likes and dislikes." "He will not respond to directions to stop disruptive behavior."

**Current.** Are the dates on the records recent enough to give a report of your child's present behavior and functioning? Records generated within the past three years are generally useful for making good decisions. Older ones should be used with caution.

**Understandable.** Is the language used meaningful, clear, and understandable to you? If technical terms (jargon) are used, have they been defined or made understandable to the non-specialist? (Example of an unclear statement: "She appears to have a psychological learning disability, calling for treatment involving a moderation of the special focus on interpersonal sensitivity she has received so far." What does that mean?)

**Consistent.** Is there consistency among the descriptions of your child given by each evaluator or teacher? Or do you find contradictions and differences of opinion? Considering the record as a whole, does it make sense and lead to the given recommendations?

An example of the analysis sheets of the Record Decoder Sara's parents worked out are found on pages 65-66.

By completing your own Record Decoder analysis sheets, you will become thoroughly familiar with your child as seen through the close-up lens of her school records. The information in these records provides the basis upon which crucial decisions will be made concerning your child's education. The importance of organizing, reading, analyzing, and evaluating your child's school records cannot be overemphasized. Therefore, before continuing to the next phase of the maze, make sure the information in your child's file paints an accurate picture of her.

## ■ EVALUATION TROUBLESHOOTING ■

After you have reviewed your child's latest evaluation reports and examined past evaluations in the school file using the Four-Step Record Decoder, you will conclude one of two things. Either you agree that the evaluation results are accurate, complete, consistent, and up to date; or you believe they are deficient in some respect. If you believe the evaluation materials are satisfactory, you move to the next corridor of the special education maze—eligibility determination. But what if you think the evaluation findings are inadequate? What steps do you take next?

You can select one of two paths in attempting to correct the defects you find with the evaluations. One path is informal; you informally ask school officials to remove the faulty evaluation from the record, or undertake additional evaluations, or add materials you provide to the file, or possibly just clarify for you the deficiencies you see in the evaluation findings. Should this approach fail, you can seek to resolve your difficulties through a more formal approach.★

If your problem involves earlier evaluations that are now a part of your child's official school file, you can seek to amend the records through the formal process for correcting records described earlier in this chapter. If your concern is the inadequacy of the school's most recent evaluation, you can request that an independent evaluation of your child be made at public expense.

Both federal and state law provide parents the opportunity to obtain an independent evaluation of their child when they believe the school's evaluation is inadequate. An independent evaluation is one made by professionals not employed by the school system. Some local school systems maintain a list of professionals or organizations whose personnel meet the licensing criteria for conducting independent evaluations. Sometimes these evaluations may be conducted by the county or state departments of health or mental

**EVALUATION**

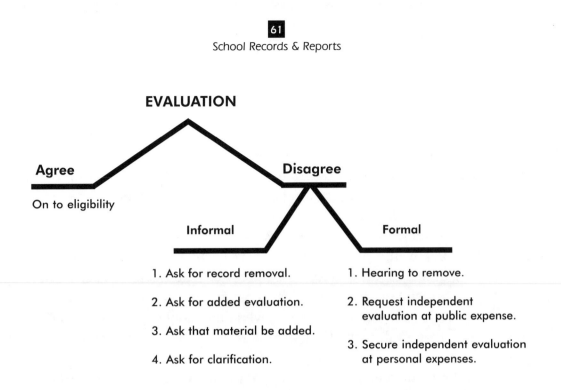

Agree

On to eligibility

Disagree

**Informal**

1. Ask for record removal.

2. Ask for added evaluation.

3. Ask that material be added.

4. Ask for clarification.

**Formal**

1. Hearing to remove.

2. Request independent evaluation at public expense.

3. Secure independent evaluation at personal expenses.

health. The steps you should follow to secure an independent evaluation are outlined in your state regulations. But remember! An independent evaluation paid for at public expense does not mean that you, the parent, can choose whomever you wish to evaluate your child. The evaluators must meet the licensing criteria of the school system.

Will school officials agree to pay for an independent evaluation? Not always. Before they can deny your request, however, they must hold a due process hearing as described in Chapter 9 and must prove to the hearing officer the appropriateness of their evaluations. Otherwise, the school system cannot deny your request for an independent evaluation. Remember! You don't have to prove that the school's evaluation results are incorrect before asking for an independent evaluation—you are entitled to an independent evaluation if you merely believe the school system's findings are inadequate. If school professionals don't wish to pay for the independent evaluation, they must initiate the hearing procedure to justify denying the request.

An alternative to the independent evaluation at public expense is the independent evaluation at private expense. If you can obtain an independent evaluation at public expense, why would you ever want to pay for one out of your own pocket? There are several reasons. First, you can personally choose the professionals who will make the evaluation. This often gives you greater confidence in the findings and allows you to select the specialist most appropriate for working with your child. Second, when you pay for your own evaluation, you can control who sees the results. When an independent evaluation is made at public expense, the findings must be considered by the school system in making educational decisions regarding your child. Further, the independent, publicly financed evaluation may be presented as evidence in a due process hearing. If you feel that the independent evaluation is also incorrect, you have no way to stop its being used by the school system or the hearing officer. In contrast, if you pay for the evaluation of your child, you determine how those results are used and who gets to see them. Thus, if you conclude that the results accurately describe your child, you may submit the results for consideration by the school system or a hearing officer. If you are not confident of the findings, you do not have to submit them to the school or at a hearing unless required to do so by the hearing officer.

Although there are many benefits to paying for your child's evaluation, you must weigh these benefits against several potential costs before deciding to have your own evaluation. One major cost is the dollar outlay itself. Complete educational evaluations may cost $800 or more. When the evaluation merely confirms the school's findings, it may still be beneficial—it gives more reason to believe the initial testing results—but it is an expensive procedure for securing such confirmation. Still another cost occurs if you introduce findings from your own specialists, and these findings are given little or no significance by school officials or the hearing officer. The reason sometimes given for downplaying the importance of such evaluation data is reflected in the comments made by one school official in a due process hearing. According to that school administrator, "Parents can shop around until they find a psychologist or other professional who will say exactly what they want to hear." If the school official or hearing officer with whom you are working has this attitude, the benefits of the evaluation you pay for may not equal their costs.

One last word about obtaining your own evaluations. Never have the evaluation results sent to school officials before you have examined them. On more than one occasion parents have done this to save time, only to discover that the evaluation results worked to their child's disadvantage. Therefore, discuss the evaluation findings with the professionals who developed them first. Then, and only then, decide whether you want the results sent to the school system or the hearing officer.

# FOUR-STEP RECORD DECODER

| Data | Source | Date |
|---|---|---|
| **MOVEMENT**<br>Strengths:<br><br>Problems: | | |
| **COMMUNICATIONS**<br>Strengths:<br><br>Problems: | | |
| **SOCIAL RELATIONSHIPS**<br>Strengths:<br><br>Problems: | | |
| **SELF-CONCEPT/INDEPENDENCE**<br>Strengths:<br><br>Problems: | | |

## FOUR-STEP RECORD DECODER

| Data | Source | Date |
|---|---|---|
| SENSES/PERCEPTION<br><br>Strengths:<br><br>Problems: | | |
| THINKING SKILLS<br><br>Strengths:<br><br>Problems: | | |
| LEARNING STYLE<br><br>Strengths:<br><br>Problems: | | |
| RECOMMENDATIONS: | | |

# FOUR-STEP RECORD DECODER

| Data | Source | Date |
|---|---|---|
| **MOVEMENT** | | |
| Strengths: 1. She can catch a bounced ball. 2. She can kick a stationary ball. 3. Walks forward on a four foot walking board. | 1-3) Mr. Terrance, Adaptive P.E. Specialist | 1/97 |
| Problems: 1. fine motor—trouble drawing and integrating complicated figures. 2. gross motor—large for her age; gives appearance of being uncoordinated. 3. difficulty in integrating motor skills to form motor plan act. | 1-2) Mrs. Lothian, psychological test  3) Mr. Terrance, P.E. | 1/97  2/96 |
| **COMMUNICATIONS** | | |
| Strengths: 1. Sara has significant improvement in syntax. 2. She eagerly participates in class using appropriate vocabulary. | 1) Mrs. Find, Speech Therapist  2) Ms. Chase, spec. ed. teacher report | 6/97  6/97 |
| Problems: 1. The problem may be in processing or word finding. 2. There is a lag in expressive language—difficulty expressing ideas. 3. Poor word finding, sequencing, auditory memory, and association skills. | 1) County Health Dept. Report  2) Ms. Lacey, spec. ed. teacher report  3) Mrs. Find | 8/95  5/96  1/96 |
| **SOCIAL RELATIONSHIPS** | | |
| Strengths: 1. She seems happy, is generally accepted by classmates—has maintained friendships in school. 2. Sara is people oriented, although on an observing type basis. | 1) Ms. Chase, spec. ed. teacher report  2) Mrs. Lothian, psycho-logical test | 6/97  1/97 |
| Problems: 1. She frequently tells peers what to do, and makes negative comments about herself when she makes mistakes. | 1) Mrs. Lacey, spec. ed. teacher report | 5/96 |
| **SELF-CONCEPT/INDEPENDENCE** | | |
| Strengths: 1. She works well in a small, structured, positive environment and needs to continue to build a positive self image | 1) Ms. Chase, spec. ed. teacher report | 6/97 |
| Problems: 1. Sara's biggest difficulty is that she feels different, abnormal and rejected. 2. Extreme need for nurturance and to feel good about herself. | 1-2) Mrs. Lothian, psychological test | 1/97 |

## FOUR-STEP RECORD DECODER

| Data | Source | Date |
|---|---|---|
| SENSES/PERCEPTION<br>Strengths: 1. On Bender-Gestalt test she could copy figures and make them recogniz-able, despite difficulties she experienced with integration and distortions. | 1) Dr. Hackett, private psychologist | 3/97 |
| Problems: 1. She doesn't remember details from pictures she sees or stories she has read.<br>2. On Bender-Gestalt her planning is haphazard and unorganized, her production inconsistent. | 1) Ms. Chase, spec. ed. teacher report<br>2) Ms. Lothian, psychologi-cal test | 6/97<br>1/97 |
| THINKING SKILLS<br>Strengths: 1. In reading, her decoding skills are excellent, she has a good sight vocab.<br>2. She has learned addition and subtraction facts—is now learning 2's, 3's, 5's, and 10's in multiplication. | 1-2) Ms. Chase, spec. ed teacher report | 6/97 |
| Problems: 1. She has difficulty following multiple oral directions.<br>2. Her poor memory has caused problems with remembering math process. | 1-2) Ms. Chase, spec. ed. teacher's report | 6/97 |
| LEARNING STYLE<br>Strengths: 1. She needs a small, structured environment.<br>2. She is eager to complete her work but often perseverates on favorite assignments. | 1-2) Ms. Chase, spec. ed teacher report | 6/97 |
| Problems: 1. Her planning is haphazard and disorganized. | 1) Ms. Lothian, psychologi-cal test | 1/97 |
| RECOMMENDATIONS:<br>1. Help her break down oral and written directions: repeating them to her, and having her repeat them are helpful techniques.<br>2. In reading use sight approach, context clues, language experience stories. | 1) Ms. Lothian, psychologi-cal test<br>2) Ms. Lacey, spec. ed teacher | 1/97<br>1/97 |

# 5. THE ELIGIBILITY DECISION

## PASSPORT TO THE MAZE

**Y**ou have passed through the educational planning cycle's first two phases—referral and evaluation. You have gathered data at home and examined your child's school records with the Four-Step Record Decoder. Now comes phase three—eligibility. This is the part of the special education process where a multidisciplinary group determines whether your child's disability affects his learning to the extent that he will need special education.

The eligibility decision is made by a committee. The committee is known by different names in different states; for example, Eligibility Committee, Multidisciplinary Team (M-Team), Placement Advisory Committee (PAC), or Admission, Review, and Dismissal (ARD) Committee. The exact name for this committee and its composition and procedures will be found in your local or state regulations. Some states require, and many encourage, parent participation in the eligibility committee meeting. Whatever the practice in your school system, you will want to be involved in this important meeting.*

The procedure followed by the committee to determine your child's eligibility for special education is simple to describe in theory, and often impossible to describe in practice. In theory, here is how the committee operates. Most state regulations for special education include a series of definitions of disabilities. These definitions vary from state to state. Children who are served in special education programs are children:

    1. who have mental retardation, hearing impairments including deafness, speech or language impairments, visual impairments including blindness, serious emotional disturbance, orthopedic

impairments, autism, traumatic brain injury, other health impairments or specific learning disabilities, and

2. because of their disability require special education in order to benefit from their educational program.

For children ages 3-8, states have the option to use the term "developmental delay." This refers to children who have problems with the development of their physical, cognitive, communication, social/emotional, or adaptive skills.

The definitions of disabilities found in federal and state regulations are not always easy to understand. For example, mental retardation is defined in the federal regulations as "significantly subaverage general intellectual functioning, existing concurrently with deficits in adaptive behavior and manifested during the developmental period, which adversely affects a child's educational performance." If you don't understand this definition or any of the others, which may be equally obscure, ask the school professionals to translate them for you. A translation of the preceding definition of mental retardation might read as follows: "An IQ remaining below a score of 70 for several years. In addition to the low IQ score, the child also shows problems in language, social skills, and other behaviors, all of which have adversely affected the ability to learn."

Remember, if you don't understand the definition of the disability your child is believed to have, ask to have the definition clarified. You may be surprised to learn that school personnel are themselves sometimes uncertain as to the exact meaning of the definitions. If this is the case, it is important to keep asking until you find someone who can explain the definition to your satisfaction. This way you can ensure that your child's learning problems are accurately identified.

Each member of the eligibility committee receives copies of the evaluation reports and other relevant information contained in your child's official school file. The evaluation reports will either suggest the presence of one or more disabilities or imply the absence of conditions severe enough to require special education services. The job of the eligibility committee is to compare the results and conclusions of the evaluation against the definitions of the disabilities that qualify for special education services. If the results correspond with one or more of the definitions, your child will be eligible for special education services. If the committee concludes that the results of the evaluation do not meet the eligibility criteria, your child will be found ineligible for special education. In either case, you will be notified in writing of the committee's decision. If your child is found not eligible for services, you can appeal the committee's decision through due process procedures as described in Chapter 10.

If your child is found ineligible for services under the criteria for special education under IDEA, he may still be able to receive some services under Section 504 of the Rehabilitation Act or the Americans with Disabilities Act. See Chapter 11, which discusses the requirements of Section 504 and ADA.

# ▪ *ELIGIBILITY IN ACTION: A CASE STUDY* ▪

Robert Boswell is seven years old. When he was two, his parents first noticed that his development was slow. Robert always has taken longer and expended much more effort to learn most of the things his brothers and sisters seem to pick up with ease. He has speech problems and uses only short, simple sentences. From the time he entered school, he has received private speech lessons. Because of Robert's continuing problems in school, his teacher suggested he be evaluated for special services. Mr. and Mrs. Boswell agreed with the recommendation and signed permission for the evaluation to take place.

Tests of general intelligence showed Robert to have an IQ of 105. Other tests showed him to have difficulties in coordinating his eyes and hands when copying geometric figures; problems coordinating his hands to catch a ball and his feet to stand on one leg; and difficulty in remembering things he had heard or read. Academic achievement tests found Robert to be more than two years behind his peers in reading and arithmetic.

In the state where Robert lives, the regulations governing special education define specific learning disability as:

> "a disorder in one or more of the basic psychological processes involved in understanding or in using language, spoken or written, which may manifest itself in an imperfect ability to listen, think, speak, read, write, spell, or do mathematical calculations which adversely affects the child's educational performance. The term includes such conditions as visual-motor disorders, dyslexia, and developmental aphasia. The term does not include children who have learning problems which are primarily the result of visual, hearing, or motor disability, of mental retardation, of emotional disturbance, or of environmental, cultural, or economic disadvantage."

When the eligibility committee compared Robert's evaluation reports with the preceding definition, they found that the results matched the definition. He displayed problems in language, reading, and arithmetic. The evaluation results indicated he had difficulty copying various shapes and was unable to distinguish left from right. These and other results showed he had perceptual impairments, as well as problems with his movement or motor control. None of these problems could be explained by mental retardation. His IQ, at 105, was in the normal range. Emotional problems, visual or hearing deficits, or environmental, cultural, or economic disadvantages were not found to be the source of Robert's problems. All the signs of the evaluation pointed to language problems and perceptual difficulties. Robert was therefore declared eligible for special education services because of his specific learning disabilities.

Had Robert's IQ fallen below 70, his disability would probably have been identified as mental retardation. With an IQ in this range and the other characteristics found in the evaluation, his learning problems would have matched those in the definition for mental retardation given earlier in this chapter. He would still have been eligible for special services, but he would have been eligible because of his mental retardation rather than because he had specific learning disabilities.

In the preceding case, the child was found to have only one major disability. But what happens if evaluation results indicate that a child has two or more disabilities; for example, specific learning disabilities and emotional problems? Usually the eligibility committee will try to identify the primary disability responsible for inhibiting the child's educational growth. If both conditions contribute equally to the child's learning problems, the committee may declare that the child has multiple disabilities. The identification of the primary disability and the secondary problems will determine the types of special education and related services the child requires.

## ■ ROLE OF PARENTS AT THE ■ ELIGIBILITY MEETING*

School systems differ significantly in the extent to which they allow parents to participate in eligibility meetings. Some invite parents to attend the meeting, present their views, bring professionals who can give expert opinions, ask questions of committee members, and be present when the committee takes its final vote. At the other extreme are school systems that fail even to notify parents when the eligibility committee is going to consider their child's case.

Your state and local regulations describe the procedures your school system must use and the timelines it must follow. Regardless of how the regulations read, you should ask to be notified, preferably in writing, when the eligibility committee plans to meet. Most likely a specialist in a certain disability area, the coordinator of special education, or one of the professionals who tested your child will be designated the case manager. The case manager produces an overall picture of your child's educational needs from the individual team members' findings and often is the team's representative at the eligibility meeting. Ask that person to notify you of the eligibility committee's meeting time and place. Let him know you would like to discuss your opinions with the committee and participate with the committee as they make their decision.

The school system may balk at allowing you to sit with the committee as it discusses your child's case and makes its final decision. While you would hope public schools would not choose to work in such a closed manner, they still may do so. Federal and state laws tend not to require parent participation in final decisions on eligibility. The spirit of these laws, however, is one of openness and increased parent participation. Therefore, more and more school systems are opening eligibility meetings to parents and allowing them to present their opinions. In fact, some states' procedures combine the eligibility determination meeting with the Individualized Education Program meeting, thus requiring parent participation.

When you attend your child's eligibility meeting, you might want to take the following steps:

1. **Get another person—spouse, friend, or professional—to attend the meeting with you.** At the eligibility meeting you will find anywhere from four to ten school officials in attendance. If you attend by yourself, you may feel threatened and overwhelmed. You should acquaint the person accompanying you with what you plan to do at the meeting. That person should then make sure you do what you said you would do. He should also be another pair of ears at the meeting listening to what is going on and bringing to your attention any important points you may have missed. Be certain to inform the committee ahead of time that this person will be coming with you to the meeting.

2. **After the participants in the meeting introduce themselves and before the official business of the meeting gets underway, pass around a picture or two of your child for everyone to see.** Or, if possible, have your child briefly meet the committee members. Your goal is to help the committee realize that your child is more than a manila folder filled with papers and reports. You want the committee to know that this is a real person—your son or daughter—whose educational needs are in their hands.

3. **As the meeting opens, ask the chairperson what procedures will be used, who the voting members are, whether you may stay for the entire time including the deliberations and decision making, what the final outcomes from the meeting will be (i.e., will a decision on eligibility be made now or later), and when you will be informed officially of the decision.** This step is very important since it assures that everyone will proceed with the same expectations for the meeting, thus eliminating much confusion.

**4. Present your opinions to the committee in a statement which you have developed prior to the meeting.** Most of the material for your presentation may be drawn from the analyses you made using the Developmental Achievement Chart and the Four-Step Record Decoder.

    a. Begin with a carefully written opening statement in which you set forth your conclusions regarding your child's disability and cite all relevant evaluations and records supporting your point of view.

    b. Describe your child's learning style as well as the developmental problems related to his disabilities.

    c. Refute or explain, where necessary, contradictory data, biases, etc. that you have found in the evaluations and records.

    d. Identify the special education program and services you believe are required to meet your child's learning needs and to build on his learning strengths. Again, cite relevant evaluations and reports supporting these recommendations.

    **5. In many instances you may wish to bring to the meeting professionals, teachers, and others who have worked with and know your child.** Prior to the meeting talk with these people to find out how their opinions and views would add to your case. Ask them to come if you think it would help. You would then develop your presentation to allow them to discuss their views at the appropriate times. Inform the school professional in charge of the meeting that these experts will be accompanying you.

    **6. Finally, if you can stay during the committee's deliberations, listen carefully to the committee's discussion.** If committee members appear to be using biased, inaccurate, incomplete, or out-of-date material or to be making incorrect statements, intervene and explain your concerns. Always remember that diplomacy and tact throughout the meeting will serve you well.

# ▪ POINTS OF CONTENTION IN THE ▪ ELIGIBILITY MEETING

Two major points of contention can arise between parents and school systems as a result of eligibility meetings. One problem occurs if the committee finds the child ineligible for services and the parents believe the child is eligible. The other problem surfaces if the committee finds the child eligible, but says the child's disability is something different from what the parents believe it is. For example, the committee may conclude that a child's primary disability is emotional disturbance, but the parents feel that it is a learning disability. Or the committee may conclude that the child has mental retardation, while the parents believe his hearing impairment is the major cause of his learning problems.

For parents and children, either of the preceding problems is serious. Both could possibly lead to ineffective educational programming that does not address the child's unique needs and strengths. Therefore, parents should participate actively in the eligibility meeting and not wait for such difficulties to occur before entering the special education maze. By following the suggestions made to this point, you will often be able to head off conflicts. And if that is accomplished, you are halfway through the maze. If, despite your active participation, either of these problems does occur, you may challenge the eligibility committee's findings through a conciliatory conference or administrative review within the school system or through an impartial due process hearing. (More about these procedures in Chapter 9.) But don't forget, if your child is declared ineligible for services, or if you feel the committee has labeled your child incorrectly, you do not have to accept these results. You can appeal these decisions.

## ■ *A Final Look at Evaluation and Eligibility* ■

Evaluation and eligibility determination are key phases in the special education cycle. An accurate, perceptive evaluation will pinpoint your child's specific learning problems and often may identify the causes of those difficulties. A valid evaluation, therefore, is essential to a fair and reliable determination of your child's eligibility to receive special education services.

Evaluation results, unfortunately, do not always provide clear, precise insights into your child's learning problems and their causes. When this is the case, the eligibility meeting takes on an even greater importance in your child's educational future. During this meeting, school professionals will review evaluation results, other records, and verbal testimony.* They will then interpret what this often confusing information means for your child's future educational placement. You cannot allow this meeting and these decisions to take place without your active participation. By following the previous suggestions for obtaining and interpreting school records, for evaluation troubleshooting, and for participating in the eligibility meeting, you will be able to exert maximum personal influence in the decision-making process. You will have an active voice in your child's educational planning, and, even if your opinion does not prevail, your systematic planning for the meeting will lay the groundwork for seeking a remedy through the appeals procedures described in Chapter 9.

# 6. The Individualized Education Program
## Road Maps, Sign Posts, One-Way Streets

**Y**ou have gained your passport to the maze! With the help of the valuable information you developed by observing your child and analyzing her school records, you have successfully passed through the referral, evaluation, and eligibility stages. Now you turn a corner into another corridor of the special education maze. In this corridor, you will begin planning for the specific special education and related services to be included in your child's education program. Here again, you will use your written materials to provide information for your child's Individualized Education Program, or IEP.

## ■ What Is an IEP? ■

An Individualized Education Program (IEP) describes the special education and related services specifically designed to meet the needs of a child with disabilities. The program is developed at one or more IEP meetings, and its provisions are detailed in writing in an IEP planning document. In this chapter you will find a description of the IEP *document*—the written plan for your child's own special education program. The six required parts of an IEP are outlined and examples illustrating ways in which parents can contribute to each of the parts are provided. The concepts of least restrictive environment and appropriate education are also discussed. Chapter 7 explores the various aspects of the IEP *meeting*, including when and how the IEP is developed, procedures followed during the IEP meeting, and alternative approaches for participating in creating your child's Individualized Education Program.

# ▪ THE IEP WRITTEN DOCUMENT ▪

As a parent, you play a vital role in developing the IEP planning document—the written description of the program tailored to fit your child's unique educational needs. The IEP is developed *jointly* by parents, educators, and, often, the person for whom the plans are being made, your *child*. Goals and objectives for your child, based on her current levels of functioning, are outlined by everyone involved in planning and providing services. The IEP specifies the educational placement, or setting, and the related services necessary to reach those goals and objectives. The IEP also includes the date the services will begin, how long they will last, and the way in which your child's progress will be measured.

The IEP is more than an outline of, and management tool for, your child's special education program. The development of the IEP gives you the opportunity to work with educators as equal participants to identify your child's needs, what will be provided to meet those needs, and what the anticipated outcomes may be. It is a commitment in writing of the resources the school agrees to provide. Periodic review of the IEP serves as an evaluation of your child's progress toward meeting the educational goals and objectives jointly decided upon by you and the teachers. Finally, the IEP serves as the focal point for resolving differences you may have with the school system. For all of these reasons, the Individualized Education Program—both the document and the process through which it is developed—is a crucial part of special education. Indeed, the IEP is the cornerstone of special education. Following is a description of the document itself and what it contains.

# ▪ IEP PART 1: A DESCRIPTION OF THE CHILD ▪

The first component of the IEP answers the question, "Who is this child?" After all, everyone involved in your child's education must come to know the person described in her written program. Basic identifying information, such as name, age, and address, is included. This section of the IEP also contains a description of your child as she is right now. It shows her current level of educational and behavioral performance and describes the effect of her disability on academic and non-academic achievements.[*] This information is written in a space on the IEP document labeled *Present Level of Functioning and Academic Performance,* or simply *Present Level,* or something similar, depending upon your local school system's IEP format.

You have already collected information necessary to contribute to a description of your child's present level of performance. In Chapter 2, Strengthening Exercise #2, you filled out a column in the Developmental Achievement Chart labeled *Can Do* in each of the developmental areas. In Chapter 4, in the Four-Step Record Decoder, you recorded *strengths* and accomplishments in each developmental area. The *Can Do* and *Strengths* are the information sources for your child's present level of functioning. The following chart presents examples parents have gathered from each source.

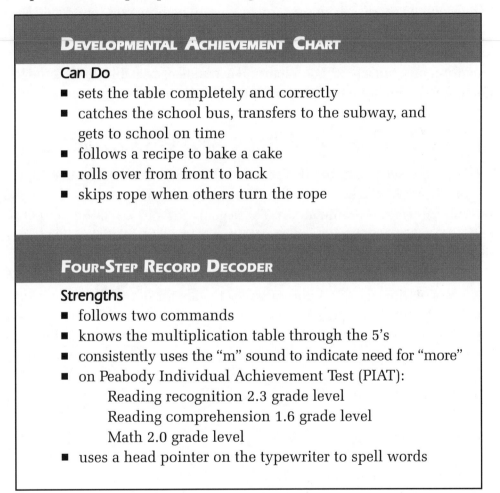

**DEVELOPMENTAL ACHIEVEMENT CHART**

**Can Do**
- sets the table completely and correctly
- catches the school bus, transfers to the subway, and gets to school on time
- follows a recipe to bake a cake
- rolls over from front to back
- skips rope when others turn the rope

**FOUR-STEP RECORD DECODER**

**Strengths**
- follows two commands
- knows the multiplication table through the 5's
- consistently uses the "m" sound to indicate need for "more"
- on Peabody Individual Achievement Test (PIAT):
    Reading recognition 2.3 grade level
    Reading comprehension 1.6 grade level
    Math 2.0 grade level
- uses a head pointer on the typewriter to spell words

Besides providing information about your child's development, in Part 1 of the IEP you have the opportunity to contribute your very important information about your child's unique learning style. Be sure to include written descriptions of your child's way of approaching a learning situation. A new teacher may need weeks or months to discover the way in which your child learns best. You can help the teacher and your child avoid some frustrations by including in the "present level" such descriptions as:

- He needs a quiet, secluded place for concentrated work.
- She learns quickly when working in a small group of children.
- He understands and learns better what he hears rather than what he sees.
- She imitates other children and learns from them.

These descriptions of *Can Do, Strengths, and Learning Style* are the substance of the first part of the IEP. Listing test scores, numerical attainment of grade level, IQ score, age equivalent, or simply naming your child's disability is insufficient. Descriptive statements are required in order for everyone involved in teaching your child to know her. The description of her present level of performance must be as complete and accurate as possible, for it is the foundation upon which the second part of the IEP, goals and objectives, is built.

# ■ *IEP PART 2: GOALS AND OBJECTIVES* ★ ■

In the second section of the IEP, you and the other members of the IEP team set goals and objectives that will help your child master the skills or behaviors you believe she should attain. These goals and objectives for your child's special education program are based upon her present level of functioning described in Part 1 of the IEP.

Before thinking about goals and objectives for your child, a look at the process of setting goals is in order. We set goals for ourselves and for others all the time. What are goals? Simply stated, goals are results to be achieved. You set goals for what you would like to do. You might set a goal to buy a new car, to lose ten pounds, to take a family vacation, or to plant a vegetable garden. In order to set specific goals, you must answer many questions. For example, to plan a vacation you might consider:

- *Who* will go with you? The whole family? Should we invite the grandparents?
- *What* will you do? Go camping? Visit relatives? Swim in the ocean?
- *How* will you get there? By car? By bus?
- *Where* will you go? To the mountains? To the beach?
- *When* will you go and how long will you stay? Early summer? Late summer? To stay forever?

After you and your family have made these decisions, you could write the following goal for your vacation plans:

**Goal:** My family will drive to the mountains to camp for one week beginning August 4.

This goal for a family vacation contains five necessary ingredients or parts. It answers *who? will do what? how? where?* and *when?* These five basic parts are necessary for all clearly stated goals.

In order to reach the goal of the family camping vacation, you must take many smaller steps. You choose a state park to camp in, arrange annual leave from your job, borrow a tent, find a kennel for Rover, and take many other interim steps to make it possible to go to the mountains. These smaller steps are *objectives.*

Goals and objectives for an IEP are structured much the same as described above. Goals are an expression of results to be achieved in the long run; objectives are the intermediate steps necessary to reach the long-range goals. Annual goals written on an IEP state what your child is expected to do in one year. Each goal must be written as:

1. a positive statement that . . .
2. describes an observable event.

A well-written goal not only tells what skill your child will achieve but also is written in such a way that you and others can observe the achievement. Many IEPs contain vague goals whose outcomes are not observable or measurable.

### Poorly Written Goals:

- Bonnie Jean will improve her self-concept.
- Edward will communicate better.
- Jamie will grow stronger.
- Kevin will learn to write.
- Nina will be cooperative.

None of these poorly written goals fulfills both criteria of being: (1) a positive statement that (2) describes an observable skill. None of these poorly written goals contains the five essential parts:

- Who? . . . will achieve?
- What? . . . skill or behavior?
- How? . . . in what manner or at what level?
- Where? . . . in what setting or under what conditions?
- When? . . . by what time? an ending date?

A well-written goal contains all five parts.

### Well-written Goals:

- Edward will use sign language to ask for help in his classroom and speech therapy by June 30.
- Nina will prepare and present an oral report in social studies with two general education classmates by May 7.

Each of these well-written goals is a positive statement describing an observable skill. They answer the questions of who? will do what? how? where? and when? When goals and objectives are written carefully and specifically, you and everyone else involved in teaching your child will hold the same expectations for her.

As mentioned above, objectives are intermediate steps taken to reach the long-range goal. Just as there are specific interim tasks necessary to make your vacation run smoothly, there are small steps or accomplishments your child needs to make in order to reach the annual goals written on her IEP. Short-term objectives are the steps to be taken between the "present level of performance" and the "annual goal." Short-term objectives contain the same five basic parts as annual goals—the who, what, how, where, and when.

An example of a well-written goal, based upon the present level of performance, with appropriate short-term objectives, is found below. This goal, written by Jamie's parents and teachers, is in the developmental category of movement.

### Annual Goal:
Jamie will walk upstairs, using one foot per tread, without assistance, at home and at school, by June 1.

### Present Level of Performance:
Jamie walks steadily on flat ground but goes up the stairs on her hands and knees.

### Objective:
Jamie will walk upstairs with two feet per tread, holding the handrail and an adult's hand, by October 15.

### Objective:
Jamie will walk upstairs with two feet per tread, holding only the handrail, by December 1.

### Objective:
Jamie will walk upstairs one foot per tread, holding the handrail and an adult's hand, by March 15.

The goal and each of the objectives fulfill the requirements for well-written goals and objectives. They describe milestones for Jamie's accomplishment that can be observed within a specific timeframe as she works toward the goal of climbing stairs unassisted.

You may have many questions as you think about goals and objectives for your child. For example:

**1. How can I know if a goal is reasonable to expect of my child? Does it demand too much or not enough of her?** The answer to this question lies in part with the IEP meeting. At the IEP meeting, a group of people, including parents, specialists, and past and present teachers who are knowledgeable of the child and knowledgeable of child development and disabilities, are brought together to discuss reasonable expectations. Goals are set while looking at present levels of performance—what she can do now—at the rate your child has been developing thus far, and at the sequence and timing of normal growth and development. These considerations are helpful in setting appropriate goals and short-term objectives. You, or the teacher, do not have to set goals and objectives alone. A group works together.

**2. How do goals and objectives in the IEP relate to the instructional plans of educational personnel?** There should be a direct relationship between the IEP goals and objectives for a specific child, and the instruction, or curriculum, the child is receiving in the classroom. The IEP, however, is not intended to be as detailed as an instructional plan. The IEP is to provide the general direction that is to be taken and serves as the basis for the instructional plan for each child.

**3. Must goals and objectives be written on the IEP for the parts of her program in the general education classroom?** Generally, goals and objectives are required only for special education services. Goals and objectives cover those areas of development in which your child has special problems. If any changes or modifications are necessary for your child to participate in a general education program, however, those modifications must be described in the IEP. This requirement applies to all regular classes in which your child might enroll—vocational education, social studies, science, art, music, and physical education. For example, a child who has a visual impairment may need to use a tape recorder in a lecture class, or sit close to the lecturer. This adaptation must be noted in her IEP.

A related question is whether the regular teacher is required to be informed of the contents of a student's IEP.* The policy of the U.S. Department of Education states that the general education classroom teacher should have a copy of the IEP, or at the very least be informed of its contents.* In some instances school systems have gone beyond the minimum requirements. They require the general education teacher to participate in the development of the IEPs for special education students in their classrooms. At the very least, parents should

---

\* "Department of Education Policy Interpretation: IEP Requirements," *Federal Register,* March 31, 1981.

request the active participation of the general education teachers. In addition, the school system should provide time for the special educator or other specialist to consult or give assistance to the regular classroom teacher.

In practice, school districts vary as to how much information flows between regular teachers and special education teachers. As parents, you will want to talk to each of your child's teachers to make sure they are informed of her educational needs. You may find it necessary to request a joint conference with all of your child's teachers and specialists in order to coordinate the various aspects of the IEP.

**4. Is it necessary for parents to learn to write goals and objectives?**
Some parents have found they are able to acquire this skill by understanding the essential requirements for writing goals and objectives and by applying them to their child. Other parents prefer to leave the actual writing of goals and objectives to the educators who have the training and experience to develop them. They are careful, however, to know in which developmental areas they feel their child needs special attention. Knowing how goals and objectives are structured, they are able to critique and offer suggestions concerning the goals and objectives written by the educators. In either case, the better you understand the nature of goals and objectives and your child's abilities and problems, the more effective you will be as a member of the educational planning team. With your help, goals and objectives can be written very specifically for your child's needs and can allow you and her teachers to assess her rate of growth and her developmental progress.

# ▪ IEP PART 3: RELATED SERVICES ▪

In addition to the goals and objectives for your child's special education program, the IEP describes related services to be provided at no cost to you, the parents. Related services supplement the educational services provided in the classroom. They must be designed to assist the child with a disability to benefit from special education in the least restrictive environment.* The regulations which implement IDEA define related services. These developmental, corrective, or other supportive services might include, but are not limited to, one or more of the following:

## ASSISTIVE TECHNOLOGY

IDEA defines an assistive technology device as "any item, piece of equipment, or product system, whether acquired commercially off the shelf, modified, or customized, that is used to increase, maintain, or improve functional capabilities of individuals with disabilities." Assistive technology service is "any service that directly assists an individual with a disability in the selection, acquisition, or use of an assistive technology device." Examples of assistive devices include language boards, a special chair, a voice output computer, and a head pointer. As assistive devices become more and more available for people with disabilities, schools are faced with decisions to: a) identify and acquire technology devices appropriate to the needs of their students with disabilities; b) train staff in the use of the devices; c) identify appropriate use of computers, communication devices, and other technology in the classroom; and d) finance the cost of the related service.

## AUDIOLOGY

Audiology services are generally provided by audiologists who screen, assess, and identify children with hearing loss. Additionally, they:

1. determine the range, nature, and degree of the hearing loss;
2. make referrals for medical or other professional attention for the improvement of hearing;
3. provide for language improvement, auditory training, speech or lip reading, speech conservation, and other programs;
4. determine the child's need for group or individual amplification, select and fit an appropriate hearing aid, and evaluate the effectiveness of amplification.

Based on the results of the hearing assessment, audiological services are provided by school-based audiologists or by other professionals such as speech pathologists or educators.

## COUNSELING SERVICES

School counselors work with students to improve their behavioral adjustment and their self-control, to develop their career awareness, and to improve their understanding of themselves. The goal is to make students with disabilities better able to participate in the educational program. The school counselor may also:

1. identify and refer students who may be eligible for special education;
2. secure parental permission for referral and evaluation.

## MEDICAL SERVICES

Licensed physicians provide these services to determine if a child's medically related disabling condition results in the need for special education and related services. Medical services under IDEA are limited to diagnostic services and do not include such activities as routine visits to the pediatrician, immunizations, and surgical correction of problems.

## OCCUPATIONAL THERAPY *

Occupational therapists assess and treat disabilities in children that impair their daily life functioning. Treatment is provided to strengthen and develop fine motor functions; to build the working of muscles such as in the face, arms, hand, and upper trunk; and to perform tasks for independent functioning, such as eating, placement of the tongue and mouth for speech formation, eye-hand coordination, and manual dexterity.

Occupational therapists work in such areas as:

1   activities of daily living, such as hearing and dressing;
2. school and work skills, such as writing, using scissors, managing books and papers, and sitting and paying attention in the classroom;
3. skills in play and leisure, such as participating in art and physical education or playing with children at recess.

## PARENT COUNSELING AND TRAINING

Parent counseling addresses the needs of the parents of a child with disabilities and recognizes the vital role they play in the education and development of the child. Counselors can assist parents in understanding the special needs of their child; provide information about child development; and refer parents to support groups, to resources for financial assistance, and to professionals outside of the school system.

## PHYSICAL THERAPY

Qualified physical therapists assist students with their physical activities and development. Physical therapy generally concentrates on gross motor functioning as it relates to postural control and daily living routines. Sitting, standing, moving, and sensory processing are examples of skills that can be improved by physical therapy.

## PSYCHOLOGICAL SERVICES

School psychologists provide services to students by:

1. administering psychological and educational tests and other assessment procedures;
2. interpreting assessment results;
3. obtaining, integrating, and interpreting information about child behavior and conditions relating to learning;

4. consulting with other staff members in planning school programs to meet the special needs of children as indicated by psychological tests, interviews, and behavioral evaluations; and
5. planning and managing a program of psychological services, including psychological counseling for children and parents.

## RECREATION

Recreation services, provided by a recreation therapist, physical education teacher, or general education teacher, include:

1. assessment of leisure or play skills;
2. therapeutic recreation services;
3. recreation programs in schools and community agencies; and
4. leisure education.

## REHABILITATIVE COUNSELING SERVICES

Rehabilitative counseling services are provided by qualified personnel in individual or group sessions and focus specifically on career development, employment preparation, achieving independence, and integration in the workplace and community of a student with a disability. The term also includes vocational rehabilitation services provided to students with disabilities by vocational rehabilitation programs funded under the Rehabilitation Act of 1973, as amended.

## SCHOOL HEALTH SERVICES

School health services are provided by a qualified school nurse or other qualified professional. They can include giving routine medications or clearing a breathing passage for a student with cystic fibrosis.

## SOCIAL WORK SERVICES IN SCHOOLS

School social workers assist students and families by:

1. preparing a social or developmental history on a child with disabilities;
2. providing group and individual counseling for the child and family;
3. working with problems in a child's living situation (home, school, and community) that affect the child's adjustment in school; and
4. coordinating school and community resources to enable the child to receive maximum benefit from his or her educational program.

## SPEECH PATHOLOGY

Speech and language therapists are responsible for:

1. identification of children with speech or language disorders;
2. diagnosis and appraisal of specific speech or language disorders;
3. referral for medical or other professional attention necessary for the improvement of speech or language disorders;
4. providing speech and language services for the improvement or prevention of communicative impairments; and
5. counseling and guidance of parents, children, and teachers regarding speech and language impairments.

## TRANSPORTATION

Schools are responsible for students':

1. travel to and from school and between schools;
2. travel in and around school buildings; and
3. specialized equipment (such as special or adapted buses, lifts, and ramps), if required to provide special transportation for a child with disabilities.

In the same way that present level of performance, goals, and objectives are individually determined for children during the IEP process, so, too, are related services. Goals and objectives are required for all special education services, including related services. If your child has been declared eligible for related services such as speech therapy or a special adaptive physical education program, goals and objectives must be written in each specialized area. "Bonnie Jean will receive speech therapy" or "Bonnie Jean will be in adaptive P.E." are not acceptable ways to describe the services. Goals must be written to describe what she will accomplish in language or physical development. For example, if Bonnie Jean's present level of performance in language describes her use of two-word phrases, an example of a goal might be: "Bonnie Jean will speak in three-word sentences using noun, verb, object construction in the classroom and speech therapy by May 15." This goal, built on her present level of functioning, alerts all teachers and her parents to work consistently toward the next step in her growth in communication skills.

Once you and school people have determined through the evaluation process that your child needs certain related services and have included them in the IEP, the school system has a legal duty to provide those services in the least restrictive environment. This duty exists even when the particular related services are not, for any reason, currently available within the school system. For example, if physical therapy, social work services, or speech therapy were not provided by school employees but your child needed them to benefit from her program, the school system would have to provide these services by contracting with outside professionals.

As you think about possible related services the school might provide your child, many questions will probably arise. What kinds of services are needed? For what length of time each day or week? Who will provide the services? How can I ensure that my child does not have to leave the classroom to receive related services so often that it interrupts her regular school program? How can I make certain that therapists and teachers talk together so there is consistency in my child's program?

To answer these questions, you will need to discuss your child and her needs with teachers, therapists, administrators, and other school personnel. You may also find it helpful to consult specialists outside the school system, discuss your child's need for related services with physicians, and talk to other parents whose children require similar services. Information and materials on related services available from the professional and other organizations listed in Appendix C may also assist you in answering these questions.

After you have accumulated information from a variety of sources, you will be able to weigh and balance the needs of your child for related services, the different ways and times for integrating services into your child's program, and the potential benefits your child will receive from those services. In this manner you can determine your priorities for your child's related services as you prepare for and participate in the IEP meeting.

## ▪ *IEP PART 4: SPECIAL EDUCATION PLACEMENT* ▪

It is all well and good to have specific goals and objectives for your child— but goals and objectives are not enough! Next come decisions concerning placement. Part 4 of the IEP describes the special education placement to be provided your child. Placement refers to the educational setting in which the goals and objectives for your child's special education and related services may appropriately be met. If this placement is in a resource room or separate class, the IEP must also state the amount of participation your child will have in the general education classroom.

In years past, children with special education needs were placed in classrooms solely on the basis of disability groupings. For example, all children who used wheelchairs to move about were placed in the same classroom.

Similarly, students who had learning problems associated with Down syndrome or other mental retardation were automatically grouped with students with the same disabilities. The IEP requirements under IDEA call for changes in the ways children are grouped. The IEP focuses the attention of parents, teachers, administrators, and therapists on *ability* as well as on disability. Goals and objectives are formulated in order to use the student's learning strengths to overcome or compensate for the disabilities. Clearly, the intent of IDEA is to determine a student's placement only after the IEP goals and objectives have been worked out mutually with parents, educators, and, whenever possible, the student. The placement decision is then made on the basis of the strengths and needs of the student, by choosing a learning environment in which the educational goals and objectives can appropriately be carried out. But, you ask, on what criteria is this placement decision based? Two equally important factors must be weighed and balanced as you participate in making the placement decision:

1. the appropriate educational program, and
2. the least restrictive environment.

Bold language in the original P.L. 94-142, now the Individuals with Disabilities Education Act (IDEA), heralds these two provisions which are the heart of the opportunities for our nation's children with disabilities.

"It is the purpose of this Act to assure that all children with disabilities have available to them . . . a free, appropriate public education which emphasizes special education and related services designed to meet their unique needs. To the maximum extent appropriate, children with disabilities, including children in public or private institutions or other care facilities, are educated with children who are not disabled."

## WHAT IS APPROPRIATE EDUCATION?

What exactly is meant by the words "appropriate education"? How will you know if your child is receiving an *appropriate education?*

For years parents, educators, and even judges have disagreed as to what is required under the law to meet the standard of an appropriate education. In 1982 the U.S. Supreme Court provided some clarification when it concluded that an "appropriate education" means the provision of personalized instruction with sufficient therapies or specialized services reasonably calculated to permit a child with disabilities to "benefit from special education." While programs and services that provide only *minimal* academic achievement do not meet the requirement of an appropriate education, the

Supreme Court stated that an "appropriate education" did not require programs and services designed to *maximize* a child's potential. Some state legislative standards may exceed the federal requirements. It is important to check your own state's requirements for what is an "appropriate education."

The Supreme Court's clarification is important for you because it reinforces the idea that an appropriate education is personalized to the individual needs of your child. Children in special education are not to be given identical programs just because they have the same disabilities. Further, an appropriate program requires that your child receive programming and services that are reasonably calculated to permit her to benefit from them. This means that the proposed program and services must be designed in terms of content, procedures, and duration to lead to the student's continuing development. Finally, a program which would appear to result in only minimal academic achievement would fail to meet the standard of an appropriate program.

The planning activities you have completed for evaluation, eligibility, and the development of IEP goals and objectives will help you to develop the personalized education program to which your child is entitled. Your close work and contact with teachers and other school professionals during these activities will allow you to determine whether your child's program and services will reasonably allow her to make more than minimal progress in the coming year. As the year progresses, you will be able to assess the appropriateness of the program by comparing your child's development with anticipated goals and objectives. Should your child's progress appear minimal or nonexistent after a period of months, you may well question the appropriateness of the program. This situation might call for a special meeting of the IEP committee, as will be discussed in the next chapter.

## LEAST RESTRICTIVE ENVIRONMENT (LRE) AND INCLUSION

Once you have designed an appropriate program for your child, you must next determine the "least restrictive environment" in which this program can be provided. The least restrictive environment for a child with disabilities is defined by the extent to which the child will be educated with students who do not have disabilities and in the school building nearest to home. *

Rather than being in separate special education classrooms or a separate school with special teachers, more and more children with disabilities are now being included in general education classrooms in their home schools. The special education teachers and specialists work alongside the general education teachers. In integrated classrooms, all children—both the children with disabilities and those who do not have disabilities—enjoy friendships and the opportunity to learn from one another. Further, following graduation from school, young people with disabilities are more often ready to move into community jobs and independent living if they have had opportunities to work and learn with their nondisabled peers.

In addition, IDEA and Section 504 of the Rehabilitation Act require opportunities for students with disabilities to participate in all nonacademic and extracurricular activities on a nondiscriminatory basis and in the least restrictive environment. These activities include meals, recess, athletics, assemblies, and special interest groups and clubs. You will want to make sure your child is able to take advantage of these activities with children who do not have disabilities. Chapter 11 discusses the provisions of Section 504 and the Americans with Disabilities Act as they pertain to children's extracurricular activities.

Many school systems, advocacy groups, and families now emphasize that *all* students with disabilities can be successfully placed in a general education learning environment if appropriate modifications and related services are provided. This move to educate all children in the general education setting is often called "inclusion," or sometimes, "supportive inclusive education." IDEA, however, requires school systems to provide a "continuum of alternative placements" to meet the special education and related services needs of individual children. School districts are required to offer a variety of settings in which a child with disabilities may be placed. These settings range along a continuum from general class placement, to resource room assistance, to separate classrooms, to private schools, to residential facilities, hospitals, homebound instruction, and correctional or detention facilities.

When determining the least restrictive placement for children eligible for *preschool* programs, the options are somewhat different. As in all placement decisions, the overriding rule is to determine what is appropriate for each individual child. If a school district has any programs for preschool aged children who do not have disabilities, the district is required to consider placing the children with disabilities in these classes. If the district does not have general education preschool, the IEP team first considers placement in other public preschools, such as Head Start or publicly run daycare. Sometimes, the least restrictive placement for a child can be in a private preschool, with the school system providing support services to the child as needed. Any public preschool special education class should be located in a regular elementary school, to give the preschoolers with developmental delays or disabilities the opportunity for education with children who do not have disabilities.

An IEP team, using the concept of a continuum of alternative placements, must go through a series of steps to arrive at a recommended placement.

After formulating the IEP goals and objectives, the first question to be answered is, "What are the specific services needed by the student?" The question of *what* services are needed comes before the second question, which is, "In what place can these services best be provided?"

A discussion then focuses on the question, "Is the general education classroom, with no changes or modifications, the place where the services can be provided?" If "yes," then that is the placement. If "no," then the consideration becomes, "How can the general education classroom be modified with supplementary services or aids to accommodate the student and the services?" At each level of the continuum of placements, the questions are asked, "Is this level, with no changes or modifications, the place where the services can be provided?" If not, "Can this level be changed or modified with supplementary services or aids to accommodate this student and the services she needs?"

The IEP team must always strive to keep the student at the highest level possible and, therefore, with the greatest opportunity to be educated with other students who do not have disabilities. The *burden* lies with the school system to prove why your child, with or without aids and supports, cannot receive appropriate, individualized education in the general education classroom in your neighborhood school. An LRE Worksheet is on page 92.

For the first three years of school, for example, Juanita was placed in a separate classroom for children with mental retardation. Her parents and the school people decided that this placement was too restrictive. Now Juanita is in the general education classroom with children her own age. She has a resource teacher come into the classroom to give her special help in reading and math. In all other subjects she participates with her class. The classroom aide is there to help both Juanita and all of the other children as well. Juanita's program was based on the two requirements of IDEA:

1. **The Appropriate Educational Program.** The IEP goals and objectives include academic achievements, physical milestones, and social/emotional growth. Juanita will receive the resource service of a special education teacher thirty minutes every day to assist her in reading and math.

2. **The Least Restrictive Environment.** Juanita's goals and objectives can be realized in the general education program, which provides maximum time for Juanita in a classroom with children who do not have disabilities. She will not be separated from her classmates who do not have disabilities for any of her academic, social, or extracurricular activities.

## LEAST RESTRICTIVE ENVIRONMENT (LRE) WORKSHEET *

### Part 1—Primary Placement

❑ Can the child's needs be met in the general education class without any additional support?          ❑ Yes  ❑ No

❑ Can the child's needs be met in the general education class with additional supports or modifications?          ❑ Yes  ❑ No

❑ Can the child's needs be met in the next, more segregated class with services in place now?          ❑ Yes  ❑ No

❑ Can the child's needs be met in the next, more segregated class with additional supports or modifications?     ❑ Yes  ❑ No

Considering the continuum from least restrictive to most restrictive, the IEP team should ask and answer the last two questions above only until a "yes" answer is obtained.

Primary Placement _____

### Part 2—Additional Opportunities for Inclusion

Even after the primary placement is determined, consider additional opportunities for part-time integration. (List all that apply.)

❑ During the school day (at same school)

❑ At a different school

❑ After school

❑ Community activities

❑ Employment or job training opportunities

❑ Other _____
_____

* Adapted from Champagne, J., Decisions in Sequence: How to Make Placements in the Least Restrictive Environment, EDLAW Briefing Paper, Vol. II, Issues 9-10, March-April 1993.

In every special education placement for every child, the appropriate education and the least restrictive environment must be given equal consideration. Many people believe the least restrictive environment means that all children with disabilities will be put into the mainstream, or general education classroom. The least restrictive environment concept, however, must always be coupled with what is an appropriate education for each individual child.

Sally is a fourteen-year-old girl who has a disability which causes her to be in constant physical motion and to talk in a loud voice incessantly and inappropriately. The least restrictive environment for her is a special day class. Sally's IEP team decided that behavioral goals should be the primary focus of her IEP. Because she is so easily distracted, the IEP team believed she would most likely achieve her goals in a small, structured class, without the many distractions of the general education classroom. Her involvement with children who are not disabled is with peer tutors from general education classrooms, attendance at assembly programs, regular physical education, and daily lunch in the cafeteria.

Occasionally, public school systems find that they simply do not have the programs or services required to provide a child with an appropriate education. For example, a small rural school system might find it impossible to hire or to contract with professionals needed to deliver highly specialized programs. Even in situations like these, IDEA requires school systems to provide the child with a free, appropriate public education. But, how might the school system do this?

When there are no public programs within the state to meet the child's educational needs, school systems place children in private day or residential schools. These private placements are legally more restrictive than special schools in the public school system because they separate the child both from peers who are not disabled and from her public school classmates. According to IDEA, the private school placement is considered a last alternative placement in which a child is to receive special education. The law requires that before choosing this placement option, school officials and parents explore every way possible for delivering a free, appropriate education within the public school system.* If an appropriate education cannot be provided within the public schools or through other public institutions within the state, then the school system has a duty to provide the child with an appropriate education in a private school at no expense to the parents. If the local school system does not have the resources to provide an appropriate education according to the child's IEP, they must ask the State Education Agency to provide the services either directly or through a contract with an outside agency.

In this way the local school system will not offer an *inappropriate* IEP for an individual child.

Below are three examples of special education placements planned in IEP meetings for children.

**Example 1.** Robert will be in the general education classroom throughout the school day. The itinerant teacher for children with visual impairments will provide talking books, consultation with the teacher about classroom adaptations, and individualized instruction on a one-to-one basis for Robert.

**Example 2.** Martha's homeroom is the third grade classroom. She will participate in social studies, science, music, and art with her classmates. Reading, arithmetic, spelling, and handwriting goals will be met in a learning disabilities resource classroom. Special physical education will be provided by a teacher trained in working with people with physical disabilities.

**Example 3.** Claudia will attend a special school for children who are deaf. She will participate in a community recreation program where she is on the swimming team and she will be a member of a scout troop.

Although these three special education placements seem very different, they all fulfill two major requirements under IDEA. They are specifically designed to provide each particular child an appropriate education in the least restrictive environment.

## ▪ IEP PART 5: TIME AND ▪ DURATION OF SERVICES *

You have moved through four stops along the IEP corridor in the special education maze. The fifth stop guarantees you won't get stuck in one place. In this section of the IEP, the starting times and duration for your child's program are determined. Once the goals and objectives are written and the services decided upon, the school system has a duty to begin these services without undue delay. Most states specify the number of days within which a program must begin once parents have signed permission for the program. At no time is a child to wait at home for special education services to begin, unless an agreement has been reached between you and the school system for a temporary homebound program. Occasionally, a temporary or interim placement is required, to which parents and the school system must agree.

Under ordinary circumstances, a date is determined in the IEP meeting for the beginning of each of your child's services. In addition, the expected duration for each service is recorded. The expected duration might be six weeks for a related service of counseling with a social worker, to be followed by an assessment of progress and a recommendation for either continuing this service or ending it. Or the expected duration may be a nine-month school year for such parts of the program as classroom placement.

Some children with severe disabilities might require more than the usual number of school days in order to receive an appropriate education. Children eligible for an extended school year include those who show significant regression during breaks in their education and those who regain their losses so slowly that they would be unlikely to attain their potential level of self-sufficiency and independence without a sustained program. In each case, provision of additional schooling beyond the normal school year must be determined on an individual basis and written into the IEP.

In general, the long-term duration for services should be projected no further than one year. This is because IDEA requires an annual review of the services provided in the IEP. Once a year at the IEP meeting, your child's special education services are reviewed to determine whether they are still appropriate and are provided in the least restrictive environment. This annual review, discussed more fully in Chapter 11, ensures that no child will be left in special education without a careful examination of her changing needs.

In addition to specifying the long-term duration of your child's services, Part 5 of the IEP should also include short-term, daily hours for each service. For example, "Jessica will attend speech therapy twice a week, for one-half hour each session." Certainly, parents will want to get specific information on the times and timing of all parts of their child's school program. Too often children who receive special services miss some of the most important parts of the instruction in their classroom. For example, when Willie went to the learning disabilities resource room for special instruction in math, he missed his reading group in the general education classroom. He was falling behind in reading until his parents talked to his regular class teacher and the resource room teacher. As a result, both teachers adjusted their schedules in order to accommodate Willie's instruction in reading and in math.

## ▪ IEP PART 6: EVALUATING THE IEP ▪

How do you know if your child is making progress? To find out, you and your child's teachers periodically need to conduct evaluations to determine if short-term objectives are being met. Part 6 of the IEP—called "Objective criteria and evaluation procedures"—allows you to plan the dates these evaluations will take place and the evaluation procedures that will be used.[*]

The critical element in evaluation comes in writing clear, measurable, observable goals and objectives. When a goal such as "Suzy will improve self-esteem" is written, parents and teachers will be hard pressed to know when and how Suzy has arrived at this improved state of well-being. A specific annual goal for Suzy might be, "Suzy will demonstrate pleasure in her own accomplishments by planning and completing classroom projects on time by June 30." A short-term objective might be, "Suzy will choose two classmates with whom she will cooperatively plan and complete an art project to illustrate a story in the fifth-level reader, by January 14." To evaluate the objective, parents and teachers might ask the following questions:

1. Was the art project completed on time?
2. Did Suzy read and comprehend the story?
3. Did the teacher observe and note incidents to illustrate Suzy's cooperation with classmates?
4. What indications show that Suzy made plans for the project? What were the materials chosen? Who took responsibility for what parts of the project?
5. How did Suzy demonstrate pleasure in her accomplishments? Did she urge her parents to come to open house to see it? Was she eager to show and tell about the project?

Specific goals or objectives such as those written for Suzy allow parents and teachers to ask critical questions about a child's growth and development. When Suzy completes the objective, her parents and teachers could conclude that she would have good feelings about her school work, about herself, and about her relationships with her classmates.

At least once a year, and at any other time when a teacher or parent requests it, a meeting is held to review progress toward goals and objectives. Very often in the space on the IEP for "objective criteria and evaluation procedures" you will see written "teacher-made tests" or "teacher assessment." You may wish to inquire about these tests. What will they be? When will they be given? Are there other ways of measuring progress? Tape recordings, examples of schoolwork, classroom observations, completed projects, standardized tests, and many other techniques are useful in evaluation. By using information from a variety of sources, the teaching team comprised of teachers, specialists, and parents can measure progress in a student's growth and learning.

# ■ A Planning Chart for the IEP ■

Now that you have passed the five stops in the IEP corridor, you may wish to copy and complete the following chart to prepare for the upcoming IEP meeting. Concentrate on those areas of development in which your child has particular problems and needs special services to help in overcoming or compensating for those problems. In the first column, write a brief description of the problem, followed by the "Present Level of Functioning" in the second column. Columns three and four are spaces for your ideas for long-range goals and short-term objectives to help your child with the problem. In the fifth column you can note the special education and related services that you believe can best help your child reach those objectives. Finally, the sixth column provides a space for your ideas for checking progress on the goals and objectives. Following the blank chart, you will find an example of an IEP Planning Chart filled out by Sara's parents before they attended her IEP meeting. A sample of Sara's IEP is found on pages 102-103.

# ■ Conclusion ■

Once your planning is completed, you will be well prepared to attend the IEP meeting. The work you have done in filling out the IEP Planning Chart will lay the foundation for your active, informed participation in the important decisions to be made about your child's education. The next chapter will show you how best to use your valuable insights into your child's growth, development, and learning style so you and your child's teachers can plan an appropriate special education program.

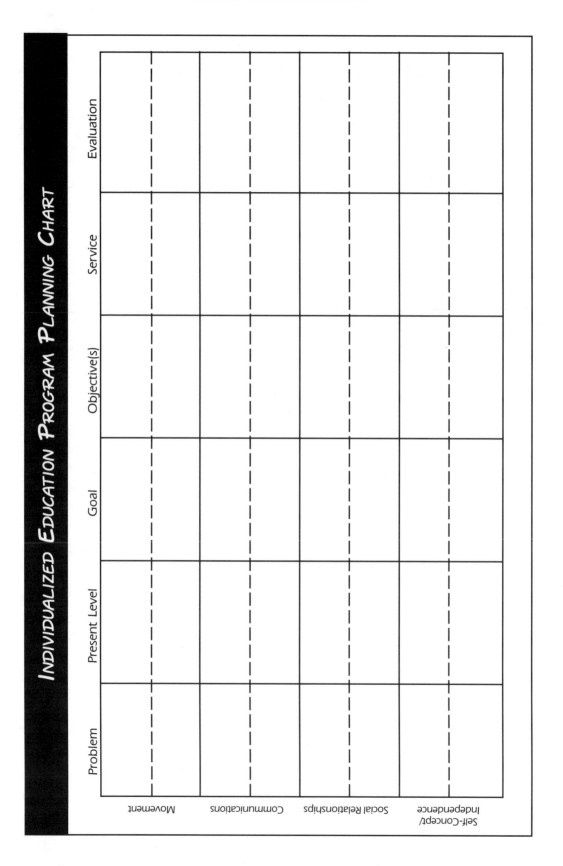

INDIVIDUALIZED EDUCATION PROGRAM PLANNING CHART

| | Problem | Present Level | Goal | Objective(s) | Service | Evaluation |
|---|---|---|---|---|---|---|
| Self-Concept/ Independence | | | | | | |
| Social Relationships | | | | | | |
| Communications | | | | | | |
| Movement | | | | | | |

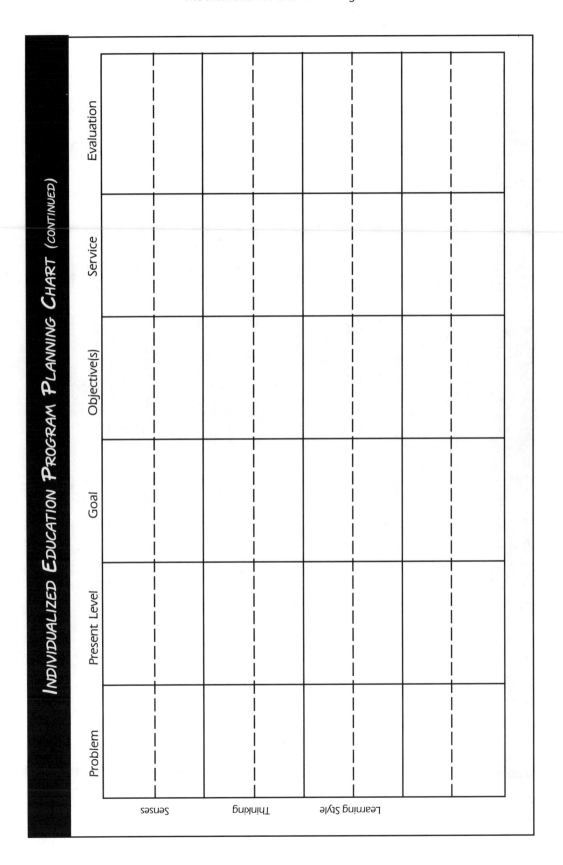

INDIVIDUALIZED EDUCATION PROGRAM PLANNING CHART (CONTINUED)

| | Problem | Present Level | Goal | Objective(s) | Service | Evaluation |
|---|---|---|---|---|---|---|
| Senses | | | | | | |
| Thinking | | | | | | |
| Learning Style | | | | | | |

## INDIVIDUALIZED EDUCATION PROGRAM PLANNING CHART

| | Problem | Present Level | Goal | Objective(s) | Service | Evaluation |
|---|---|---|---|---|---|---|
| **Movement** | Uncoordinated | She gives up in the middle of an obstacle course | To find her way across an obstacle course | 1. Practice skills for individual sections of course 2. Understand what to do on an entire course | Adaptive PE | By June 30 she will complete obstacle course unassisted |
| **Movement** | Trouble drawing human figures | Draws simple shapes and people figures | To draw more complex figures in a recognizable way | 1. Draw shapes using a stencil 2. Draw shapes without using stencil; add on features | Special Ed. Classroom and reg. ed. art class | By June 30 Sara's human figure will include 10 specific parts |
| **Communications** | Can't think of common words | Forgets names of common household items—hairbrush, ketchup, radio | To increase her ability to use the right words | 1. Work with new vocabulary words 2. Use new words correctly and spontaneously | Special Ed. Classroom | Tape recorded conversations |
| **Communications** | Poor sequencing skills | Talks about daily activities with no attention to the proper order | To tell about her day or weekend in sequential order | 1. Sara will talk about single experiences 2. She will keep an activity calendar | Special Language Therapy | Tape recordings (compare to 9/96 tape) |
| **Social Relationships** | Frequently tells peers what to do | Insists her friends play Barbie dolls or she won't play | With a classmate, will plan a project in a "give and take" way | 1. Plan with a friend under adult direction and praise 2. Work with classmate independently | Special Ed. Classroom | Observation of Spec. Ed. teacher |
| **Social Relationships** | She feels different from others | Asks why she is in special class and her sister is not | Sara will describe ways she is same/different from a friend | 1. Describe same/different clothing 2. Identify some different personality traits | Special Ed. and regular classes; home with family and friends | Observation: Notes |
| **Self-Concept/ Independence** | Makes negative comments about herself when she makes mistakes | She says "I hate myself" when she does something wrong | Sara will praise herself verbally for a job well-done | 1. She will smile when praised 2. Imitate a shoulder shrug when she makes mistakes | All teachers and family | Teacher and parent observations |
| **Self-Concept/ Independence** | Always wants mom to be around | Sits and waits alone on front porch for long periods if mom is not home on time | To make independent decision to go to neighbors when she gets home from bus alone | 1. Make a chart describing plan for alone time 2. Explain plan to teacher and neighbor | Spec. Ed. teacher, home and neighbor | Parent observation: Chart completed |

## INDIVIDUALIZED EDUCATION PROGRAM PLANNING CHART (CONTINUED)

| | Problem | Present Level | Goal | Objective(s) | Service | Evaluation |
|---|---|---|---|---|---|---|
| **Senses** | Doesn't remember details of picture | Remembers vaguely the whole picture but not details | To look at picture and describe more than 2 details | 1. Identify missing details in picture by drawing them in 2. She will name missing details | Spec. Ed. classroom | Oral test |
| | Difficulty following oral directions | Follows one direction at a time | To carry out 3 directions given at one time | 1. Follow one command correctly 2. Repeat directions aloud before acting | Spec. Ed. classroom; Speech Therapy; Home | Informal teacher made tests |
| **Thinking** | Disorganized way of describing a story she has read | Tells about story in a disorganized way; no attention to proper order | To understand and tell main ideas in short stories | 1. Describe main character 2. Describe one event 3. Decide on main ideas | Spec. Ed. classroom; Oral Book report time | By June she will present an oral book report and accurately tell main ideas |
| | Does not understand value of coins | Confuses nickels, dimes, and quarters, both value and name | To buy something and count the change | 1. Learn the name and value of each coin 2. Count money with mixed change | Spec. Ed. classroom | Demonstrate use of money |
| **Learning Style** | Haphazard planning | Leaves one homework subject to start another, then leaves both unfinished | To plan alone how to do her school work | 1. With adult help, she will learn to break tasks into small steps 2. Make her own charts | Spec. Ed. classroom | Completed planning charts showing accomplishment |
| | Very concrete—not able to think abstractly | Doesn't understand jokes or puns that are the least bit subtle | To learn to tell a joke | 1. Read a riddle—explain meaning to teacher 2. Tell riddle from memory | Speech/Language Therapy | Tell the class a joke or riddle |

# INDIVIDUALIZED EDUCATION PROGRAM

Student Name  Sara Austin
Student ID#  72348        DOB  10/8/88
Current Assignment  Queensbury School
_____  4th grade  _____

**DATES**
Initial IEP  9/94
Current IEP  9/97
IEP Review  6/98

| EXCEPTIONAL EDUCATION ASSIGNMENT(S): | INITIATION DATE | ANTICIPATED DURATION | PERSON RESPONSIBLE |
|---|---|---|---|
| Learning disability resource room 15% of time/week at Queensbury School | 9/97 | 6/98 | Roberta Chase |
| | | | |
| (Location / Program / Organization / Time) | | | |

**RELATED SERVICES:**

| | INITIATION DATE | ANTICIPATED DURATION | PERSON RESPONSIBLE |
|---|---|---|---|
| Speech and language therapy ½ hr.  3x/week | 9/97 | 6/98 | Phyllis Find |
| Occupational therapy ½ hr.  2x/week | 9/97 | 6/98 | Paul Cecil |
| | | | |

**EXTENT TO WHICH STUDENT WILL PARTICIPATE IN GENERAL OR VOCATIONAL EDUCATION:**  85% in general education
_____  program  _____

**REQUIRED SPECIAL AIDS, SERVICES, OR EQUIPMENT:**
N.A.

| Subject    Hours/% of time | Subject    Hours/% of time |
|---|---|
| English, Social Studies, | Art/Music  1 hr./week |
| & Science  20 hrs/week | |
| Vocational Education | |
| Physical Education  X Regular  ___ Adaptive | |

**IN ATTENDANCE AT IEP MEETING:**

| | Signature | Date | | Signature | Date |
|---|---|---|---|---|---|
| LEA Representative (Title: Principal | _Louise Fischer_ | 9/97 | | | |
| Parent(s), Guardian(s) or Surrogate Parents (s) | _Lisa Austin_ | 9/97 | _Robert Austin_ | 9/97 | |
| Student | | | | | |
| Teacher(s) | _Anna Chase_ | 9/97 | | | |
| Evaluator(s) | | | | | |

Student Name   Sara Austin
Student ID#   72348
Exceptional Education Assignment  LD Resource Room

PERFORMANCE OR SUBJECT AREA: Math

PRESENT LEVEL: Adds and subtracts 2 digit numbers
Counts to 50 by 5's
Identifies penny, but confuses nickels, dimes, quarters

ANNUAL GOAL:
Sara will be able to make change for a dollar using pennies, nickels, dimes and quarters by June.

SHORT-TERM INSTRUCTIONAL OBJECTIVES

EVALUATON OF SHORT-TERM INSTRUCTIONAL OBJECTIVES

| SHORT-TERM INSTRUCTIONAL OBJECTIVES | Criterion for for Mastery | Evaluation Procedures and Schedule to be used | Results/ Date |
|---|---|---|---|
| 1. Sara will discriminate between the 4 different coins. | Accurately name the coins -- 100%. | Teacher observation using real coins by Oct. 29. | |
| 2. Sara will identify the coin and its value. | Write number value under picture of coin. | Worksheets on coins completed accurately in independent work by Jan. 1. | |
| 3. Sara will make change for a dime in three ways. | Demonstrate with real coins. | Teacher observation by March 1. | |
| 4. Sara will make change for a quarter in three ways. | Use pennies, nickels & dimes to make a quarter accurately -- 100%. | Teacher observation by April 6. | |
| 5. Sara will purchase a box of crayons at school store and count change. | Purchase completed with 100% accuracy. | Crayons and correct change given to teacher by May 27. | |

NOTE: Additional performance
or subject area pages would be
completed for Sara Austin's IEP.

# 7. THE INDIVIDUALIZED EDUCATION PROGRAM MEETING

## SELECTING THE ROUTE

**Y**our child's Individualized Education Program (IEP) is the cornerstone of his special education program. The IEP meeting is an opportunity for you and the school system to combine your separate areas of expertise and jointly come up with the appropriate education program for your child.

Because your contributions to the IEP meeting are so important, IDEA requires schools to follow specific procedures and timelines to ensure your participation. The school district must tell you, in writing, and in ways that you understand: 1) when the meeting will be held; 2) its purpose; and 3) who will attend. When your child reaches age 14, the schools are required to invite him in the IEP meeting when plans are being made for his transition services and life after high school. Most parents find that including their child at much earlier ages helps them understand expectations for them and to be a part of their own planning and decision making.

According to IDEA, the school is required to schedule the IEP meeting at a time that is agreeable both to you and the school personnel involved. This meeting must be held within 30 calendar days of the date the school finds your child eligible for special education services. Additionally, IEP meetings are to be held at least once a year; more often if requested by a teacher or parent.

Building on the suggestions given in Chapter 6, the following section offers hints for preparing for the meeting and for making your contributions once you are there. Each time you are notified of an IEP meeting, you may want to reread this section to decide which of the many suggestions made you will want to follow as you prepare for the meeting.

# ■ SOME THOUGHTS ON PREPARING FOR AND ■ PARTICIPATING IN AN IEP MEETING

## CONSIDERATIONS PRIOR TO THE IEP MEETING

**1. Upon notification of the IEP meeting, call the person who is in charge of the meeting and find out:**

      a. who will attend the meeting, if that information is not included in the notification, and

      b. how long the meeting will last.

**2. The following people are required to attend IEP meetings:**

      a. a representative of the public school qualified to provide, or supervise the provision of, special education;

      b. a teacher*; and

      c. one or both parents.

If the meeting concerns your child's initial evaluation, a member of the evaluation team or a person qualified to interpret evaluation results must be there. Other individuals may be invited by the parents or the school system. Your child can be included if you feel it is appropriate. If the purpose of the IEP meeting includes discussion about transition goals for a student 14 years or older, the student must be invited. If anyone who provides services such as speech therapy to your child has not been invited to the meeting, ask that he be invited. If he cannot attend, make arrangements to meet with him and obtain his ideas to include in the final IEP document.

**3. If you feel the time allotted for the IEP meeting may be inadequate to discuss all your concerns, make arrangements to meet a second time or to make the first meeting longer.**

**4. Referring to your personal observations, the Record Decoder, and the IEP Planning Chart, make notes on the goals, objectives, and evaluation criteria you want included in your child's IEP.** Alternatively, you may wish to design your own IEP to bring with you to the meeting, using the sample IEP in the previous chapter as a guide.

**5. For each developmental area, rank order the goals and objectives you want your child to achieve.**

**6. Talk with other persons—teachers, parents, professionals, and so on—about the special education and related services they feel your child**

**needs.** Identify and write down in rank order the special education and related services you want your child to receive.

7. **Determine the extent to which you feel your child should participate in general education programs in light of his learning style and special education needs.**★

8. **Develop a written agenda of everything you want to discuss at the IEP meeting,** including your rank ordering of goals and objectives, the extent of your child's participation in the general education program, and the special education and related services you want your child to receive.

9. **If school professionals are working with your child for the first time, develop a plan for making your child's presence felt at the beginning of the IEP meeting.** Telling a short anecdote or bringing photographs of your family, tape recordings, examples of schoolwork, or your child himself can help people unacquainted with him realize that he is far more than a stack of papers!

10. **While you and the school professionals will most often agree about your child's IEP, you might want to think of potential areas of disagreement and develop plans to address those problems.**

    a. Identify the data in the records and elsewhere supporting your position on the potential problem areas.

    b. Identify the data in the records and elsewhere supporting the school's position.

    c. Identify information to counter the school's position.

    d. Develop alternative proposals for achieving your goals and objectives for your child which school officials might accept more readily.

    e. Prior to the IEP meeting, determine the minimum special education program and related services you will accept for your child before appealing the IEP.

11. **Determine the role you feel most comfortable assuming during the meeting.**

    a. *Very assertive role:* taking charge of the meeting early and guiding it. If you choose a very assertive role, a way to ensure that your own agenda is covered is to have it carefully written out and even rehearsed with your spouse or others who support your point of view. To help guide the meeting in the directions you wish, provide a copy of your agenda for each member of the IEP team.

    b. *Assertive role:* allowing school officials to lead the meeting but ensuring that all items on your agenda are covered completely to your satisfaction.

   c. *Less assertive role:* permitting school officials to lead the meeting and pressing only for a few specified items.

**12. Ask someone to attend the meeting with you.** Often it is very helpful to have someone else to listen, take notes, and support you. Prior to the meeting, discuss with him what you hope to do in the meeting and what you want him to do.

## CONSIDERATIONS DURING THE IEP MEETING

**1. If school officials are working with your child for the first time, take steps at the beginning of the IEP meeting to make your child's presence felt in that meeting, as previously suggested.**

**2. Ensure that each item required for an IEP is fully discussed.**[*] These include:

   a. a description of your child's present level of educational performance in all areas, including movement, communications, social relations, self-concept/independence, senses/perception, thinking, and learning style;

   b. a statement of annual goals and of short-term objectives for each of those goals;

   c. a statement of the special education and related services to be provided to meet each of the goals and objectives;

   d. a statement of the extent to which your child will participate in general education programs;

   e. a statement of transition services for a student 16 years or older, or age 14, if appropriate;

   f. the projected dates for starting services and the anticipated duration of the services; and

   g. a statement of the objective criteria, evaluation procedures, and schedules for determining, on at least an annual basis, whether your child is achieving his short-term objectives.

**3. Whether you have chosen a very assertive, assertive, or less assertive role, make sure that everything you want to discuss is covered to your satisfaction.** If the school personnel begin the meeting by reviewing their recommended goals and objectives, anticipated services, and evaluation criteria for your child, you should follow their discussion by identifying how these items relate to the IEP you envisioned before the meeting. Where you agree with the proposed program, express your agreement and check off the item from your list. Where disagreements arise, explain your objections and try to reach an acceptable solution. If disagreements cannot be resolved immediately, make a note of those areas, express your desire to come back to these issues later, and move on to new goals and objectives.

Another approach is for you, the parents, to begin by reviewing the elements of the IEP you have developed and to have the school people comment on each item either as you bring it up or after you have finished your presentation. Then you can proceed to deal with areas of agreement and disagreement as described above.

**4. As the meeting progresses, keep participants focused on the elements of the IEP and on your child.** Do not let the discussion wander off to unrelated matters.

**5. As the discussion comes to an end, review the agenda of concerns you developed prior to the meeting.** Make certain that everything on your agenda has been covered. If you disagreed earlier over any aspects of your child's IEP, return to those matters now and seek to resolve them.

**6. At the conclusion of the meeting you will probably be asked to sign the IEP document.** Your signature may have a different meaning in different school systems. Sometimes parents are asked to sign the IEP merely to indicate their presence at the IEP meeting. When this is the case, you should sign the document as requested. Remember, however, that your signature in this case does not mean you agree with the IEP as written.

In some school systems, your signature on the IEP indicates that you agree with the document and consent to proceed with the proposed placement. Certainly if you are satisfied that the IEP meets your child's needs to the fullest extent possible, you may now signify agreement by signing the IEP or the permission for placement document, whichever your school system requires. If, however, you want to examine the IEP without time pressure, tell the school officials you would like to review the IEP over the next day or two. Request that they provide you with a copy and tell them exactly when you will give them your final decision regarding the program and placement described on the IEP. And if you do not accept portions of the IEP, identify clearly to the school officials those portions that you find unacceptable. If they will not change those items, tell them you want additional time to consider the IEP. Ask them to give you a copy, and tell them exactly when you will make your final decision.

**7. Whether or not you request extra time to examine your child's IEP, review this final checklist before signing the IEP or permission for placement document:**

    a. Does the IEP accurately and fully describe your child's present level of educational performance in all relevant developmental areas? Does it accurately portray your child's learning style?

    b. Do the annual goals describe the skills you would like your child to develop within the next year?

c. Are annual goals written to build on your child's present level of educational performance?

d. Is there at least one annual goal and short-term objective for each related service your child will receive?

e. Are goals and objectives written as positive, measurable statements?

f. Do goals and objectives contain the five essential parts of **who** will do **what, how, where,** and **when?**

g. Do the annual goals and short-term objectives meet the priorities you have established as essential for your child?

h. Are all special education and related services clearly identified, along with projected dates for beginning services and the anticipated duration of the services?

i. Does the IEP clearly describe the extent to which your child will participate in general education programs?

j. Are necessary transition services described?

k. Does the IEP include appropriate and understandable criteria and evaluation procedures and schedules for determining, at least on an annual basis, whether the short-term instructional objectives are being achieved?

l. Have you asked all teachers and therapists who are providing services to your child whether they agree with the IEP and will provide these services? If these professionals attended the IEP meeting, they will have already answered these questions. If they did not attend the meeting, you should talk with them before signing the IEP.

8. **If you do not find the IEP totally acceptable, decide which of the following actions you will take:**

a. Sign the IEP or permission for placement document but note which parts of the IEP you find objectionable and indicate in writing your plan to appeal those parts. This option should allow your child to receive the special education and related services on his IEP pending appeal of the part to which you object. (See Chapter 11 for information about ways to resolve disagreements with the school.)

b. Refuse to sign the IEP or permission for placement document and indicate in writing your intention to appeal the IEP. Before doing this, ask what educational services your child will receive if you follow this option.

c. Sign the IEP or permission for placement document and indicate in writing the parts with which you disagree but write nothing about a plan to appeal. This option at least puts you on record as feeling that the IEP does not adequately meet your child's needs.

# ■ VISITING PLACEMENT OPTIONS ■

Before you agree to a classroom placement for your child's special education program, you will want to visit the school. Occasionally there is more than one classroom within the school system appropriate to meet the goals and objectives and to provide the related services outlined in your child's IEP. In the same way you offered educators unique, valuable knowledge of your child during the evaluation, eligibility, and IEP phases, you will also be able to give them particular insight into the kind of environment suited to your child's learning style. By visiting school classrooms, talking to administrators and teachers, eating in the cafeteria, and observing playground activities, you can assess the educational program with the needs of your child in mind. You will be able to ask questions and perhaps offer suggestions about adjustments or modifications necessary to respond to your child's unique ways of learning.

Many parents feel uncertain when they visit schools. They wonder what to look for as they observe school programs. The outline below serves as a guide for your observations. It provides questions to ask and guidelines to follow in assessing the classroom's activities, materials, methods, and physical layout. This guide can help you decide whether the suggested placement is compatible with your child's educational needs and his learning style. It can also help you decide if the classroom environment will enable your child to build on his strengths, allowing him to learn in ways he does best. You should find this guide useful when you visit a school or classroom before giving permission for your child to be placed there; you should also find it valuable when you have questions and concerns at parent-teacher conferences.

# ■ GUIDELINES FOR PLACEMENT OBSERVATIONS ■

## I. CLASSROOM ORGANIZATION
### A. PHYSICAL ENVIRONMENT
1. Layout
   a. How is furniture arranged? (Desks lined up in rows? Tables and chairs for small group work?)
   b. Are there large open areas or is the room divided into smaller components?
   c. Is the furniture the right size for the students? Is

special equipment available (e.g., chairs with arm supports, individual study carrels, balance stools, bathroom fixtures at appropriate levels, etc.)?

    d. Where is the classroom located in relationship to the cafeteria? The bathroom? Outdoor areas? The special services?

2. General atmosphere

    a  Is the general atmosphere relaxed or formal? Soothing or stimulating?

B. DAILY SCHEDULE

  1. Sequence of Activities

    a. What is the daily schedule? Do students seem to understand the schedule?

    b. Are related services scheduled at times that do not interrupt a child's participation in the ongoing school work?

    c. How does the teacher indicate that one activity is over and another beginning?

  2. Consistency

    a. Is the schedule generally the same every day?

  3. Variety

    a. Does the daily schedule include active times and quiet times?

    b. Is there provision for daily outdoor activity?

    c. How frequently does the teacher change the pace of activities?

C. SOCIAL ENVIRONMENT

  1. Peer interactions

    a. Are students allowed to interact spontaneously with one another? When? How often?

    b. Does the teacher encourage students to cooperate with one another? During schoolwork activities? During free time?

  2. Teacher-child interactions

    a. How does the teacher relate to the students?

    b. Does the teacher tolerate and adjust to individual students?

c. Does the teacher enter into conversations or play situations with students?

3. Values

a. What values do the teacher and the students seem to hold? Success? Creativity? Social manners? Enthusiasm? Docility? Physical prowess?

## II. Curriculum

A. GOALS AND PRIORITIES

1. What developmental areas are included in the curriculum (i.e., movement, communications, social relationships, independence/self-concept, thinking skills, etc.)?
2. What developmental areas receive emphasis in the classroom? What is not a curriculum priority? Where do academics fit in? Are life skills emphasized?

B. MATERIALS

1. Are the teaching materials concrete or abstract?
2. Are the teaching materials appropriate to the developmental level of the students?
3. Do the materials teach through various senses—vision, touch, hearing? Through movement?
4. Are the materials physically accessible to students?
5. Are the materials designed to interest students?

C. METHODS

1. Groupings

a. Do students work individually, in small groups, or as a total class?
b. Are the students grouped homogeneously (all at the same skill level) or heterogeneously (different skill levels in the same group)?
c. Are the groupings different for different curriculum areas?

2. Teaching style

a. Does the teacher take a highly structured approach, leading all learning activities? Or does he also allow for spontaneous learning situations?
b. Does the teacher work individually with students or does he focus more on groups?

    c. Performance expectations
        (1) Does the teacher expect all students to perform at approximately the same level?
        (2) Does the teacher expect students to wait for their turns or to volunteer answers spontaneously?
        (3) Does the teacher expect students to listen to and follow group verbal instructions?
        (4) Does the teacher expect students to work independently? Without interrupting with questions for the teacher?

# ■ CONCLUSION ■

Obtaining the results you wanted for your child has taken time and energy as you negotiated the special education maze. Your hopes and those of the school system are that your son or daughter will make educational and developmental strides with the program you have jointly designed. If your child is still an infant or toddler, you will need to be aware of other considerations due to your child's young age. Special laws and regulations have been passed for very young children. The following chapter will assist you in making decisions for your baby and your family that are different from the ones you might make for an older child.

    If your older son or daughter is approaching the end of school, you are most likely wondering what lies ahead. It is never too early to begin exploring passageways in the maze that lead to maximum independence in work life, living arrangements, recreation, and community activities. In Chapter 9 you will find suggestions of ways to work with school professionals to prepare your child for his life as an employee, citizen, and contributing member of society.

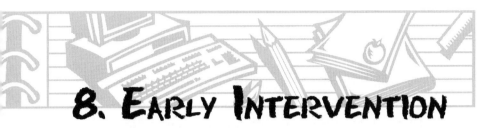

# 8. EARLY INTERVENTION

## BEGINNING THE JOURNEY

## ▪ A PROGRAM FOR INFANTS AND TODDLERS ▪

For his first six months of life, Brian was a healthy, typically developing baby. Suddenly, he developed seizures and was taken to the pediatrician for observation and treatment. His family felt quite overwhelmed and anxious. A nurse suggested to his mother that she call HUGS, the early intervention program in her community. Before long, the Ellis family was receiving some much needed support both for Brian and for the rest of the family. How did this come about?

In 1986, the U.S. Congress recognized the importance of getting help as early as possible for children with special needs and their families. Legislation was passed to encourage states to set up programs for infants and toddlers with disabilities and for their families. This program, referred to as *Part H—Early Intervention for Infants and Toddlers with Disabilities and their Families*,* was added as an amendment to the Individuals with Disabilities Education Act (IDEA).

Early intervention provides services that are designed specifically to meet the individual needs of a child and her family, to enhance the development of the young child, and to minimize the need for future special education. These services are jointly selected by the parents and a team of service providers. The services may be provided in the child's home, school, hospital, or other central location. Services may be provided on an individual basis, or in a small group that might include other children with developmental problems, as well as others who do not have disabilites. Early intervention services assist families in meeting their own child's needs.

Since the enactment of Part H, states have made significant progress in setting up early intervention services. All states now guarantee early intervention to eligible children and their families. The Part H amendment specifies the U.S. Department of Education (DED) as the responsible agency for early intervention at the national level. That is, the DED sets policies and procedures that the states must follow. Each state then assigns a public agency, called the lead agency, to administer the program. In some states, the lead agency for early intervention is the education department; in others, it may be the department of health, mental health, or social services. Regardless of the lead agency, all public agencies that provide services to infants and young children must be involved.

Early intervention services can begin at birth and last until a child turns three. At the age of three, if eligible, the child can begin receiving preschool special education services from the local public school. Families can enter the early intervention system in a variety of ways. When a child is identified as having a disability or being at risk of a disability at birth, medical professionals often tell the family about early intervention services in their community. Other families learn about early intervention from friends, social workers, or pediatricians. Every state has a central directory that parents and professionals may call to find out about resources in their community. Appendix B has that telephone number for each state.

There are several ways infants or toddlers can qualify for Part H services:

- They may be identified as having developmental delays in one or more of the following areas: cognitive development; physical development; language and speech development; social or emotional development; or self-help skills.
- They may be diagnosed with a physical or mental condition that has a high probability of resulting in developmental delay.
- In some states, babies or toddlers who might develop substantial developmental delays due to one or more risk factors are eligible for early intervention services.

More information about how children qualify for early intervention is found on page 118-120 of this chapter.

## ■ A FAMILY SERVICE SYSTEM ■

When the Part H program was enacted, Congress found that in order for early intervention to be successful, services must focus not only on the baby but on the whole family. It recognized that services must go beyond those which meet a baby's developmental needs. Early intervention services can include:

1. Help to families that will encourage their baby to learn and grow.
2. Assistance in getting services that will help the child and family (service coordination, social services, medical assistance), or benefits (insurance, food stamps or Supplemental Security Income—SSI).
3. Social work, nutrition, nursing, or psychological services for the child or family.
4. Family training, counseling and home visits.
5. Occupational, physical, and speech-language therapy for the child.
6. Planning and assistance as a child prepares to leave one program and move on to new programs or services.

Other services available under the Part H legislation include, but are not limited to: audiology; medical evaluation and diagnosis; early identification, screening and assessment services; health services necessary to enable the infant or toddler to benefit from the other early intervention services; assistive technology services and devices; vision services; and transportation and related costs that are necessary to enable a child and family to receive services.

## FAMILY CENTERED EARLY INTERVENTION SERVICES

Families and early intervention professionals have come to recognize the importance of family members as key decision makers for their infant or toddler. Families and professionals together have learned that certain principles must guide them as important decisions are made. The principles are:

1. A child with disabilities, like all children, is first a member of a family within a community.
2. The family is the child's first and best advocate.
3. Families decide what services they need.
4. A family's perspectives and values are shaped by life experiences, including their ethnic, racial, and cultural background.
5. Family support is an integral part of meeting a child's special needs.
6. Effective early intervention services make families feel welcomed and are shaped by the families.
7. Families and professionals must work together in a climate of mutual respect and trust to be successful.

Families and professionals working together, keeping the family centered principles in sight, are helping infants and toddlers with disabilities grow and develop to their fullest potential.

# ▪ THE PATH TO EARLY INTERVENTION ▪

Just as there is a special education planning cycle, there is also a prescribed pathway to early intervention services. Family members and service providers together plan and coordinate the services along each step in the pathway.

> 1. Identifying and Screening
> 2. Assigning a Temporary Service Coordinator
> 3. Evaluating by a Multidisciplinary Team
> 4. Determining Eligibility
> 5. Developing the Individualized Family Service Plan

## 1. IDENTIFYING AND SCREENING

If you suspect your baby or toddler has a disability or developmental delay, or potentially has such problems, you or anyone helping your family can request a screening. A telephone call to your local school system will most likely help you find where to go. Many communities conduct periodic screening clinics to help identify children who might need early intervention. These screenings, often called Child Find, are advertised in local newspapers, on grocery store bulletin boards, at schools, and at health departments.

Screening methods vary from place to place, but can be done in clinics, in your home, by your observation or report, or through a check-up at your pediatrician's office. The purpose is to pick up potential difficulties and to identify children who need further evaluation and diagnosis.

If your child does not appear to meet the eligibility requirements for Part H Early Intervention Services, you may be asked to come back at a later date for a follow-up screening, or be referred to other services your child or family might need. Regardless of the outcome, if you believe your child is eligible for early intervention, you may request a multidisciplinary assessment and evaluation. If your child's diagnosis or condition is likely to qualify her for Part H services, you may just bypass the process and move directly down the next step in the pathway—the assignment of a temporary service coordinator.

## 2. ASSIGNING A TEMPORARY SERVICE COORDINATOR

Once the early intervention agency has received a referral of a baby or toddler, either directly from a parent or from a screening program, two things must happen. First, arrangements must begin for evaluation and assessment. Second, a temporary service coordinator must be assigned to the family to work with them throughout the evaluation process. Both of these steps must be accomplished within two working days. The temporary service coordinator is responsible for pulling together the appropriate team to evaluate your child's development and for gathering information from you and from the professionals who have worked with you. The temporary service coordinator is the primary person with whom you will talk during the evaluation process. You must give written permission before the next step—evaluation—can take place.

## 3. Evaluating by a Multidisciplinary Assessment Team

Within forty-five days of the referral, an evaluation must be completed and a service plan put in place if your child is found eligible for early intervention. Evaluation is the word used to describe all of the procedures used to determine your child's unique strengths and weaknesses. The evaluation includes various procedures—observations, tests, interviews, and other means of gaining knowledge about the child. Family members may participate in planning the types of tests and evaluation the child might need. If you choose, you may provide information about your child's growth and development; about your family's concerns, resources, and priorities; and about what types of early intervention services might be needed by your child and family.

Based upon the screening information, your temporary service coordinator will plan with you the procedures used in the evaluation. The evaluation will be multidisciplinary, which means there must be people with various professional backgrounds to evaluate your child. Later in this chapter you will find suggestions for making the evaluation go well for you and your child.

## 4. Determining Eligibility

Following completion of the evaluation, you and members of the multidisciplinary team will meet and decide whether your child and family are eligible under Part H criteria to receive early intervention services. Eligibility will be based upon the information you provide and upon whether the tests given indicate that your child meets any *one* of the three criteria below:

- the child has developmental delays, as measured by appropriate diagnostic instruments and procedures, in one or more of the following areas:
  –cognitive development;

–physical development, which includes vision and hearing;
–communication development;
–social or emotional development;
–self-help or adaptive skills.

**Example:** Elsa was born with a cleft palate. Her speech and language development was delayed, so she was found eligible for early intervention services.

■ the child has a record of a diagnosed physical or mental condition which has a high probability of resulting in delay of development.

**Example:** Khoi was diagnosed at birth with mild cerebral palsy. His development measured within normal limits, yet his family and doctor felt that extra help and carefully planned activities would enhance his physical and communications development.

■ the child is regarded as being at risk of having substantial delays in development if early intervention services are not provided. This is an optional criterion which not all states have adopted.

**Example:** Tommy's mother was fourteen when he was born two months prematurely. Concern for Tommy's development led to his receiving early intervention services, for in the state in which he lived, children at risk of having substantial delays are eligible.

## 5. DEVELOPMENT OF AN INDIVIDUALIZED FAMILY SERVICE PLAN (IFSP)

If your baby or toddler is found to be eligible for early intervention services, you and a team will meet to write a plan for addressing the unique needs of your child and your family. The Individualized Family Service Plan (IFSP), like an IEP, has certain requirements. The required parts of an IFSP are:

**1. Information about your child's current development.** Included in this section is information you provide, as well as the evaluation results about her health, vision, hearing, language, speech, social, emotional, self-help, and intellectual (cognitive) development.

**2. Information about your family's resources, priorities, and concerns.** You will be asked about ways in which your family strengths can contribute to your baby or toddler's development. Example of "family strengths" might be an extended family nearby to help with child care, a strong religious belief, or a network of family and friends who give emotional support. You may choose whether or not to give this family information.

**3. The outcomes expected, which include your hopes and dreams for your child and your family, and how you might make progress toward reaching the outcomes.** Examples of outcomes are found later in this chapter on a sample IFSP.

**4. The early intervention services needed to help your child and your family reach the outcomes discussed and acted upon.** This section also must describe where, when, how, and for what length of time each session of the services will be given, as well as payment arrangements, if any, for the services.

**5. Statement about the natural environment in which services will be provided.** The natural environment includes home and community settings in which children who do not have disabilities learn, play, and grow. Some babies or toddlers receive early intervention services in day care centers, others at home, while others go to a special center for infant education.

**6. If appropriate, other services are included, which might address medical or other special needs of your child but which are not required under the IFSP.** By including other services, the team can help you plan and secure such services needed by your child and family members.

**7. The dates and duration of services.** This section states when the services will begin and how long they will last.

**8. Naming of the service coordinator.** This person will help you coordinate the various services required by your child and family, including helping to obtain the services identified in the IFSP, arranging for evaluations and assessments, and facilitating review meetings for the IFSP.

**9. A transition plan for your child.** The plan includes the steps that will occur to support the transition to whatever preschool services your child will receive, including either public or private preschool. The transition plan must be written 90 days before your child's third birthday. In addition, this part of the IFSP indicates the procedures you need to follow if your child will require **special education** preschool services. You may be asked to sign permission to have your child's record sent from the early intervention program to help the local school system with the referral process. Further information on transition is found on page 143-144 in this chapter.

The actual format for a written IFSP differs among various states and localities. The elements described above, as well as your consent for the services, however, are required under the federal law. IFSPs are reviewed every six months or more often if needed. A formal evaluation of the IFSP is done each year as your baby or toddler grows and changes.

# ▪ PROVISION AND COSTS FOR SERVICES ▪

Under Part H of IDEA, several early intervention services must be provided at *no cost* to the family. These include evaluations or assessments, the development of IFSPs, and service coordination for eligible children and their families. Part H, however, does *not* require that all services be provided at no cost to families. Although many early intervention programs do not charge families for any services, early intervention programs *can* charge families for services included in the IFSP according to a sliding fee scale.

Besides being required to pay for some services, families sometimes also find that public services included in their child's IFSP are not available. Unfortunately, when a community has limited availability of services, waiting lists may form.

If you encounter problems related to the costs or availability of early intervention services, contact your service coordinator. Your service coordinator is responsible for informing you of options for finding alternative services and for helping you to arrange for the payments. For some families, Medicaid or a private insurance carrier may pay for early intervention services. Other families pay on the sliding fee scale. You cannot, however, be denied early intervention services if you prove an inability to pay. One thing to remember is that you can say no to any service recommended, including one or more that you don't want to pay for.

Remember, Part H was designed to involve many agencies in a coordinated effort to establish a comprehensive early intervention system at the local level. The multiple agencies have a responsibility to work together in providing services for families and their babies. When waiting lists and other problems with service delivery arise, the interagency body should address these problems. As parents, you can present your problem to the interagency committee and ask for a solution.

# ▪ PREPARING FOR YOUR PARTICIPATION ▪
# IN THE IFSP PROCESS

Do you, like most people, come away from a visit to your doctor thinking, "Why didn't I ask this question?" "I wish I had told my doctor about this when I saw her." All too often we find anxiety gets in the way of full participation in our own care. This, too, can happen when you are working with professionals who are helping you with your child.

One of the unique aspects of the IFSP process is that parents' wishes and concerns are considered first and foremost. With assistance from a team of experienced professionals, you are in the driver's seat. At each of the five steps along the pathway to your child's early intervention services, you will find yourself feeling more in control if you make careful preparations. You will feel better prepared for your role if you get information about your child's condition, prognosis, and effective interventions. Parents and other family members participate more fully by thinking through their perceptions of their infant or toddler's development and writing down information they wish to share with the people helping them.

## ■ BEFORE AND AFTER THE EVALUATION ■

Evaluation procedures provide useful information about your child's developmental levels. Taken together, the evaluation results are used to determine if your child is eligible for early intervention. Tests and observations identify areas that you and the professionals may want to focus on. You also can look objectively at your child's progress and see milestones she has reached and levels mastered. Even so, going through various evaluations and assessments can be trying for you and your child. To get the most accurate results and to reduce your stress, you may find some of the following ideas helpful.

*Before evaluations* people have various ways of getting ready. One family asked a professional to guide them through the process by explaining unfamiliar concepts and terminology. Another family visited programs and talked to other parents to get their advice and to learn about their experiences in early intervention. A third family prepared for the evaluation by writing down what they wanted to say and deciding what they wanted out of the meeting. A fourth family did all of the above!

As you decide how to get ready for your baby's or toddler's evaluation and assessment, consider some of the following questions:

- When is my child at his best? For example, after he eats, when I am out of the room, in the early afternoon?
- Who will be conducting the procedures?
- What are their roles?
- What types of tests will be used? What do these tests measure?
- How are the evaluations and assessments usually conducted? Is there any flexibility if I have suggestions?
- Do I need to bring anything? For example, food, toys, immunization records, other reports?
- What role do parents usually play? What role should I play?

- How soon will I know the results of the tests? In what way is this information usually given?
- How do the evaluators use information if my child does something at home that she does not do during the evaluation?

*After the evaluations* the professionals will often give you the preliminary results. You may be pleasantly surprised about your baby or toddler's progress . . . or disappointed that your child's progress has been slower than you had hoped. In some cases you may disagree with the people who conducted the assessment or feel as if they have not developed a complete picture of your child. How do you handle these kinds of situations?

Questioning the professionals carefully can help you. For example, parents often hear only the things that are wrong with their child. You will want to ask what they found that is right—the positive things—to provide the rounded picture needed. Many parents find that talking about the evaluation with other family members, trusted professionals, or friends can help them sort through their feelings and their information. In addition, a special event for the family, such as eating a meal out or going on a picnic, can help in gaining perspective.

Another source of help may be the parent-to-parent groups located in many states and local communities. These groups link parents who have had similar experiences in order that they can support one another. National Parent-To-Parent is listed in Appendix C in the back of this book. By contacting this group, you can learn more about parent-to-parent groups in your community.

## ■ ORGANIZING INFORMATION ■

Keeping track of the paperwork can feel daunting. Not long after you learn that your child needs special help, you may find yourself buried in a mountain of papers. There are bills, reports, notes, questionnaires, and appointment slips. You will want to take charge of all of these papers before they take charge of you! You also will come in contact with an array of new people—parents, specialists, physicians, insurance claims adjusters—to name only a few. How can you stay on top of all of the information?

The following forms, kept in a three-ring binder, can help you organize your information. An organized notebook helps you keep important information at your fingertips. You may feel quite discouraged if you start rummaging through the drawer where you *know* you put a copy of a special report about your baby or toddler, yet be unable to find it!

# KEY PEOPLE CHART

## I. HEALTH

| Name | Address | Telephone |
|------|---------|-----------|
| Primary Care Physician | | |
| Other Specialists | | |
| | | |
| | | |
| | | |
| Hospital | | |
| Nursing Advice Line | | |
| Public Health Nurse | | |
| Pharmacy | | |

## II. EARLY INTERVENTION

| Name | Address | Telephone |
|------|---------|-----------|
| Service Coordinator | | |
| Specialists | | |
| | | |
| | | |

## III. FAMILY SUPPORT

| Name | Address | Telephone |
|------|---------|-----------|
| Parent Support Line | | |
| Sitter or Other Helper | | |
| | | |
| | | |

## KEY PEOPLE CHART (CONTINUED)

### IV. FINANCIAL

| Name | Address | Telephone |
|------|---------|-----------|
| Insurance | | |
| Medicaid | | |
| Supplemental Security Income | | |
| Emergency Services | | |
| Other | | |

### V. OTHER CONTACTS: FRIENDS, CHURCH, FAMILY, CONSULTANTS

| Name | Address | Telephone |
|------|---------|-----------|
| | | |

# PHONE CALL RECORD

Who: _____    Date: _____

_____    Phone: _____

_____

Notes:



Need to follow up? _____ No    Who: _____

_____ Yes    When: _____

Who: _____    Date: _____

_____    Phone: _____

_____

Notes:



Need to follow up? _____ No    Who: _____

_____ Yes    When: _____

Who: _____    Date: _____

_____    Phone: _____

_____

Notes:



Need to follow up?

____ No    Who: _____

____ Yes    When: _____

# ▪ The IFSP Meeting ▪

## Getting Ready for the IFSP Meeting

As you think about your child's services, remember that you are the primary decision maker on the team. The service coordinator and the other professionals are there to help *you* think through your situation, and to solve problems, and to assist your child's growth and change. No services will be provided without your written consent. As an IFSP team member you will discover ways that your family can care for your child who has special needs, while at the same time preserving a family life that is as normal as possible. Decisions will be made during the meeting about the kinds of help and services you require.

To prepare for the IFSP meeting, you can fill out the *Hopes and Dreams Exercise* found on page 129. The first section helps you think of goals you have for your child in the near future—perhaps six months down the road. It allows for your hopes for your baby or toddler in four major developmental areas. As you think about these areas, also consider what kinds of assistance you will need to fulfill the hopes and dreams.

The second section asks for hopes and dreams for your family now and in the next six months. In each of these parts you are asked to think about services and means of support you will need to realize these dreams now and in the future. On page 130 you will find the *Hopes and Dreams Exercise* filled out by a mother prior to attending an IFSP meeting. Following that is a blank form that you can use.

The *Hopes and Dreams Exercise* helps you plan for the IFSP meeting. Your family values and routines are an important part of the planning process. Others on the team need to know what you want for your family so they can respond to your family's strengths, areas of concern, and priorities. The plan must respect your family routines and values. If possible, all planning will be in your family's primary language so that you and the other team members can understand the plans and outcomes.

## Participating in the IFSP Meeting

Your child's IFSP meeting will be called by the temporary service coordinator or by the person who has been designated as your service coordinator. Also in attendance will be the other members of your child's team, including one or both parents, and people who provide or can help you gain access to various services.

# HOPES AND DREAMS EXERCISE

## HOPES AND DREAMS FOR MY CHILD IN SIX MONTHS

Independence (i.e., feeding, toileting, doing things without help):

Movement (i.e., grasping, creeping, using motorized wheelchair, etc.):

Social (i.e., smiling, recognizing mother, having friends, sharing toys, etc.):

Communication (i.e., understanding words, letting you know when hungry, using a touch-talker, etc.):

Services and supports my child will need to realize these hopes and dreams:

## HOPES AND DREAMS FOR MY FAMILY RIGHT NOW

Things we can do together:

What I can do with individual children:

Things just for my partner and me:

Supports we need to realize our hopes and dreams (i.e., service providers, relatives, church, other assistance, etc.):

## HOPES AND DREAMS FOR FAMILY IN SIX MONTHS

Things we can do together:

What I can do with individual children:

Things just for my partner and me:

Supports we need to realize our hopes and dreams:

# HOPES AND DREAMS EXERCISE

## HOPES AND DREAMS FOR MY CHILD IN SIX MONTHS

Independence (i.e., feeding, toileting, doing things without help):

*Eat with a spoon.*
*Decide which toy to play with.*

Movement (i.e., grasping, creeping, using motorized wheelchair, etc.):

*Hold onto cart and walk across the room.*

Social (i.e., smiling, recognizing mother, having friends, sharing toys, etc.):

*Play with children at nursery school (at church).*

Communication (i.e., understanding words, letting you know when hungry, using a touch-talker, etc.):

*Point at object or food that he wants.*

Services and supports my child will need to realize these hopes and dreams:

*Maxwell will need someone to help him hold his spoon correctly and encourage him to make his own choices. Nursery school teachers will need to help him participate in activities with other children.*

## HOPES AND DREAMS FOR MY FAMILY RIGHT NOW

Things we can do together:

*Go to church on Sundays; go to restaurants together.*

What I can do with individual children:

*I want some time to play with Sarah and not worry about Maxwell.*

Things just for my partner and me:

*We need some time on our own once in a while.*

Supports we need to realize our hopes and dreams (i.e., service providers, relatives, church, other assistance, etc.):

*Nursery school teachers need some help so they can care for Maxwell during church. We need help so Maxwell won't scream through every meal. We need a trained— dependable—babysitter.*

## HOPES AND DREAMS FOR FAMILY IN SIX MONTHS

Things we can do together:

*Take a week's vacation at the beach this summer.*

What I can do with individual children:

*I want to help Sarah's soccer team; maybe coach a little.*

Things just for my partner and me:

*We'd like to go somewhere alone overnight.*

Supports we need to realize our hopes and dreams:

*We need some help for Maxwell so he can sit and play in the sand and water and enjoy it. We need reliable, trained babysitters.*

You may choose to take a family member or friend with you as a support person—to listen with you, to help you explain some of your points of view and wishes, and to take notes that you might need later. Prior to the meeting, go over the *Hopes and Dreams Exercise* with your support person so that both of you will go with the same agenda in mind. Following the meeting you might go out for pizza or coffee so that you and your support person can talk about what happened at the meeting.

The contents of your child's IFSP are determined at the meeting, considering the points of view of all participants. You, as the parent, are the one who makes the final decision about accepting or rejecting the proposals. The team, including you, decides what the final IFSP contains. If you want something different from what is recommended by other team members, you may follow procedures described later in this chapter to resolve any disagreements. Without your consent the IFSP will not be put into effect.

IFSP meetings must be conducted annually and reviewed every six months. Meetings can be held more frequently if necessary, or if the family requests a review or change.

## FAMILY-CENTERED IFSP MEETINGS

The IFSP is more than simply a written plan. It is a process which leads parents and professionals toward a mutual understanding of the child's needs and the family's wishes. The written IFSP is a guide leading to the future. Families and service providers suggest that the following steps be taken to ensure productive and constructive IFSP meetings:

1. Families and service providers agree to a convenient time and place for the meeting so that parents and other important family members or friends may attend. The meeting is scheduled at least one week in advance to allow everyone time to prepare.
2. Families receive copies of all written reports before the meeting so they can understand the information and be ready to discuss it. If this is not possible, it may be necessary to schedule a second meeting soon after the first.
3. Parents and the service coordinator meet before the IFSP meeting to prepare information and plan ways for the family to be active participants in the meeting.
4. Enough time is allowed for the meeting so that no one feels rushed and participants have time to discuss what they consider the most important outcomes for the child and the family.

5. The meeting determines what the family believes is important for their child to do or to accomplish. The IFSP outcomes (goals) are the result of what the family identifies.

6. The outcomes for the child and family are developed at the meeting, giving full opportunity for parents and other members of the family to participate in their development. Parents may not know what aids or therapies will help their child reach these outcomes. Professionals contribute knowledge about specific ways to accomplish an outcome identified by the family.

On the following page is an IFSP prepared by the Jackson family and their IFSP team. The format may be different in your locality, but the required parts will be the same.

## ▪ WHEN SERVICES BEGIN ▪

You might think that once you have written the IFSP you can sit back, relax, and let things happen. But not so. Now is the time for the important work outlined in your baby or toddler's IFSP to start. You and other family members will be involved in helping your child and family move forward on the pathway toward growth and change.

Early intervention services take many forms. Families whose babies have specialized health care needs often feel that services should be in their homes, in part to avoid exposing their child to colds or other infections. Generally, service providers also recommend home-based services for fragile children. Yet other families want their child to face the rough and tumble of everyday life and request center-based infant education for their child. They want the exposure to other children and their families both for themselves and for their child. While you may or may not have a choice as to whether your child receives services at home or at a center, Part H requires that services be provided in the child's natural environment, which may mean for your child that she be with other children without disabilities. If choices are available, you can express your preferences at the IFSP meeting.

The different services on your child's IFSP may be provided for an hour a week, twice a month, or at other intervals. Between times, parents practice activities such as speech and language games, physical exercises, or eating skills with their child. Each session, either at a center or at home, offers opportunities for discussion between the service provider and the family.

Families in which the single parent or both parents work can find themselves in a bind at their workplace if participation with their child in early

# INDIVIDUALIZED FAMILY SERVICE PLAN

## IDENTIFYING INFORMATION

Child: *Martha Dee Jackson*

Parent/Guardian: *Bernice Jackson*

Address: *4421 Main Street*

Home Phone: *(218) 467-9999*

Foster Home: [ ] yes [X] no

Date: *8/23/97*

Birth Date: *8/20/95* [ ] M [X] F

Work Phone(s):

Language Spoken in Home: *English*

## DATES

Present Meeting: *8/23/97*

Anticipated Six Month Review: *2/98*

Anticipated Annual Review: *8/98*

## IFSP MEETING INFORMATION

Type of Meeting:  [X] Initial

[ ] Six Month Review

[ ] Annual Review

[ ] Interim

Amendment of IFSP          Dated:          [ ] To add or [ ] delete

Information Update

[X] Identifying Information

[X] Family Concerns, Priorities, & Strengths

[X] Child's Strengths and Needs

[X] Outcomes

[X] Other Services

[ ] Transition Plan

[ ] No longer eligible

[ ] Moved out of county

[ ] Parent withdrawal

[ ] Whereabouts unknown

[ ] Transition to: _____

[ ] Other

## ELIGIBILITY

1. [X] Child is eligible for Part H services based on *"at risk" status* _____

   Functional Description of Disability: *Spina Bifida* _____

2. [ ] Specific eligibility undetermined; recommend: _____

3. [ ] Child does not meet eligibility for Part H services _____

# INDIVIDUALIZED FAMILY SERVICE PLAN (CONTINUED)

## IFSP PARTICIPANTS

The following individuals participated in the development of the IFSP. Each person understands and agrees to carry out the plan as it applies to their role in the provision of services.

Service Coordinator: *Mary E. Morgan*   Representing: *Early Intervention*   Date: *8/23/97*

Name: *Bernice Jackson*   Representing: *Mother*   Date: *8/23/97*

Name: *Ann Adams*   Representing: *Easter Seals*   Date: *8/23/97*

Name: _____   Representing: _____   Date: _____

Name: _____   Representing: _____   Date: _____

The IFSP was developed with telephone consultation from the following people:

Name: *Nina Baxter*   Representing: *Parent Center*   Date: *8/24/97*

Name: _____   Representing: _____   Date: _____

Name: _____   Representing: _____   Date: _____

## FAMILY APPROVAL

[X] I had the opportunity to participate in the development of this IFSP. I agree with and support the outcomes and services in the IFSP for my child.

[ ] I have had the opportunity to review the proposal of the IFSP Team and I do not agree with the outcomes or services selected. I do not give my permission for it to be implemented.

Parent/Legal Guardian _____*Bernice Jackson*_____ Date *8/23/97*

Parent/Legal Guardian _____ Date _____

## FAMILY'S CONCERNS, PRIORITIES, & RESOURCES (AS DESCRIBED BY PARENTS)

*Martha Dee's gross motor and language development are the primary concerns of the Jackson family. Martha Dee speaks 4-5 words and responds well when her brother plays and talks with her. They believe that consulation by a language therapist will increase Martha Dee's speech.*

## CHILD'S STRENGTHS AND NEEDS (AS DESCRIBED BY PARENTS)

*Martha Dee has made significant progress in her gross motor development. She sits, crawls and now uses a "stander" at home 2 times per day, half hour each time. Her mother plays with her with a large "therapy ball" 15 minutes, 3 times a day. Martha Dee and her brother sing and play together. Her language development is her major area of need.*

# INDIVIDUALIZED FAMILY SERVICE PLAN (CONTINUED)

## OUTCOME #1—Part H Services

Martha Dee will identify pictures in familiar picture books and will increase her vocabulary to 15 words by 2/98. She will receive broad-based infant development programming to address her special developmental needs, particularly in motor and language skills.

1.1 Home-based infant development services—3 hrs./month
1.2 Center-based services—16 hrs. per month at Easter Seals
1.3 Speech language teacher to consult with both home and center teacher

### SERVICES/ACTIONS (HOW WILL OUTCOMES BE REACHED AND SUCCESS DETERMINED?)

Teachers at the center and in the home and Martha Dee's mother will reinforce new words and keep a vocabulary list as she learns new words

PROVIDERS: Easter Seal Society
LOCATION: 1:1 teaching at home; 1:3 Easter Seal Society
FREQUENCY: home-based; 3 hrs./month; center-based
DURATION: 9/6/97—8/20/98
RESPONSIBLE AGENCY: Travis County Early Intervention Services (TCEIS)
SIGNATURE OF RESPONSIBLE AGENCY PERSON: Marye Morgan    DATE: 8/23/97

## OUTCOME #2—Not Funded by Part H

Martha Dee has a VP shunt and requires catheterization for urine every 3 hours. These needs will be medically monitored, along with her regular pediatric needs.

2.1 Spina Bifida and Urology Clinics will monitor the neurological and urological development
2.2 Ongoing medical monitoring and treatment to be given at Greenway
2.3 Martha Dee's mother will administer catheterization every 3 hours as directed by a physician

### SERVICES/ACTIONS (HOW WILL OUTCOMES BE REACHED AND SUCCESS DETERMINED?)

Physician and Martha Dee's mother will discuss the ongoing catheterization needs.

PROVIDERS: Spina Bifida and Urology Clinic and Greenway Children's Clinic
LOCATION: San Jacinto
FREQUENCY: semi-annually and as needed
DURATION: 9/6/97—8/20/98
RESPONSIBLE AGENCY: Medicare
SIGNATURE OF RESPONSIBLE AGENCY PERSON: Marye Morgan    DATE: 8/23/97

(MARTHA DEE'S IFSP WOULD HAVE THREE ADDITIONAL OUTCOMES DEVELOPED IN THE AREAS OF MOTOR DEVELOPMENT, PARENT SUPPORT GROUP AND CASE MANAGEMENT.)

intervention services cuts into their work day. Some families ask another relative to go with the baby to the center-based services, or arrange for their in-home care giver to be the primary person who works with the baby as the teachers or therapists suggest. Other families try to arrange for sessions at times that minimize time lost from work; for example, before work or during their lunch hour. Remember, parents should be the primary decision makers as these types of issues are discussed and resolved with the multidisciplinary team.

Depending on the services described in the IFSP, your active involvement will help to ensure positive results. Working as a partner with service providers helps you build a support group. Your service coordinator or a parent-to-parent program can also link you to other families who are living and dealing with a family situation similar to yours. This can help, too, in expanding your network of support.

Different families find different ways to become partners with people who are there to assist them. The most important way to build a partnership with people who will be helping you and your family is by practicing good communication techniques. Often infant intervention services are given at home. You may find that having a friend there at the end of the therapy session to play with your child will give you time to have a discussion with the therapist. Or you might set up a separate time when your child can be cared for by someone else, so that your full attention can be on the conversation about your child's progress and development.

Good communication requires careful building of relationships. There are many ways to strengthen relationships with professional people—most take little time. A "thank you" in person, on the telephone, or in a short note shows your appreciation. Professional people, like all people, like to know you care.

## FAMILY INFORMATION FORM

The Family Information Form found on the next page can be helpful in beginning discussions about your child and family. Getting a session off to a positive start is easy if you use an ice breaker. Showing the picture of your baby or a family picture can help. Or telling a humorous story about your child can provide a link to the more serious issues to be discussed.

The relationships you build will help you to check on your child's progress and to solve problems that may arise later. The time and effort you take to write a short note, to telephone and celebrate some progress your baby or toddler has made, to have a service provider over for a cup of tea, or to write a positive letter to the person's supervisor or board president will pay off in the long run for you and your child.

# FAMILY INFORMATION FORM

Date _____

My Name _____

My Child's Name _____

Please Call Me _____

Child's Birthday _____

Photograph or sketch of
your child or family.

1. Description of our family (parent(s), brothers and sisters, grandparents, special

friends and relations): _____

_____

2. What we enjoy doing as a family: _____

_____

During these family times my child: _____

_____

3. My child's favorite activity is: _____

_____

Because _____

4. My child's least favorite activity is: _____

_____

Because _____

## FAMILY INFORMATION FORM (CONTINUED)

5. What I enjoy most about my child is: _____

_____

6. What my child and I enjoy doing the most is: _____

_____

7. I am most frustrated when caring for my child when _____

_____

8. My child lets me know when he/she needs something by _____

_____

9. I could do more for my child if I had _____

_____

(transportation, someone to talk to and listen to me, time to myself, time for the other children, more information about my baby's condition and about ways to help her, help with medical and other expenses, housing, Supplemental Security Income (SSI), food stamps, etc.)

10. Some changes or progress I've recently noticed in my child: _____

_____

11. What I would like to see my child do in the next six months: _____

_____

12. How my family, friends or I can help my child do these things _____

_____

13. Some of my hopes for my child and family are _____

_____

# ■ WHEN DISAGREEMENTS ARISE ■

Even in the best of relationships, disagreements can arise. When you have made the effort to build positive partnerships with professionals, however, disagreements have a good chance of being resolved quickly and satisfactorily.

You and your infant or toddler have certain rights under the early intervention law. You have assurance that:

- parents and families are served by programs that are conducted in a voluntary and nondiscriminatory way;
- parents and family members have access to the information they need to know in order to participate in early intervention programs and to make clear decisions; and
- family members' preferences and choices are respected regarding the services for their child and their family.

You, your child, and family have the right to:

- give written consent when your child is to be assessed or evaluated;
- be given written notice in your native language, if possible, of actions proposed by the service providers;
- see copies of and correct records about your child and family;
- keep confidential any private information about your child or your family;
- have a service coordinator who will assist you in pulling together the information and the people needed to develop an IFSP; and
- go through a mediation or formal hearing process if there are disagreements or complaints that can't be resolved informally with the service provider.

Families are involved in all steps of the early intervention process. While the process is designed to minimize conflict, disagreements may occur. Examples areas of possible disagreement between parents and professionals are:

- *Professionals* believe an initial assessment and evaluation are not necessary.
- *Parents* believe an initial evaluation is not necessary.
- The family and service providers do not agree on the type, frequency, or duration of services.

- The family and service providers have difficulty getting the help needed for the child and the family.

What happens when the process does not go smoothly? What should parents and professionals do when differences of opinion persist?

## INFORMAL PROBLEM SOLVING

You may reach a point where you can't think your way through a difficult situation, either in relationship to another person or as you make choices for your child and family. If so, a problem solving approach can be very helpful. First, clarify the situation, identifying what you believe to be unsatisfactory. Second, make a plan of action by exploring various alternatives and deciding which of these to pursue. If you can find a partner to go through these steps with you, and/or write them down, you may find the situation under control.

### Problem Solving: A Case Study

Brendan's speech and language are delayed. He was born with a cleft palate that was corrected by surgery when he was six months old. In his community there are three early intervention programs. At his IFSP meeting the professionals recommended the Tiny Tots program, which provides the least intensive services of the three. Brendan's mother agreed reluctantly, although she felt the services at I & T Center were more appropriate both for Brendan and for her family.

After six weeks at Tiny Tots, Ms. Lindsay decided a change was necessary, as she felt that Brendan's progress was much too slow. She needed more assistance in learning ways to work with him at home. She visited the I & T Center program, talked to early intervention specialists and parents, and made notes about what she learned. The babies seemed much more like Brendan in their development, and the family training to help the babies was much better.

She then talked to her service coordinator, sharing her thoughts and observations. Together they went to the teachers at Tiny Tots and described the level of services Ms. Lindsay felt Brendan needed. The Tiny Tots staff was unable to increase their services for the Lindsays. Luckily, there was an opening at I & T Center. Ms. Lindsay and the service coordinator reconvened the IFSP team and all agreed that the change would benefit Brendan and the family. Ms. Lindsay and the professionals felt good about their informal way of solving the problem.

## OTHER OPTIONS FOR RESOLVING DISAGREEMENTS

If informal problem solving does not resolve a disagreement, the law provides other procedures that allow families and service providers to reach a resolution. Most states have both mediation and due process hearings. In addition, court proceedings are an option. Chapter 10 explains in detail the procedures to be followed to resolve differences through a hearing by an impartial hearing officer. Most families find, however, that a formal due process hearing or court proceeding takes such an enormous amount of time, money, and energy, that these actions are not practical for an infant or toddler. In most states and localities a helpful means of dispute resolution is *mediation.*★

## What Is Mediation and How Does it Work?

When the people involved in a disagreement are unable to reach a solution through informal problem solving, they may decide to try mediation. Mediation is a process for resolving conflicts between two or more parties using a trained, impartial person to help solve the problem. It is structured, but is far less formal than a due process hearing or court proceeding. In mediation, each party is directly involved in talking with the other to reach a solution. They retain control of the issues and how they are settled. Mediation begins with the present and focuses on the future. Rather than examining past actions or wrongs, the parties concentrate on how to resolve the current dispute and move forward.

The mediator may be able to guide the parties to a compromise they were unable to reach on their own. The role of the mediator is to focus attention on the *problem,* rather than on the participants. This allows the group to work toward a solution to the problem.

Mediation is not restricted by legal rules of evidence or other rules of procedure. It is not dependent on the presentation of facts by attorneys or others not directly involved. Mediation is scheduled and completed in a short period of time, permitting the parties to concentrate on a resolution rather than preparation of a case for a hearing.

Mediation is increasingly used to solve disagreements between parents and public school officials arising under the Individuals with Disabilities Education Act (IDEA). This process can also be useful to parents and professionals who work with infants and toddlers in the early intervention system. You will find that mediation is faster, less expensive, less stressful, and more constructive than due process hearings. Families and service providers continue, after the present disagreement is resolved, to work together to provide services to a child. Mediation can be a win/win solution, where nobody loses, and where the parties work together to develop flexible solutions.

Mediation does not mean that you give up the right to a due process hearing at a later time if attempted mediation fails. Mediation *does not* eliminate any rights a child or family has under IDEA; it is an available alternative.

Each state that provides for mediation has certain provisions. For example, in one state mediation must be completed within fifteen calendar days of the request. When the parties have reached an agreement, the mediator then writes it out in language acceptable to both parties, who then sign the written agreement.

## Mediation: A Case Study

Amy Wilson was born two months prematurely. At six months of age, she could not turn over or make "cooing" noises, and she had suffered from several ear infections. At her pediatrician's recommendation, she began to participate in an early intervention program. After evaluation, her multidisciplinary team determined that she was developmentally delayed and enrolled her in a program one morning a week. The services Amy received included speech, physical, and occupational therapy, offered in an informal play setting with two other infants.

Amy's parents, the Wilsons, were very concerned about her delayed development, especially when they compared her with her older brother. They asked that she attend three times a week and engaged private therapists to come to their home as well. The staff encouraged the Wilsons to play with Amy at home and demonstrated exercises they could do, but declined to add two more mornings to her schedule. The Wilsons felt strongly that Amy needed the additional time and that the outcomes on her IFSP could not be met without it. The center staff told Amy's parents that they believed the additional time would not benefit Amy. After several unhappy meetings, the staff and family decided that they were at a standstill and could no longer have constructive meetings. They agreed to meet again, with a mediator present.

The Wilsons telephoned the Early Intervention Office in their state to request a mediator. The mediator telephoned both the center staff and the Wilsons to set a convenient time for the meeting and explained the mediation procedure. At the meeting, the mediator opened the session by explaining its purpose, emphasizing its confidentiality and the necessity to focus on the future, rather than on past events.

The mediator listened as Amy's family explained their wish to provide their child with as much assistance as possible early in her life to help her compensate for her developmental delays. Their hope was that Amy would not require special assistance once she entered preschool. The staff supported the Wilsons' goal, but explained to the mediator that they rarely recommended that infants under one year of age come to the center more than once a week, because it is often too stressful.

The mediator pointed out that both parties shared the same goal for Amy, but differed on how to reach that goal. The mediator guided a discussion which helped to clarify the staff's reasons for one-day-a-week therapies, and the family's concerns about Amy's development. The Wilsons agreed that additional therapy provided by the specialists would not necessarily benefit Amy. Center staff offered to meet once a week with the Wilsons at home and help them with activities that could further Amy's development. With this assistance, the family agreed to once-a-week sessions with the additional weekly meeting, and to re-evaluate Amy's progress in four months.

# ■ *TRANSITION INTO PRESCHOOL SERVICES* ■

Just as you feel life is settling down into some kind of pattern, things change. When your toddler nears age three, a new program looms on the horizon. How do you prepare yourself and your family for the next step in your child's life? Each Individualized Family Service Plan (IFSP) must spell out the steps in the transition from the early intervention services to whatever preschool services are appropriate for your child. The steps must include discussions with, and training of, parents regarding future placements and other matters related to the child's transition. Additionally, there should be a description of the help the child will receive to prepare for changes in service delivery, including steps to help her adjust to and function in the new setting. With your permission, information about your child—including evaluations and assessments and copies of the IFSPs that have been developed—can be sent to the local school system. The transition plan must provide for a smooth transition into preschool special education or other appropriate services when your child turns three.

New evaluations and assessments are done to establish your child's eligibility for preschool special education. In some states the early intervention system will do evaluations, while in other states the school system wants to do their own. No matter who does the evaluation, the school system depends upon up-to-date information to make its eligibility decision. An Individualized Education Program (IEP) will be written for your child following the evaluation. This will occur either in the early intervention system with a local education agency person as a member of the IEP team, or by the education agency with the assistance of an early intervention specialist.

Steps can be taken by your family to ease the change both for you and your child. Families may choose from among the following steps:

- Gather as much information as possible about the next program.
- Explore possible alternatives in order to select one or two of the best choices.

- Locate another family whose child has been in the proposed program and learn about their experiences.
- Talk to the person who is in charge of the proposed program.
- Visit the proposed program in advance.
- Talk to teachers and administrators of the program, describing your family's experiences in early intervention and your expectations for the new situation.
- Ask for written materials and learn the procedures for entering and participating in the new service or system.
- Evaluate the proposed program carefully and realize that you are in charge and can say either "yes" or "no" to the services recommended for your child and family.

When the time comes for the actual change, you may want to prepare yourself, your child, and your family for the new routines. For example, you can visit the new program or service in order for your child to become acquainted with the new people and the new environment. Perhaps sending a favorite toy with your child might make her more comfortable in the new situation. And maybe other family members may need to be alerted to the new routines brought on by the change.

As time goes on, you will find that changes or transitions present many of the same problems you have previously worked through with success. The past certainly can help prepare you for new experiences. What you have learned in the early intervention program can be applied if your child enters a preschool special education program. As in all of the decisions you have made and will be making, the more information you gather and the stronger the relationships you develop, the easier the transition will be for you and your family.

# 9. TRANSITION

## PATHWAYS TO THE FUTURE

Can my child really learn to live away from home? Will he have a job in the community? What are his chances for further education after he leaves the public school system?

No matter how young your child is, these and many other questions most likely have already come to your mind. As your child grows older, your family will continue to be faced with many perplexing concerns regarding his future. As the years go by, these concerns often cause increasing anxiety about what life will hold. With your hands full just coping with day-to-day life, planning to address future concerns is often difficult to do. Without a crystal ball to provide a vision of what lies ahead, you may question whether you have anything to gain by putting forth the time and effort required for such planning.

Whatever a child's disability, steps you take now can help create a more positive future for both you and your child. Probably the best way to reduce the anxiety and stress associated with future uncertainty is through careful planning, beginning early enough in your child's school life to use the resources of the school to assist you. You have an important role to play to ensure that your child with disabilities—as with all of your children— will have as independent and self-sufficient a life as possible. This chapter will help you understand the concept of transition and the ways transition planning can help your child move toward a future of maximum independence.

# ▪ HOPES AND FACTS ▪

Families of children with disabilities are now accustomed to the educational entitlement provided by IDEA and its amendments, including a free, appropriate, public education in the least restrictive environment. You may assume that a similar entitlement to publicly funded services will continue for your child upon graduation from school. Unfortunately, this is not the case. Once a young adult with disabilities leaves the public school system, there is no guaranteed program that takes up where IDEA leaves off. No current federal or state laws provide all young adults with disabilities with rights to continuing education, or to the housing, jobs, or support services needed to help them live independently.

School personnel, parents, advocates, and community-minded people have been working hard in recent years to address the problems faced by young people who leave school between the ages of eighteen and twenty-one with nowhere to go. In particular, amendments to IDEA in 1990 require transition services for all students with disabilities. As a result, all students in special education—beginning at age sixteen or as early as fourteen when appropriate—should have plans and services in place to help them achieve or continue working toward their lifelong goals.[*]

# ▪ ONE FAMILY'S TRANSITION PLANS ▪

Early in life, Mary Connors showed strong interest in caring for pets, young children, and her elderly grandfather. She often pretended to be a nurse or veterinarian with her dolls and pets. Her family gave her every opportunity they could to be with other children and adults and to help with household chores, especially when company was coming. As the years went by, they began to perceive that Mary's interests and strengths might lead to a possible career for her.

When Mary was fourteen, Mrs. Connors arranged for her to work with a teenage family friend as a baby sitter's helper. When her friend Carla had a sitting job, Mary would accompany her and help put the young children to bed. At school, Mary's Individualized Education Program included a goal for her to visit four different jobs to observe people at work and learn about the various occupations. She was also taking a home economics course to learn to plan and prepare simple meals.

In high school, Mary was in a work experience program that allowed her to spend part of her day in the community, participating in a special nursing assistant program. Students in this program worked in a variety of settings, providing care to others for several hours each day. First, Mary worked with the nurse in an elementary school, keeping the equipment clean, putting fresh sheets on the cots, and staying with young children as they waited for the nurse. Six weeks later, she worked in a nursing home alongside a skilled nurse's aide. Her final experience during that school year was at the pediatric unit in the local hospital, learning to make beds, to sterilize toys and equipment, and to be a companion for young sick children.

With help from her high school counselor, Mary and her family located a junior college with a two-year nursing assistant program. The program provides Mary with instruction and support in living on her own, as well as training for her chosen career.

Mary and her family were able to plan for her life after high school and get services in place with the help of the transition requirements of IDEA.

## ■ *Transition and IDEA* ■

To prepare children with disabilities for their next steps after high school, schools are to provide, according to IDEA, ". . . a coordinated set of activities . . . based upon the individual student's needs, taking into account the student's preferences and interests." In other words, several activities should be included as a part of your son or daughter's plan, and your son or daughter should be directly involved in choosing those activities. The activities need to be planned with certain results, or outcomes, in mind. These include: *postsecondary education, vocational training, integrated employment (including supported employment), continuing and adult education, adult services, independent living and community participation.*

What are these outcomes? For what are students with disabilities being prepared?

### 1. Post-secondary Education

Colleges, whether they are two-year junior or community colleges or four-year colleges and universities, offer an opportunity for students with disabilities to continue their education and earn a certificate or a degree. Under the Americans with Disabilities Act (ADA) and Section 504 of the Rehabilitation Act, post-secondary institutions are prohibited from discriminating against otherwise qualified students with disabilities in the provision of education programs. (See Chapter 11 for more information about the requirements and protections provided by Section 504 and the ADA.)

## 2. CONTINUING AND ADULT EDUCATION

Continuing education courses offer opportunities for personal enrichment in areas such as cooking, gardening, and woodworking, as well as courses for enhancing career goals, such as business management. Adult education programs are designed to provide instruction to any person sixteen years of age or older who is no longer being served by the public education system. The programs may include vocational education courses, course work to prepare people to take the General Education Development (GED) exam, and English as a Second Language instruction. You can find information about continuing and adult education through your local school district, recreation department, or community college.

## 3. VOCATIONAL TRAINING

**Trade and Technical Schools.** These schools prepare students for employment in recognized occupations such as secretary, air conditioning technician, beautician, electrician, welder, and carpenter. Course work can take anywhere from two weeks to two years, and the schools generally require a high school diploma or high school equivalency degree to enter. Again, under the ADA and Section 504, trade and technical schools must provide reasonable accommodations and modifications for persons with disabilities, so as not to unfairly discriminate against them in the provision of their programs. For example, a young man with mild mental retardation wants to take auto mechanics. Through tape recordings of the manuals required for the course, he is able to learn the materials and participate fully in the vocational education program.

**On the Job Training.** On the job training is short-term training that enables a person to work on a job site while learning the job duties. Many vocational rehabilitation agencies, disability organizations, and large corporations provide this type of training and job placement.

## 4. INTEGRATED EMPLOYMENT

**Competitive Employment.** Competitive employment includes everyday jobs in the open labor market, such as health care worker, data entry clerk, legal assistant, waiter/waitress, service station attendant, retail clerk, secretary, and mechanic. These jobs pay wages at the going rate, and can be either on a part-time or full-time basis.

**Supported Employment.** Supported employment is paid employment for workers with severe disabilities which enables them to work with people who do not have disabilities. Your son or daughter would work either individually or as a part of a small work crew, always integrated, however, into the mainstream of work life. A job coach provides support by helping the employee to improve his job skills, interpersonal relations, or any other job-related needs. Job coaches generally "fade back," or reduce their involvement, as the worker becomes more skilled in his job. Salaries for supported jobs are at or above the minimum wage. Examples of supported jobs include grounds keeping, assisting at a veterinarian's office, working in medical laboratories to keep equipment ready for the scientists, or assembling electronic circuit boards.

## 5. ADULT SERVICES

Adult service programs, which include adult day programs, work activity centers, and sheltered workshops, provide a work environment in a supervised setting without integration with workers who are not disabled. In **adult day programs**, participants usually receive training in daily living skills, social skills, and recreational skills. **Work activity centers** offer similar training, but may also include training in vocational skills. In **sheltered workshops**, workers do contract work such as preparing bulk mailings, refinishing furniture, or assembling bicycle brake parts. Each worker is paid on a piece rate basis according to the number of items he or she completes.

## 6. INDEPENDENT LIVING

Independent living requires that young adults learn the skills they need or obtain the support they require to live on their own. This usually means managing several parts of daily life, obtaining food and clothing, learning to manage time and money, and knowing ways to have fun.

Depending upon their financial independence and independent living skills, young people with disabilities may continue living with their parents, other relatives, roommates, or paid companions, or they may live on their own. Options for young people who need significant support in independent living include family care, supervised living arrangements, and facilities that provide intensive care. **Family care** is provided by individuals who are licensed by the state to provide family-like settings for elderly people and adults with disabilities. **Supervised living arrangements,** such as group homes, are managed by public or private agencies that own or rent homes or apartments. Paid staff supervise the residents and assist them with daily living such as budgeting, food preparation, and transportation. Many people with severe disabilities are living under supervision in small apartments with roommates of their own choosing. They are supervised and supported by paid staff from human service agencies in the community. **Specialized Nursing Homes and Intermediate Care Facilities** are licensed facilities operating under strict regulations and providing intensive support for people in the areas of personal care, communication, and behavior management.

## 7. COMMUNITY PARTICIPATION

Community participation takes many forms—volunteering at the local hospital, planting trees in the neighborhood park, attending church, serving on the board of a nonprofit agency, and walking the neighbor's dog. Young people with disabilities who take part in the community make new friends, possible work contacts, and contribute to the life and well-being of the community. Transition plans and activities are to be developed in order to ensure that young people with disabilities can be a part of their community and participate to the fullest extent possible.

## ■ *THE IMPORTANCE OF SELF-ADVOCACY* ■

In the past, the predictable transition for students with disabilities was from segregated school settings to specialized adult day programs or workshops restricted to people with disabilities. Thanks to creative parents and professionals, innovative programs, and laws such as IDEA and the ADA, this is no longer true. Today's young people are more fully included in all aspects of school life and, therefore, are learning to make choices about their adult lives. They expect that they will have opportunities to be workers, students, family members, friends, and community participants. Legislation, research, and best educational practices emphasize that a young person's transition to adult life must be based upon his unique interests, capacities, career goals, and needs for support. Your child most likely would welcome encouragement from you and his teachers to make decisions about his future and to express his own views about his interests and preferences.

When you think about your child, you may feel that he will not be able to learn to make responsible decisions and speak up for himself. Certainly, the amount of independent self advocacy a young person is able to demonstrate varies depending upon his abilities and the degree of disability. While some young people are not able to speak verbally for themselves, they communicate their preferences in many other ways. All young people need the involvement and support of their family members, friends, teachers, and others as they learn to solve problems, be assertive, and make their own plans for transitions from high school. IDEA recognizes the importance of self-advocacy skills by requiring that decisions about transition activities be based upon the student's preferences and interests.

# ■ PLANNING TRANSITION WITH THE SCHOOLS ■

As you consider ways to plan for your child's entry into the work world, the logical place to begin is with the school. By using the school system's resources wisely, you can go far in preparing him for the transition into adult life. You, your child, school professionals, and people from adult service agencies all possess important knowledge and perspectives. If everyone works together as a team, your child will be able to develop the skills, find the opportunities, and obtain the support services that will be necessary for him to participate successfully in work and community life.

Transition planning is meant to be a part of the special education process—not a side trip or detour on the circle road map of the special education cycle. Most of the same people who develop your child's IEP are involved in the meetings to plan for his transition. In fact, in many school systems, IEPs and transition plans are discussed and written at the same time. Additional people may attend the meeting, depending upon the types of transition services your son or daughter may need.

## WHO ATTENDS THE TRANSITION MEETING?

IDEA requires that **students** be invited to any meeting where transition plans are discussed. Mary Connors began attending her IEP meetings when she was fourteen and made sure her ideas were a part of the plan. She shared her thoughts about the future, her interest in child care, and her hopes for a future of working with children or elderly people.

**Parents** are also crucial members of the transition planning team. You can help your child explain his ideas and questions to the other team members. The team needs to hear your unique perspective of your child's strengths, interests, and needs for support.

**School personnel** are, of course, part of the transition team. Your child's teacher(s), guidance counselor, vocational coordinator, and school administrator may attend the transition meeting. Many school districts appoint at least one transition coordinator who manages transition services for students with disabilities and would probably attend transition meetings. Any other school staff that you or the school thinks would be helpful can be included as a part of the team as well. The transition coordinator was an integral part of Mary Connors's transition teams, managing the work experience program for her and ensuring the activities were consistent with her career goals.

Adult service agency staff, such as vocational rehabilitation counselors or staff of an independent living center, may attend if your child requires services from such an agency. Because Mary needed some assistance with using public transportation, the "On-The-Move" program coordinator from the Independent Living Center attended several of Mary's transition planning meetings.

Other individuals, at the request of you, your child, or school staff, may also take part in the transition meeting. For example, Carla, the friend Mary helped with baby sitting, attended all of her transition meetings. As Mary was preparing to graduate and apply for a two-year college program, her employer from the day care center attended to offer her thoughts and insight.

## EVALUATION AND TRANSITION PLANNING

One important part of transition planning is to ensure that the plans and services are based upon your child's interests, aptitudes, and preferences. Evaluations can provide helpful information in these areas, although not all assessments will be appropriate for all students. You will want to choose which type of testing will provide you and your child with the information that is most useful. And, like Mary Connors, your child will have some ideas of his own about transition activities and plans for the future. Evaluation information for your child comes from a variety of sources, some of which are described below.

As a part of the high school curriculum, all students are offered testing, usually in the ninth grade, that will give them a better understanding of their unique interests and career strengths. Your child's school guidance counselor can provide information regarding these tests.

Through your child's high school career/vocational technical center, he can participate in vocational assessments and other opportunities to explore possible career paths. Mary Connors participated in community-based instruction that was both an assessment opportunity and a job-training program. She learned skills while she tried out a variety of jobs to assess her preference and suitability for each.

For students enrolled in special education, schools are required to offer vocational assessments. These assessments typically include paper and pencil activities, interest assessments, and actual samples of work activities to determine physical abilities, current skills, and areas for skill development. Formal testing and informal observations should be included to get a full picture of your child's abilities, interests, and preferences.

In most states, the local rehabilitation services agencies can provide vocational assessments before students leave school. Some have special programs where they work with students who have disabilities, providing them with opportunities to undergo intensive assessments in a setting away from home. Your school transition specialist or special education director can provide you with more information about the availability of these types of programs in your community.

### Vocational Assessment

Under IDEA, vocational assessment can be considered a related service and written into your child's IEP when he reaches middle school or early high school years. The purpose of a vocational assessment is to obtain a picture of your child's aptitudes and interests as they relate to careers he might want to pursue. Many school systems have their own procedures for conducting formal vocational assessments, while others work cooperatively with rehabilitative service agencies to provide them. No matter who conducts the assessment, it should help you and school personnel with vocational planning for your child.

Vocational assessments provide information about a particular student in order to design, implement, and evaluate an appropriate vocational program. They may also be used to provide information necessary to determine eligibility for certain programs or services, such as those provided by school vocational programs or vocational rehabilitation agencies. In addition, they should help your child explore career possibilities, assist teachers in determining his skills and learning styles, and target those areas where he can benefit from further training.

Vocational assessment generally consists of three major components:
1. work sampling;
2. standardized tests; and
3. behavioral observation.

First, **work sampling** tests a student's hands-on performance in certain simulated and actual work environments. The more closely the work sample resembles an actual job, the more easily a student and the evaluator can judge whether or not such a job would fit the student's abilities and interests. Examples of work samples include assembling gears for bicycles or filing papers in alphabetical order.

Second, **standardized tests** evaluate such areas as the student's interests, aptitudes, manual dexterity, clerical ability, and mechanical ability. These tests are designed to give some prediction of how a student is likely to perform in jobs calling for certain interests and skills.

Third, **behavioral observation** is a systematic way of observing, recording, and interpreting the behavior of a student as he works. Most vocational educators agree that skilled observation of a person on the job gives a far better idea of the person's vocational abilities than any standardized tests or work samples. Therefore, in many schools vocational assessments include observations of students in a variety of community-based work settings over a period of months. From these observations, the vocational evaluator gains a broad picture of the student's interests and abilities. These experiences also provide a real work environment in which students can practice work behaviors and learn the expectations of various jobs.

Ideally, a vocational assessment should use a combination of work samples, standardized tests, and behavioral observations to develop a picture of your child's vocational interests and potential. Parents or professionals, however, should never allow vocational assessments to be the sole factor in determining the suitability of a job or career pathway.

Vocational assessments can be valuable for your child when combined with additional input about his interests, hopes, and vision of the future. Likewise, employers and adult service providers recognize that vocational training alone seldom fully prepares a person for a job. If you wait until a young person is "ready" for a job; if you wait until he has learned in school all the requirements for a job; if you wait until some service provider has prepared him to move from a sheltered, segregated job to a job in the community; the day may never come. It is now widely acknowledged that young people with disabilities are able to get and to keep jobs for a longer period of time if they are placed in jobs that interest them, are trained on the job, and then are given the supports they need to keep the job.

## INDIVIDUALIZED EDUCATION PROGRAM AND TRANSITION

IDEA requires students' IEPs to include statements describing necessary transition services when the student is age sixteen, and as early as age fourteen, if appropriate.* In some school districts, students have separate Individualized Transition Plans; other school districts incorporate transition goals, objectives, and services within the regular IEP. Schools are responsible for coordinating transition plans and providing the services the school agrees to in the plan. If an agency, other than the school system, does not provide the services the agency agreed to in the transition plan, the school is to reconvene the IEP meeting to identify other ways to meet the transition objectives.

When developing plans for transition, the team discusses services that your child might need in the areas of: instruction, community experiences, the development of employment and other post-school adult living objectives, acquisition of daily living skills, and functional vocational evaluation.

(Functional vocational evaluation usually consists of formal and informal observations of students in a work setting.)

If the team—which includes you and your child—decides that the student does not need services in any of those areas, a statement must be included as to why and how that decision was made. For example, a student working towards a high school diploma with the hopes of entering a four-year college would most likely not have "learning daily living skills" as part of his transition plan.

## PLACEMENT AND TRANSITION

For some students transition services will be incorporated into their current high school classes. Others will attend specific programs to prepare for their lives after high school. Mary Connors's transition plan included both "regular" high school classes and a specialized program. Examples of specific programs include:

**Work-Study Programs in the Community.** Here, your child would receive training leading to employment and also receive credit toward graduation for the work experience. Work-study programs sometimes involve paid employment, and the students are supervised on the job by their work supervisor, not school employees. For example, Mary Connors's friend Katy was employed as a physical therapy assistant four hours per day, and attended English and History classes two hours per day in her senior year of high school. She received credit toward graduation for her entire day of work and classes.

**Regular Vocational Education Courses/Programs.** These are designed to prepare students for jobs in areas like construction, cosmetology, food service, or electronics. Some school districts have separate vocational centers; others incorporate the vocational programs within their high schools.

**Special Education Vocational Programs.** These programs are designed specifically for students with disabilities and include vocational training, work adjustment, and social skills development. They often include training in such areas as food service, gardening, and janitorial services.

**Community-based Instruction.** Students participating in community-based instruction—sometimes called cooperative vocational education—receive supervision and instruction from school staff on their jobs in the community. Part of Mary's school program included community-based instruction in various locations and settings as she was learning skills to be a nursing assistant.

**Centers for Independent Living (CILs).** If your child needs to develop skills in the area of self help, self advocacy, and independence, she may be able to attend a CIL program as a part of her school day or in addition to her school activities. Mary Connors supplemented her school home economics class with a nine-month independent living skills program at her CIL. She learned to balance her check book, plan and cook healthy meals, and do her own laundry.

# ■ *Person-Centered Planning* ■

How do you begin to plan for the future? If your child is a teenager and has been enrolled in special education for a number of years, you are used to the IEP process. Transition planning, however, is different. Rather than emphasizing a person's shortcomings and working toward remediation, transition planning focuses on the future. It is centered on your child's interests and preferences for his future. It requires exploring what is involved in learning a job and living on one's own.

One method that is helpful in preparing for the development of transition plans is a process called person-centered planning. In person-centered planning, the person with disabilities helps choose members of his planning team and often runs his own meeting. His hopes and dreams for the future and other important information such as strengths, talents, goals, and needs for support are identified during the person-centered planning process. The results of the planning process provide the basis for the more formalized transition plan.

Mary Connors's first person-centered planning meeting took place when she was fourteen years old. She invited her mom, dad, and Uncle Fred. Her friends Carla and Katy, her mom and dad's friend Jane, and her favorite teacher from middle school also were invited. One of her high school teachers, also a family friend, ran the meeting.

During the meeting, the group answered questions together, including:
- Who is Mary?
- What is her dream for the future?
- What are her strengths, talents and unique needs?
- What are her needs? What do we do to meet these needs?
- What is her nightmare?
- What can we do to make the dreams come true?
- What can we do to prevent the nightmare from happening?

During the course of the meeting, Mary spoke for the first time of her strong desire to learn more in school; to be able to take more challenging courses such as algebra and biology. She and her parents talked about Mary going to college, of living on her own someday. Everyone agreed that the strong family friendships the Connors enjoyed were an important part of Mary's life and needed to be a central part of her future. Mary talked about her desire for work that involved helping people, possibly older people, or maybe young children.

In subsequent meetings, Mary and her transition planning team refined their thoughts and developed a formal transition plan. They used a planning chart, like the one that follows, to write down their ideas. Mary and her team meet frequently to review her progress and solve any problems that may arise. At a minimum they know her transition plan needs to be reviewed and updated annually. The practical insight and information provided by Mary, her parents, and other family members and friends are vital when planning successful transitions from school to the workplace.

# ■ TRANSITION PLANNING CHART ■

The Transition Planning Chart on pages 160-161 is divided into five parts. Part I is Student Information. In this section, you and your child can write down information summarizing the information you and his team gathered during the person-centered planning process about his needs, strengths, talents, and gifts. There is also space to write down your child's long-range career goal. This can be as broad as "going to college" and "getting a job" or as specific as "becoming a car mechanic" or "learning to be a child care worker."

Part II is a Summary of Transition Activities to Date. Based upon information summarized in Part I and upon other observations made in the home, community, and at school, you can write your family's initial thoughts and suggestions for a transition program. In addition, transition activities in which your son or daughter has participated can be described briefly in this section.

In Part III you set priorities by ranking the areas of transition planning you believe need attention at this time. If you and your child decide that two areas are of equal importance—for example, independent living skills and employment—goals and objectives will need to be developed in both areas.

Goals and Objectives for Transition can be written in Part IV. The process for writing them is the same as for the IEP. Teachers, transition specialists, vocational educators or others familiar with transition can assist you in formulating appropriate goals and objectives. The Transition Planning Chart prepared by Mary Connors and her parents is found on page 162-163. On this chart you can see examples of transition goals and objectives.

Part V allows you to identify the Services Needed to Meet Goals. In this section you write the name of the agency that will provide the services, the contact person at the agency, the specific services, and the responsible funding party. For example, if your child needs to learn to use public transportation, the local vocational rehabilitation agency may provide and pay for that training. Any individuals who will be providing services should be a part of the transition planning meeting.

You can use the Transition Planning Chart not only to plan services for and with your child but also to monitor services once they are in place. Remember, no plan is permanent. Your child's transition plan should be reviewed and updated by the team at least annually and changed as your child's needs change. By taking the time and effort to write your ideas and hopes on the Transition Planning Chart, you will find that the planning meetings with school officials and adult service providers will be more focused on your child's and family's needs and, hopefully, will lead toward greater opportunities for your child.

Just as IEPs are different for each child, transition plans are going to vary according to the preferences, interests, and life goals of each young person with a disability. According to IDEA, transition plans are to be developed for all students enrolled in special education. Therefore, students with mild, moderate, or severe disabilities should have the opportunity to think about the future, what they would like to do once they leave high school, and obtain the supports and services they need to assist them in reaching their goals. Two sample transition plans are included at the end of this chapter to illustrate different transition activities and services.

Opportunities for further schooling or for work differ from community to community. Many families find that the best avenues into the work world for their child with disabilities are the same as for their children who do not have disabilities. What has been called the self, family, friends network is often an effective way of developing resources and programs for young people with disabilities. Calling upon family connections and contacts is one of the surest ways to explore work and training options for young people. For example, Mrs. Connors asked her friend's daughter to let Mary accompany her when Mary first expressed an interest in baby sitting. A second example comes from Mary's uncle, who owns a paint and hardware company. He has created jobs for several young men with disabilities.

Another way to explore opportunities for work, training, or further education is to seek out community service agencies and organizations serving people with disabilities. Many states have piloted "statewide system change projects" for transition and have developed model programs throughout the state which improve services for students with disabilities. Your state's Department of Rehabilitative Services or Vocational Rehabilitation, the Department of Mental Health and Developmental Disabilities, and, of course, the Department of Education can provide you with information about such programs and further direct you to programs which might be of assistance. Support, advocacy, or educational groups such as The Arc, United Cerebral Palsy, and the Learning Disabilities Association may also provide important information on post-school programs and services. These and other organizations are listed in Appendix C of this book.

Remember that all communities do not offer their citizens with disabilities every type of option described in this book or every opportunity you may have learned about from other sources. Once again, parents often find themselves on the "cutting edge" of developing programs and services for their young adult children. Planning effectively for your child's life after high school, however, requires the exploration of options that are available well in advance of your child's graduation or twenty-first birthday. Transition planning meetings can provide a source of information about eligibility criteria and the availability of programs and services. You and your child can visit the programs, assess their suitability, and understand the requirements for gaining entrance. By advance planning you can use the school years, the IEP and formal transition planning process, your child's network of family and friends, and the assistance of public and private agencies to help prepare the way for a smooth transition from school to citizenship in the community.

## ■ CONCLUSION ■

Transition planning provides a systematic introduction to the world for young people with disabilities. Through participation in planning for transition, students learn the importance of work, of continuing education, self advocacy and independent living. You, as a parent of a young person with a disability, have an important role to play in your child's transition. It is essentially the same role enacted by parents of any other young person. You are preparing your child to be as independent and self-supporting as possible. Because of the obstacles most young people with disabilities face, however, your role in planning the transition from school to adulthood becomes more critical. By planning with your child for transition, you can assist him in gaining the skills, confidence, and positive attitudes needed to participate as fully as possible as a citizen in the community.

## TRANSITION PLANNING CHART

Date _____

Student's Name_____

## I. Student Information

Interests

Strengths/Capabilities

Career Goal

## II. Summary of Transition Activities to Date

## TRANSITION PLANNING CHART (CONTINUED)

### III. Transition Priority Areas

Rank areas as High (1) Moderate (2) or Low (3) priority.

        a. Employment _____

        b. Community participation _____

        c. Independent Living\Self-advocacy _____

        d. College or Vocational Training _____

### IV. Transition Goals

a. Employment

b. Community participation

c. Independent living\self-advocacy

d. College or Vocational Training

### V. Services Needed to Meet Goals

**(Representatives should be included in Transition Planning meeting)**

| Agency | Contact Person Telephone No. | Services | Agency Responsible for Funding |
|---|---|---|---|
|  |  |  |  |
|  |  |  |  |
|  |  |  |  |
|  |  |  |  |

## TRANSITION PLANNING CHART

Date _____

Student's Name _____*Mary Connors*_____

## I. Student Information

Interests

*She likes to take care of other people and animals.*
*She plays well with young children.*

Strengths/Capabilities

*She is a good helper with pets, with young children at the Rec. Dept. and her*
*grandfather. She senses other people's needs and remembers what they like.*

Career Goal

*Mary would like to work in a day care center with young children or in a nursing*
*home for elderly people.*

## II. Summary of Transition Activities to Date

*Mary has had some job "try-out" experiences. She helped out at a day care*
*center two mornings a week, washing toys, as part of a vocational assessment.*
*Mary takes "home ec" to learn some basic cooking skills.*

## TRANSITION PLANNING CHART (CONTINUED)

### III. Transition Priority Areas

Rank areas as High (1) Moderate (2) or Low (3) priority.

      a. Employment   _1_

      b. Community participation   _3_

      c. Independent Living\Self-advocacy   _1_

      d. College or Vocational Training   _2_

### IV. Transition Goals

a. Employment

*To learn skills to become employed in a day care facility or in a nursing home.*

b. Community participation

*(Doesn't need to work on this now, as she has a large network of friends.)*

c. Independent living\self-advocacy

*To learn ways of communicating basic needs.*

d. College or Vocational Training

*Would like to be able to take some courses at the community college.*

### V. Services Needed to Meet Goals

(Representatives should be included in Transition Planning meeting)

| Agency | Contact Person Telephone No. | Services | Agency Responsible for Funding |
|---|---|---|---|
| *Recreation Dept.* | *Elizabeth Shoemaker* | *child care training program* | *Recreation Dept.* |
| *Middle County Public Schools* | *Andrew Chitty* | *Speech/ language* | *Middle County Public Schools* |

# 10. Due Process

## Detours

As you and your child participate in the special education cycle, you may sometimes find yourself disagreeing with observations, conclusions, and recommendations school people have made concerning your child and her educational program. And school people may not always agree with ideas you have about your child, either. In these situations, how are disagreements settled? Does the school system have its way by default? Must you seek appointment or election to the school board to exercise enough influence to have your way? Fortunately, a procedure known as the due process hearing exists to resolve differences that develop as you negotiate the special education maze.

This chapter describes the conflicts between parents and school systems resolved through due process. It outlines the procedures and steps followed in a due process hearing and the benefits and costs involved in such a hearing. You should also be aware, however, of your state education agency's complaint procedure for resolving disputes. The procedure allows you to write a letter to the state department of education, detailing why you believe your rights or those of your child have been violated. Because it does not involve the complicated steps of a due process hearing, it is often a very effective way to achieve the changes you think necessary for your child's education. The procedures for using the state education agency complaint process are outlined in your state's regulations governing special education.

Both the state education complaint procedure and the due process hearing described in the following pages may also be used to resolve disagreements that might arise as families seek early intervention services under Part

H of IDEA. In most instances the hearing process should be the parents' last resort for obtaining a free, appropriate public education for their infant, toddler, or school-aged child. The experiences of parents and educators demonstrate that problems are usually resolved more quickly and satisfactorily in an informal setting, beginning with the teacher, and, if necessary, moving on to include principals and other administrators.

Especially if the disagreement involves early intervention services, it is usually best handled through the mediation process. This process is less costly, less adversarial, and usually quicker than due process procedures. If your child is receiving early intervention services and disputes arise, you should consult your state's policies for the specific procedures to follow. These policies can be obtained from your local school district or early intervention program.

To encourage the informal resolution of disagreements, school systems usually provide you with the opportunity to participate in an administrative review or mediation prior to going to a formal due process hearing.* The mediation process is described more fully in Chapter 8. If all the informal approaches have failed to produce the results you believe are right for your child, you need not give up on your efforts for change. At this point, the due process hearing offers another opportunity for you to secure the educational rights to which your child is entitled.

## ■ CONFLICTS RESOLVABLE THROUGH ■ DUE PROCESS

Educational advocacy for children with disabilities has its legislative foundation in the Education for All Handicapped Children Act enacted by Congress in 1975 and reauthorized as the Individuals with Disabilities Education Act (IDEA) in 1990. This law establishes broad guidelines for local schools to follow in providing special education and in protecting the rights of parents and children entitled to those services. While state and local laws and regulations may be more detailed in their provisions than IDEA and related federal statutes, their provisions cannot conflict with the federal law. For this reason, this chapter focuses primarily on due process procedures and the due process hearing described in IDEA. Should you have to use these procedures, however, you will also need to read and understand the procedures followed by your state and local school jurisdictions.* These procedures may be readily obtained from your local director of special education.

IDEA not only describes the due process hearing procedure for resolving conflicts in obtaining special education for your child, but it also identifies the specific conflicts that may be resolved by this process. You may initiate the due process hearing procedure only when you believe the school system has not fulfilled a duty it is required to perform under the law itself. Just what are these duties IDEA requires of school systems?

**1. School systems must provide a free, appropriate public education for all children with disabilities aged three through twenty-one, unless state law prohibits or does not authorize the expenditure of public funds to educate children without disabilities aged three through five or eighteen through twenty-one.\*** In these states, a free, appropriate education is only required for children aged six through seventeen. Because IDEA specifies only the minimum requirements that states must satisfy, some states provide a free, appropriate education for children with disabilities younger than three and older than twenty-one. Check your state laws and regulations to determine the policy in your state. This education is to be provided completely at public expense.

**2. School systems must ensure that children with and without disabilities are educated together to the maximum extent appropriate.** Children with disabilities are to be placed in special classes or separate schools only when the nature and severity of their disability is such that education in general education classes, even if supported with supplementary aids or services, cannot be achieved satisfactorily. This is the legal provision mandating the education of children with disabilities in the least restrictive environment.

**3. School systems must set forth in writing in the Individualized Education Program the specially designed education and related services your child will receive to meet her unique educational needs.**

From the school's perspective, the preceding three items are duties the law requires them to perform. From the child's and parents' perspectives, these are rights IDEA gives to the child. To guarantee that these rights are exercised, the law outlines further duties for school systems and further rights for children and parents.

**4. School systems must give reasonable written notice to parents before they evaluate or place a child, change her special education placement, or refuse to take such actions.** The notice must contain a full explanation for the school system's decision and be communicated to the parents in their native language and in a manner they can understand.

**5. School systems must obtain parent consent before the initial evaluation is conducted and before the child is first placed in a special education program on the basis of the IEP.\*** After the initial placement, parents must be notified in advance of any changes, but their consent is not required. Parents can, however, initiate a due process hearing to challenge changes with which they disagree. Should parents refuse to allow the initial evaluation or initial placement of their children in a special education class, school officials may also request a due process hearing or initiate court action to override the parents' objections. Actions of this nature, however, are usually taken by school personnel only in extreme situations. Such an action might be taken when they believe special education is required to protect the physical or mental health of the child or others in the school environment.

**6. School systems must provide an evaluation of the child using a multidisciplinary team, which includes at least one teacher or other specialist knowledgeable in the area of the suspected disability.** A child's eligibility for services cannot be determined solely on the grounds of one test or the observations of one professional.

**7. School systems must ensure that evaluation tests are nondiscriminatory.** Tests and other evaluation material must be free of cultural bias. They must reflect accurately the child's aptitude or achievement level and not be biased by the child's impaired sensory or speaking skills or by other disabling conditions. A brief explanation of the tests to be used and the information they provide must be made available to the parent.

**8. School systems must make available to parents for inspection and review all records used in the evaluation, placement, and IEP processes as well as those records that are a part of the child's official school file.** These records must be maintained in strict confidentiality. (See Chapter 4 for a complete discussion of your rights regarding school records.)

**9. School systems must provide for the child to have an independent evaluation at public expense if the parents disagree with evaluation results obtained by the school system.** The only exception is if school officials believe their evaluation data are accurate and sufficient. In these cases, school personnel may request a due process hearing to prove their claim. If the hearing officer does not agree with the school system, an independent evaluation at public expense will be ordered for your child. Should the hearing officer uphold the school's position, however, you will be unable to secure a free, independent evaluation. But remember, unless school officials request and hold a due process hearing to validate their evaluation data, they cannot deny your request for an independent evaluation. They have a duty to honor your request.

**10. Upon request, school systems must provide an impartial due process hearing to parents who believe any of the preceding rights have been violated.** Conflicts concerning school records, however, do not require an impartial due process hearing. See Chapter 4. The hearing must follow procedures described by state statute, regulation, or the written policy of the state education agency. Hearings conducted at the local school system level allow both the parents and the school system a right of appeal to the state education agency.

If you believe the school system has violated any of the preceding rights and you have been unable to resolve your differences informally, you can request a formal due process hearing by writing the local superintendent of schools. Parents whose children are in early intervention programs can make their request to the administrator of the local lead agency. Remember, this process cannot be used to settle all disputes—only those arising from rights and duties provided in the federal law as outlined above or as set forth in your own state and local laws.

## EXAMPLES OF CONFLICTS RESOLVED IN DUE PROCESS HEARINGS

- Whether a child should be identified as having a learning disability or emotional disturbance (evaluation/eligibility).
- Whether a child should receive related services such as speech or occupational therapy (appropriate services and IEP).
- Whether a child should be placed in a self-contained classroom or a general education classroom with support services (least restrictive environment).
- Whether a child should be placed at public expense in a private school (appropriate education and least restrictive environment).
- Whether a specific intelligence test discriminates against young, nonverbal children (nondiscriminatory testing and the need for an independent evaluation).
- Whether a child is eligible to receive learning disability special education services (evaluation/eligibility).
- Whether a child is receiving the program outlined in her Individualzed Education Program or Individualized Family Service Plan (appropriate education/IEP/IFSP).
- Whether a child's appropriate education requires more than the normal 180 school days—an extended school year (appropriate services and IEP).
- Whether a child receives services at home or at a school (least restrictive environment).
- Whether a child receives a vocational or academic education (appropriate education/IEP).

As you can readily see, the preceding conflicts center upon some aspect of the child's right to a free, appropriate public education, outlined by an IEP or IFSP, and provided in the least restrictive environment. Disputes like these represent the vast majority of conflicts brought to due process hearings. These are the areas most crucial in determining the educational progress your child will make. At the same time, decisions regarding these matters are ones where professionals may well disagree and where school systems may be forced to spend additional money if their opinions are not upheld. If you go to a hearing, the chances are quite good that it will concern issues of this nature.

Seldom are due process hearings required to force school systems to perform their procedural duties of providing notice of proposed actions, obtaining parental consent for testing, offering appropriate evaluations, or allowing parents to review their child's records. Usually schools have standard procedures for meeting these requirements. They develop form letters for notifying parents of actions they take or propose to take and for obtaining parental consent when necessary. They normally use teams for educational evaluation and try to avoid biased evaluation methods and tests. And they usually provide opportunities for parents to see records and to obtain independent evaluations when they disagree with the results of the school's evaluation. In the event you do have a conflict with the school system on a procedural issue, however, remember, you have a right to a due process hearing.

## ▪ CONFLICTS NOT RESOLVABLE THROUGH ▪ DUE PROCESS HEARINGS

What about disagreements with the school system involving issues other than those outlined above? For example, what about other situations in which you believe your position is reasonable and that the school's position is unreasonable or just plain wrong? Often you may feel certain that an impartial third person would see the situation your way. Unfortunately, a due process hearing cannot be used to settle all conflicts. The process is only available for resolving disputes directly related to the rights and duties of parents and school systems under IDEA.

### EXAMPLES OF CONFLICTS NOT RESOLVED THROUGH DUE PROCESS HEARINGS

- You want to attend the meeting where committee members will determine your child's eligibility for special services, and state law does not require your presence at that meeting.
- You want your child to have a particular teacher, but school officials say there are other teachers with similar qualifications (and they are correct).

- You want the teacher to use a specific approach for teaching your child with learning disabilities to read, but the teacher uses another approach considered equally effective by professionals.
- You find school personnel condescending and sometimes abrasive to work with. Although you have mentioned this to them, their behavior has not improved.
- You want your child moved to another class because she has a personality conflict with the teacher, but the school will not approve the change.
- You feel that school officials could move faster in placing your child, but they always use the maximum number of days legally allowed in making their decisions.
- You dislike the school psychologist who will do your child's evaluation and would like another psychologist to do the testing. The school says no change can be made without violating the time guidelines set by the state education agency for completing your child's evaluation and eligibility determination. But you can later request an Independent Educational Evaluation at public expense or challenge the results of the testing in a due process hearing.

In each of these examples, the school system has discretion in making decisions or is not required by law to perform a specific duty. To make changes in these situations, parents must informally negotiate with school personnel or lobby for help from the local school board, PTA, or other relevant groups. Due process hearings cannot be used to resolve issues of this nature.

## ■ WHAT HAPPENS AT THE ■ DUE PROCESS HEARING

The purpose of the due process hearing is to allow an impartial third party, the hearing officer, to examine the issues upon which you and the school system disagree and to settle the dispute by making an unbiased decision. Hearing officers are usually appointed by the state education agencies and often are lawyers, educators, or other professionals familiar with special education. The hearing officer cannot be an employee of a public agency involved in the education or care of the child, nor can she have a professional or personal interest that could adversely affect her objectivity in the hearing. Each state maintains a list of persons who may serve as hearing officers. Refer to your state and local regulations to determine how hearing officers are selected to hear individual cases.

IDEA does not describe in great detail the procedures to be followed in due process hearings. Most states, therefore, have developed these procedures more fully in their own laws, regulations, and policies. States' laws differ over matters such as the degree of formality followed in the hearing; whether the hearing officer is a lawyer, educator, or other professional; whether the hearing is conducted by one hearing officer or a panel of hearing officers; and whether or not witnesses are allowed to hear the testimony of one another. Regardless of these differences, however, the basic outlines of a hearing can be described along with certain rights parents may exercise during the hearing.

## ■ RIGHTS OF PARENTS IN THE HEARING ■

As explained earlier, both parents and school systems may initiate due process hearings. Whichever party initiates the hearing, however, IDEA gives you certain rights to employ before, during, and after the hearing:

1. To be accompanied and advised by an attorney or by a lay advocate, and by individuals with special knowledge or training with respect to your child's problems.
2. To present evidence, to confront and cross-examine witnesses, and to compel school personnel to serve as witnesses at the hearing.
3. To prohibit the introduction of any evidence at the hearing that was not disclosed to you at least five days before the hearing.
4. To obtain a written or electronic verbatim record of the hearing.
5. To obtain a written copy of the hearing officer's determination of the facts of the case and the decision reached.
6. To appeal the decision of the local hearing officer to the state education agency, and, if desired, to bring suit in the appropriate state court or a district court of the United States.
7. To have your child present at the hearing.
8. To open the hearing to the public.
9. To receive from the school system reasonable attorney's fees as part of your costs when the hearing officer or judge rules in your favor in a due process hearing or civil action. These costs may only be awarded when parents have been represented by an attorney. In a few instances costs may not be awarded even when you win your case. You should ask your attorney to explain these exceptions before proceeding.

# ▪ DESCRIPTION OF THE HEARING ▪

As mentioned earlier, hearings may be formal or informal. Hearing officers, however, usually prefer informality—especially when parents are not represented by an attorney. Parents may choose to be represented by a lay advocate—a person without a law degree but with specialized knowledge in representing children and parents in due process hearings and other proceedings. The participants in the hearing will be: 1) the parents, their counsel, or advocate (where used), and the parents' witnesses; 2) the school system's representative, the school system's counsel (where used), and the school system's witnesses; and 3) the hearing officer. Also in attendance, but not participating, might be a court reporter—if the hearing is transcribed—and the public—if parents have requested an open hearing.

The sequence of events at a typical hearing varies from state to state and according to the formality of the proceedings. Basically, however, a hearing proceeds in the following manner.

## SEQUENCE OF EVENTS[*]

**1. The hearing officer checks to be sure that all is ready to "go on the record," that is, the stenographer and/or recording equipment are ready.**

**2. The hearing officer will open the hearing, usually stating:**

    a. the nature of the matter to be heard;

    b. the time, date, and place of hearing;

    c. the names of all parties and counsel, if any, and of the hearing officer;

    d. any factual matters already agreed to by the parties; and will

    e. ask for preliminary statements by the parties.

**3. The party requesting the hearing, the plaintiff, makes the first opening statement, followed by the opening statement of the other party, the defendant.** Opening statements should be brief, clear, and to the point. They explain your view of the case—the issue(s), the law, and the broad outlines of the facts. The purpose of the statement is to give the hearing officer a preview and an overview of what your evidence is going to show. A good opening statement creates an impression of clarity, organization, and control.

**4. The plaintiff calls his first witness.**

**5. The hearing officer swears in the witness and asks that his or her full name be stated for the record.**

---

[*] Barbara Bateman, *So, You're Going to a Hearing: Preparing for a Public Law 94-142 Due Process Hearing* (Northbrook, IL: Hubbard, 1980), pp.18-20.

**6. The plaintiff then proceeds with the questioning. If the witness can identify documents to be introduced into evidence, that will happen while the witness is on the stand.** For example:

*Plaintiff:* Your honor, we'd like to introduce this document, D-1.
(It is numbered then, if not previously.) What is this?
(showing D-1 to witness)

*Witness:* This is a letter I wrote to the parents on November 15 stating why Jane was not eligible for special education.

*Plaintiff:* (Shows copy to other counsel)

*Hearing Officer:* Any objections?

*Defendant:* No.

*Hearing Officer:* D-1 is admitted into evidence.

**7. The defendant cross-examines and/or questions the plaintiff's witness (optional).**

**8. The plaintiff again questions witness (optional).**

**9. The hearing officer questions the plaintiff's witness (optional).**

**10. Steps 4 through 8 are repeated for all plaintiff's witnesses, then for all defendant's witnesses.**

**11. Both parties make closing statements.** A closing statement summarizes your case, emphasizing the strong points you have made and the weaknesses in your opponent's case. The closing statement, like the opening statement, is not evidence. Rather, it is your effort to organize the case for the hearing officer so he views it as you wish it to be viewed. Keep it brief. Everyone, even in a short hearing, tends to feel tired and drained and anxious for it to be over.

**12. The hearing officer and both parties, still on the record, discuss when written arguments or briefs, if any, are to be submitted, when the decision is to be rendered, and they check that all documents are properly marked and the hearing officer has copies, and so forth.**

**13. The hearing officer closes the hearing by announcing, "The hearing is closed."**

According to IDEA, the local school system must ensure that within forty-five days after receiving a parent's request for a hearing: 1) a final decision is reached by a hearing officer, and 2) a copy of the decision is mailed to the parents. The decision of the hearing officer is final unless one of the parties appeals to the state education agency or brings civil action in court.

In practice, school systems may fail to meet the forty-five day time limit. When parents complain of these time violations at due process hearings, most hearing officers will criticize the school officials and direct them to comply with time requirements in the future. Seldom, however, will a hearing officer render a decision in favor of a parent merely because the school system has failed to observe legally imposed time guidelines. You can, however, file a formal complaint with the state education agency. Your complaint may lead to the state education agency reviewing the matter and instructing the school system not to violate these time lines in future cases. Failure to follow these instructions may ultimately result in federal and state funds being withheld from the local school system. Therefore, local school systems usually will bring their procedures into compliance and will not violate parents' rights in future cases.

## ■ DECISIONS AND APPEALS ■

The hearing officer does not make a final decision at the time of the hearing. The maximum length of time the hearing officer has to render a decision is the number of days remaining in the forty-five-day period since the hearing was requested. In practice, most hearing officers attempt to reach a final decision and notify parents within two weeks of the hearing.

The hearing officer's duty is to make an independent judgment either affirming what the school system has done or proposes to do, or directing school officials to take a specific action to correct a mistake they have made. This judgment clarifies the rights and duties of children, parents, and school officials as to exactly what must be done in order to meet the requirements of the law. The written decision must include the hearing officer's findings of the relevant facts of the case determined at the hearing and her recommendations for resolving the conflict. If you or the school system do not agree with the hearing officer's decision, you may appeal for another hearing with the state education agency, known in many states as the State Board of Education.

The review made by the state education agency will also be an impartial due process hearing. The official conducting this review will examine the record developed in the first hearing to identify the substance of the issues and to see that all procedures followed due process requirements. The reviewing officer may, at his or her discretion, provide the parents and the school system the opportunity to present additional oral or written argument, or both. Finally, the official may request a hearing to obtain additional evidence believed essential to render a fair decision. A formal hearing at this appeal may not be necessary, however, when the reviewing officer believes that sufficient evidence to decide the case was provided in the original hearing. The decision of this official is final unless you or the school system bring a civil action in court.

Federal law requires the state education agency to render its decision and to notify parties of that decision within thirty days of receipt of the appeal. Some states shorten the time for action by requiring a decision within ten to fifteen days after the initial decision. Check your own state regulations to determine the time limit in your state.

Should you or the school system believe that the decision of the state education agency is incorrect, IDEA gives either party the right to file suit in the appropriate state court or in a federal district court of the United States. If a suit is filed, the court will receive and examine the records of the prior hearings; will sometimes hear additional evidence at your request or that of the school system; will base its decision on a preponderance of the evidence (meaning the side having more than 50 percent of the evidence in its favor); and will direct the losing party to do whatever is believed appropriate to remedy the existing problem. Since courts are heavily burdened already, legal action of this nature may take far too long to serve as a practical remedy for problems you may face with school officials.

## ▪ THINK TWICE (OR MORE) BEFORE ▪ REQUESTING A HEARING

The decision to resolve your differences with the school system through a due process hearing should not be taken lightly. This step will ultimately involve significant time, money, thought, and physical and emotional energy from both you and school people. Consequently, it is seldom advisable to seek a due process hearing unless you have reached the point where you feel any further discussions with school officials are futile and the only way around the impasse is a hearing. Before you reach this point, use every possible means to resolve disagreements. Attend meetings. Request conferences with the teacher, principal, or special education director. Listen to and seriously consider all proposed solutions. Ask questions. And provide all the information you have to prove that your view or recommendation is correct. Prior to requesting a hearing, you may wish to try an intermediate step. In your state, this step may be called an administrative review, a conciliatory conference, or mediation. (See below.)

## ▪ FINAL STEPS BEFORE REQUESTING ▪ A HEARING

If you reach an impasse with school officials, most school systems provide for an administrative review, conciliatory conference, or mediation to resolve troublesome issues before going to a hearing. Usually one or more neutral third parties are brought in to hear the issues and to find an acceptable solution. These third parties are most often drawn from the ranks of schoolteachers and administrators not directly involved in the problem. Since these third parties are employees of the school system, many parents feel that a fair solution cannot be reached in these meetings. Experience shows, however, that acceptable solutions frequently *are* developed when parents and school professionals work in good faith. If you find the outcome of these conferences unsatisfactory, though, you may still go forward with a due process hearing.

The procedures followed in administrative reviews, conciliatory conferences, or mediation are outlined in state and local laws and regulations. The authority of these committees varies. In some states, the conciliatory conference committee can make binding decisions for the school system. In others, the committee functions solely as a mediator attempting to help parents and school officials find an agreeable solution to their problems. Once again, you will need to examine your own state and local laws to determine the functions of this committee in your school jurisdiction.

If you wish to go directly to a due process hearing, you can choose not to work with the principal or special education director and can bypass a conciliatory conference or mediation. The school system cannot require such conferences or mediation as prerequisites to a due process hearing, nor can they use the conference or mediation to delay the due process hearing. The danger with skipping these intermediate steps is that doing so may prejudice your case.

Most hearing officers and judges believe that parents should try all possible means for resolving their problems before coming to them. So for the sake of your child's education, you need to work as closely as possible with the teachers, principal, and other administrative officials of your school system.

## ▪ *Factors to Consider and Weigh* ▪ *before Requesting a Hearing*

As the previous sections pointed out, the decision to request a due process hearing is a serious matter. For this reason, you should consider each of the following matters carefully and thoroughly.

First, do you understand clearly the position of the school system regarding the education of your child, and do you know what evidence—facts, reports, professional testimony—the school will present to support its position? At least five days prior to the hearing, you can obtain from the hearing officer a list of the witnesses and the documents the school system will present. Without this knowledge, you will be unable to determine what issue you are questioning at the hearing, your chance of winning the hearing, and, ultimately, whether or not you should request a hearing.

Second, are you absolutely clear as to what you believe is wrong with the school system's actions or decisions? Do you possess or can you obtain evidence demonstrating that the school's actions or decisions are incorrect? Unless you can articulate precisely where and why the school system is in error, you will be unable to gather evidence to support your case. Furthermore, unless you can submit evidence at the hearing to prove the school's error, the hearing officer cannot rule in your favor.

Third, do you know exactly what services, placement, or other actions you believe the school system should take to provide your child with a free, appropriate public education in the least restrictive environment? Can you obtain evidence to support these educational recommendations for your child? Hearing officers are often not educators. Therefore, it is not enough for you merely to show that what the school system is proposing is inappropriate. You will also need to convince the hearing officer of the correctness of your own educational recommendations. This requires additional research and evidence gathering.

Fourth, when you look at the evidence supporting your position and weigh it against the evidence supporting the school's position, which is more convincing? If the evidence for both positions is equally persuasive, the hearing officer will usually give the educational professionals the benefit of the doubt. Unless the evidence is well over 50 percent in your favor, you will have a very, very difficult case to win.

Fifth, where will your child be placed during the time required to conclude the hearing? Normally, your child will remain in the existing placement pending the outcome of the hearing. If you like your child's placement and the school is recommending a placement you do not like, you may want to request a hearing merely to keep your child where she is until your disagreement is resolved. But what if you do not like your child's current placement but still want to continue with the hearing?

If you wish to place your child in a private school pending the decision of the hearing officer, you should first obtain written agreement for such action from the school officials.* If the private placement is upheld by the hearing officer, the school system will be directed to reimburse you. Similarly, if you move your child without the school's permission, you may still receive reimbursement if the hearing officer or court concurs that the placement you have selected is the appropriate placement for your child. If, however, you move your child to a private school, with or without the school's agreement, and your position is not upheld, you will have to pay the private school expenses yourself.

Sometimes even if you do not like your child's current placement, there is no alternative to leaving her in that placement until the hearing is complete. Once the hearing officer announces a decision, your child will be placed in the education program required by that decision—either the program you proposed, the program the school proposed, or yet a third alternative specified by the hearing officer. Should either you or the school system appeal the hearing officer's decision, your child will remain in her current placement.

Sixth, do you want a professional to represent your interests in the due process hearing? While you may be well informed regarding educational advocacy for your child, most parents find they are too emotionally involved to represent themselves effectively. Thus, they either obtain the services of an attorney or a lay advocate to prepare and present their case.

Whether you select a lawyer or a lay advocate, you should first make certain that anyone you are considering is experienced in the practice and procedures of special education due process proceedings. Otherwise, you will tend to increase your expenses as your attorney or advocate learns on the job and to reduce your chances of receiving competent representation. You can often find the names of experienced attorneys and advocates by contacting your state and local bar associations, organizations for persons with disabilities, members of the local special education advisory committee, or parent training and information centers in your community or state. (See Appendices B and C.)

The costs of representation in due process hearings are usually significant. Therefore, before hiring any representative, you should ask for an informal estimate of the costs likely to be incurred. While this informal estimate is not binding, you will at least have a general idea of the amount of money involved.

Although lay advocates may charge less for their services than attorneys, an amendment to IDEA makes hiring a lawyer more attractive if you win the hearing or a court action. Under this law, courts may award reasonable attorney's fees to parents or guardians of children with disabilities who have been the prevailing party in a due process hearing or civil action. These costs may be awarded only when parents have been represented by an attorney, not by a lay advocate. When costs are awarded, parents are reimbursed by the school system for most expenses involved in preparing and presenting their case. Costs may include travel expenses, fees for expert witnesses, transcripts, and the like. Should you lose your case, however, you remain solely liable for all the costs you have incurred. To understand fully your rights to reimbursement under this statute, consult an attorney familiar with your state and federal courts and laws.

Obviously, a decision to go to a hearing is a commitment of substantial time, money, and psychic energy. When two adults share responsibility for a child, they should not go to a hearing unless both agree that such action should be taken. Preparing for and participating in a hearing requires the cooperation and support of all adults responsible for the child. If both do not agree that a hearing is the only route to go, neither will probably weather the hearing process very well.

The final factor to consider in deciding whether to request a due process hearing is the benefits of winning your case. The most important benefit, of course, is that your child will receive an appropriate educational program designed to meet her specific educational needs. You could even put a dollar value on the benefit by determining how much a similar program would cost—if you could get it—from a private school. A second benefit is that you will have spared your child the harm that might have accompanied an inappropriate educational program. For example, the school system might have diagnosed your child as having an emotional disturbance rather than a learning disability. If the school is wrong and is proven so, the benefit you receive is saving your child from the inaccurate label, seriously emotionally disturbed.

Once you have examined the potential costs and benefits of a hearing and have weighed the chances of winning your case, you are ready to make a final decision. If the potential benefits are greater than the potential costs, you may well want to go to a hearing. If the potential benefits and costs are about equal, you may want to consider alternative ways to provide your child with what you believe is an appropriate educational program. For example, you may want to obtain private placement or services at your own expense. If the costs are much greater than the potential benefits, you will have to decide if you can afford those costs should the hearing officer rule against you.

The decision to request a due process hearing is not an easy one to make. By examining each of the preceding matters, you can understand more completely the implications of your choices and have greater confidence in the correctness of your final decision. One last suggestion—once you have considered all of the pros and cons you can think of, discuss them with friends, professionals, and others familiar with your situation. You will be amazed at how often someone with a fresh perspective will see potential costs and benefits that you have overlooked.

## ▪ Final Thoughts ▪

The impartial due process hearing has promoted the objectives of the Individuals with Disabilities Education Act in two important respects. First, the existence of this process has put school officials on notice that their actions may be reviewed by impartial third parties if parents feel that mistakes have been made. Consequently, school officials have become more careful, discreet, objective, and open in their work with special children and their parents. Without the cloud of the due process hearing hanging over their heads, many school systems might lapse into the practices of prior years when parents' concerns were ignored or merely tolerated.

The second way due process hearings have advanced the goals of IDEA is by actually correcting mistakes made by school systems. Considering the hundreds and thousands of children with disabilities which school systems serve each year, it is little wonder that mistakes are made. These mistakes, however, need not go uncorrected today. As parents learn how to exercise their children's and their own due process rights, they become more knowledgeable, influential educational advocates. This chapter has sought to inform you of how and when to use the due process hearing. In the final analysis, the due process hearing should be a last resort for correcting mistakes made by school systems. But because the due process hearing exists for parents to use, its use is needed less often. That is as it should be.

# II. NONDISCRIMINATION PROTECTION:

## ALTERNATIVE ROUTES THROUGH THE MAZE

In addition to IDEA, two other federal laws have proven themselves important and beneficial in advancing the educational rights of children with disabilities. These laws are Section 504 of the Federal Rehabilitiation Act of 1973 and the Americans with Disabilities Act (ADA) of 1990. Both laws have been frequently used to obtain equal access to educational services for students who are eligible for special education under IDEA. Just as important, these laws have also been used to gain equal access to educational services for students with disabilities who have been declared ineligible for services under IDEA. This chapter discusses the central features of these laws and how parents may use them to ensure their children with disabilities are not unfairly discriminated against in securing their education.

Section 504 serves a much different purpose from IDEA. Section 504 neither creates new rights for students with disabilities nor supports those rights with federal money. Rather, Section 504 prohibits agencies and organizations that receive federal funding from discriminating against qualified individuals with disabilities. They may not exclude students with disabilities from participating in, or obtaining the benefits of, any preschool, elementary or secondary education program, or activity receiving federal financial assistance.

If your child is found to have a disability under Section 504, he is to be given the aids, equipment, and accommodations that will allow him to enjoy the benefits of the school program. For example, he might receive special seating in the classroom or simplified instructions about class assignments.

One limitation to this requirement is that the accommodations must be reasonable and they must not impose an undue financial or administrative burden upon the education system. This law also prohibits technical schools, colleges, and universities from discriminating against students with disabilities when those institutions receive federal financial assistance.

The Americans with Disabilities Act (ADA), likewise, prohibits such discrimination by schools through Title II of that Act. Thus, Section 504 and Title II of the ADA are described as nondiscriminating statutes rather than as an entitlement statute such as IDEA. They provide procedures to ensure that persons with disabilities enjoy the same rights as persons without disabilities. And when those rights are thought to be violated, the laws provide a procedure for addressing the alleged violations, as described later in this chapter.

To illustrate how Section 504 and the ADA can be used to prevent unlawful discrimination against students with disabilities, here are two examples:

Judy is a general education student. She is very limited in her ability to walk and most often uses a wheelchair. When her class took a field trip, they traveled on a yellow school bus. The teacher would not let Judy ride with her classmates, even though the bus driver said it would be OK and that he could store the wheelchair in the back of the bus. As a result, Judy's mother drove her on the field trip.

After the field trip, Judy's mother filed a complaint with the Office of Civil Rights (OCR) of the U.S. Department of Education. OCR investigated the situation. They ruled that the school district had violated Section 504 and the ADA regulations when it failed to arrange transporation that would give Judy an equal opportunity to participate in the field trip. Subsequently, the district developed a two-part plan to accommodate Judy's needs to travel with her schoolmates and to counsel her teacher concerning Judy's rights of equality with other students. In this way they addressed the violation of Section 504.

Reggie was receiving special education with adaptive physical education (PE) services. Reggie's parents believed he was being denied an equal education because he had to miss the end of his math class in order to attend his special PE class. After Reggie's parents contacted the Office of Civil Rights, an investigation was conducted. OCR found that the school district violated Section 504 by requiring him to miss his math class in order to receive adaptive physical education services. The school district was required to rearrange Reggie's schedule so he could attend his adaptive physical education class and also attend his entire math class.

These cases demonstrate how Section 504 and Title II of the ADA may be used to benefit children, both those in special education and those who have a disability not requiring special education. Due to the similarity and overlap of these two laws, the U.S. Department of Education generally uses Section 504 regulations to interpret Title II of the ADA. For this reason, the following pages primarily address the educational rights and procedural protections provided for children with disabilities under Section 504 of the Rehabilitiation Act.

# ■ STUDENTS WHOSE RIGHTS ARE PROTECTED ■ UNDER SECTION 504

To qualify for protection against discrimination under Section 504 and to be provided the reasonable accommodations he may need to benefit from school programs, your child must meet three criteria.

First, he must have a demonstrated physical or mental impairment. Individuals are also protected if they are discriminated against because they have previously had such an impairment and there is a record of the impairment. In addition, persons who are regarded as having an impairment, such as testing HIV positive, enjoy Section 504 protections even if they have no impairment that would affect their education.

The second criterion requires your child to show that this impairment "substantially limits one or more major life activities, such as caring for one's self, performing manual tasks, walking, seeing, hearing, speaking, breathing, learning, and working."

And third, the services or other accommodations needed to enable your child to enjoy the benefits of the school program must be identified. A detailed discussion of these criteria is found below.

## 1. POTENTIAL DISABILITIES ELIGIBLE FOR PROTECTION UNDER SECTION 504 BUT NOT FOR SERVICES UNDER IDEA

All children who qualify for special education and related services under IDEA also qualify for the non-discrimination protections of Section 504. This factor often becomes important when access to nonacademic services and programs, such as bus transportation, after school daycare, and participation in extracurricular activities, becomes an issue. In addition, there are many children who do not qualify for services under IDEA but are eligible for protection under 504. Although all eligibility determinations must be made on an individual basis, the following list illustrates situations in which students often qualify for reasonable accommodations under Section 504 in the provision of their educational services:

- Students with Attention Deficit Disorder (ADD) or Attention Deficit Hyperactive Disorder (ADHD) who are not found to be eligibile under IDEA within the categories of specific learning disabilities, serious emotional disorder, or other health impaired.
- Students who have health needs, including insulin dependent diabetes, chronic asthma, severe allergies, or temporary disabilities after an accident.
- Students with learning disabilities who do not meet the more exacting criteria of IDEA but do meet the broader criteria for a disability under 504.
- Students who have contracted communicable diseases, including those testing HIV positive.
- Students identified as socially maladjusted but not found to be "seriously emotionally disturbed" under IDEA.
- Students dropped from the special education rolls because they no longer meet the IDEA requirements for eligibility.
- Students with drug and alcohol dependencies, so long as the students are not currently engaging in the use of illegal drugs or alcohol.

These examples illustrate how Section 504 and the ADA increase the number of children with disabilities eligible for protection under these laws. Thus, while your child may not be eligible for educational services under IDEA, educational rights and protections may well be available to your child under Section 504 and the ADA.

But remember, the presence of any of the preceding conditions alone will not make your child eligible for 504 protections. You must also: 1) show that your child's impairment substantially limits a major life activity, and 2) identify the needed aids, equipment, or accommodations that will enable your child to enjoy the benefits of the school program.

## 2. ESTABLISHING THAT DISABILITIES "SUBSTANTIALLY LIMIT" MAJOR LIFE ACTIVITIES

To qualify for protections under Section 504, your child must also show that his disabling condition "substantially limits" a major life activity. Regulations describe major life activities as: walking, seeing, hearing, speaking, learning, working, taking care of oneself, breathing, and performing manual tasks.

Regulations under the ADA define the term "substantially limits major life activities" in the following manner:

"A person is considered an individual with a disability (for purposes of the definition) when the individual's important life activities are restricted as to the conditions, manner or duration under which they can be performed in comparison to most people …taking into consideration both the duration (or expected duration) of the impairment and the extent to which it actually limits a major life activity of the affected individual.

"The question of whether a person has a disability should be assessed without regard to the availability of mitigating measures such as reasonable modifications or auxiliary aids and services. For example, a person with hearing loss is substantially limited in the major life activity of hearing, even though the loss may be improved through the use of a hearing aid. Likewise, persons with impairments, such as epilepsy or diabetes, that substantially limit a major activity are covered under the first prong of the definition of disability, even if the effects of the impairment are controlled by medication."

The definition from the ADA is not binding under Section 504, but it does illustrate the wide range of disabilities encompassed by the term "substantially limits a major life activity." For example, a child with cystic fibrosis might qualify for 504 protections because he is unable to breathe adequately in a particular classroom contaminated with mold. In practice, decisions must be made on an individual basis as to whether a student's impairment "substantially limits" learning in either academic or nonacademic activities. State and/or local education agencies are required to publish written criteria for determining the definition of "substantially limits academic or nonacademic activities," and parents should obtain these written definitions from the special education director early in their educational advocacy efforts.

## 3. Reasonable Accommodations—Aids, Equipment, Accommodations, and Services

If your child is found to have a disability under Section 504, you then must identify the kind of aids, equipment, or other accommodations that will be needed to enable him to benefit from the school program. More specifically, Section 504 regulations define an appropriate education for an eligible child as, "regular or special education and related aids or services that are…designed to meet individual educational needs of the person with disabilities as adequately as the needs of nondisabled persons are met." Types of aids, equipment, and accommodations which may be required under Section 504 include, but are not limited to:

- Use of a word processor for class and/or homework
- Extra time for all writing assignments
- Occupational therapist observation and recommendations
- Seating at the front of the class away from distractions
- Repeating and simplifying instructions about in-class and homework assignments
- Using tape recorders
- Modifying how tests are given—e.g., orally rather than in writing

Parents and school people alike need to recognize the importance of Section 504 and how it differs from the educational rights and protections under IDEA. First, Section 504 covers a broader and more inclusive range of disabilities than IDEA. Its protections apply both to students receiving special education services and to students whose disabilities fall within its more encompassing criteria. Second, the effectiveness of services provided under 504 are not held to as high a standard as those under IDEA. Under IDEA, services must be sufficient to allow the student to *benefit* from his schooling. Under Section 504, the services must merely be *comparable* to those received by students without disabilities, with no requirement that the student benefit from the services. Finally, Section 504 gives school systems the duty of ensuring that students with disabilities are not discriminated against in any program receiving federal funds.

## ■ LIMITATIONS ON THE PROVISION OF ■ REASONABLE ACCOMMODATIONS

The following factors will be weighed and balanced when deciding whether proposed accommodations are required to be made by the state or local education agency.

1. Is the equipment, aid, or service provided to general education students?
2. Is the equipment, aid, or service necessary for the student to receive the benefit of a specific activity within the instructional program?
3. Will the student, with reasonable accommodations, be able to meet all the program's or activity's requirements in spite of existing disabilities?

4. Can the proposed accommodations be made without imposing an "undue financial and administrative burden" upon the education agency?

If school officials answer "yes" to the first and second questions, they will usually provide the requested aid, equipment, or service. If the answer to question one is "no," but the answers to questions two, three, and four are all "yes," again schools will usually provide the requested accommodations. If school officials answer "no" to any of these questions, however, they will often refuse to provide the requested accommodations. Parents' options for responding to a refusal for reasonable accommodations will be discussed later in this chapter.

# ■ *PROHIBITIONS OF DISCRIMINATORY PRACTICES* ■

In addition to requiring schools to make an appropriate education available for students with disabilities, Section 504 and the ADA prohibit school agencies from discriminating against these students in the provision of general education services. The following are examples of practices that have been found to be discriminatory by the U.S. Department of Education, and in each case the school system was required to correct the practice.

■ The parent of a student who used a wheelchair complained that the bus ride for her child was longer than for children without disabilities who rode the bus. Further, the bus ride often resulted in her child getting to school after classes had started. This practice was found in violation of Section 504.

■ A school district placed a student with disabilities on homebound instruction. A violation of Section 504 was found when the school district limited the number of hours of instruction and the availability of related services without a full assessment of the child's individual needs. A further violation was found because there was no plan to provide the homebound student with opportunities to participate in nonacademic and extracurricular activities with nondisabled peers.

■ A school district scheduled graduation ceremonies for students with severe disabilities at a different time and location from all other students. A violation under Section 504 was found because there was no educational necessity for separate graduation ceremonies.

■ A school district limited its extended school year program to students with severe disabilities. Parents of other children were not notified of the availability of such services and some who obtained them were charged fees. Violations found included: services were limited to students with severe disabilities rather than considering each student's individual needs; the school system had no written policy, criteria, or procedures for determining when extended school year services were necessary; and the school system had provided no in-service training for its teachers on extended school year services.

- A school district refused to provide program modifications to a student with attention deficit disorder. A violation under Section 504 was found because the student was considered "handicapped" within the definition of Section 504.

Under Section 504, any organization or individual who is contracted by the public schools to provide services to students with disabilities must also meet the nondiscriminatory requirements of Section 504. For example, a school system contracted with a private school for services to be provided to students with disabilities. Parents of children placed in the school complained to the Office of Civil Rights that the school had no accessible restrooms, drinking fountains, and ramps or elevators to allow students in wheelchairs access to programs or activities conducted on the upper or lower levels of the two-story building. When OCR investigated, they found that the school system had violated Section 504 and the ADA by contracting with an organization that subjected individuals with disabilities to discrimination. If a public school is paying for your child to attend a private school, residential facility, or other special program, he is entitled to reasonable accommodations and nondiscriminatory treatment by the contracting organizations and the individuals who work there. Should discrimination occur, you have a right to challenge the alleged violations. The procedures for doing so are discussed later in this chapter.

# ■ PROCEDURAL REQUIREMENTS OF SECTION 504 ■

The Office of Civil Rights (OCR) of the U.S. Department of Education has the duty of ensuring that school systems comply with the requirements of Section 504. In enforcing these requirements, OCR tends to focus on reviewing school systems' policies and procedures for implementing the law rather than on violations in individual cases. What, then, are the procedures the public schools are required to follow?

# 1. Self-Evaluation and Signed Assurances

Under both Section 504 and the ADA, school systems were required to have completed a self-evaluation by January 26, 1993 to determine whether their policies, practices, and procedures discriminate on the basis of disability. Where discrimination is found to occur within policies, practices, or procedures, steps must be taken to make the necessary modifications. During the evaluation process itself, disability organizations should have been given the opportunity to submit comments. The final evaluation should include: a list of the interested persons consulted; a description of areas examined and any problems identified; and a description of any modifications made.

For school systems employing 50 or more employees, the ADA requires that the self-evaluation be retained and made available for public inspection for at least three years following its completion. In addition, school systems must sign annual assurances that they have read the Section 504 regulations and that they promise to comply fully with them. Parents can obtain a copy of their school system's 1993 self-evaluation, or a more recent evaluation, to assess the results, procedure, and thoroughness with which the evaluation was undertaken. Your local director of special education should be able to tell you how to obtain copies of these self-evaluations.

# 2. Required Notices

Schools must provide *general notice* of the availability of special education and related services to students who are eligible for services under Section 504. The notice will usually be in newspapers, in general mailings that are sent to all students, in student handbooks, or in parent newsletters. A school must not wait until eligibility for special services is established before notifying parents or guardians of the availability of these Section 504 services.

Under the requirements of IDEA, every school system must plan and implement procedures for identifying, locating, and evaluating children within the district who may have disabilities and may need special education. When schools carry out their annual "child find" activities, they are also required to provide an explanation of the specific procedural safeguards they have developed to meet their Section 504 responsibilities. Since the rights and procedures under Section 504 are somewhat different from those provided under IDEA, parents should ask school officials for information pertaining specifically to Section 504 rights, responsibilities, and procedural safeguards.

School systems must identify one or more individuals responsible for receiving complaints and coordinating the grievance processes required by Section 504 and the ADA. In addition, school systems must adopt and publish written procedures that govern the grievance process under both Section 504 and the ADA and that explain parental rights in the grievance process. These procedures must be published along with the name, office address, and telephone number of the grievance coordinator.

## 3. EVALUATIONS, ELIGIBILITY DECISIONS, AND THE INDIVIDUALIZED PLAN

As discussed earlier, the definition of a child with a disability under Section 504 and the ADA is broader and covers more children and circumstances than IDEA's definition. Therefore, school systems may often find they must evaluate students under Section 504 even though these same children would appear ineligible for special education under IDEA.

Unfortunately, many school systems in the past have not provided for Section 504 evaluations and have restricted evaluations only to students they believed possibly eligible for services under IDEA. Likewise, when students were evaluated but found not to meet fully the requirements for services under IDEA, school officials often told parents they could not legally provide additional educational services to their children. Both of these practices are clearly wrong.

Section 504 *specifically* requires school systems to evaluate children who are believed to have a disability significantly limiting their ability to learn. And when these students are found to be disabled under the definition of Section 504 and the ADA, school systems are required to provide an appropriate education for these students even if they are not eligible for special education services under IDEA.

School systems implementing Section 504 must have written procedures which provide for:

    a. determining students' eligibility under Section 504;

    b. ensuring that the evaluation procedures employ non-biased tests and materials which accurately reflect the students' abilities; that the evaluations are administered by trained personnel; that the evaluations assess specific areas of educational need; and that the tests are selected and administered to reflect accurately the factors the test is supposed to measure;

    c. identifying the persons who must attend the evaluation meeting to discuss the evaluation and determine students' eligibility for services and/or accommodations; and,

    d. describing the elements of the individualized plan (sometimes called the 504 Plan or the Individualized Determination Plan) designed to implement an appropriate education as required under Section 504.

Section 504 does not require school systems to allow parents to participate actively in either the evaluation or eligibility processes. If your school system does provide opportunities for participation, you can beneficially follow the steps described earlier in this book for contributing your unique knowledge to evaluation and eligibility decision making. If your school system does not allow substantial participation, you should contribute as much information as possible to the decision processes, review the procedures and data used to reach final decisions, and use the appeals process if you believe inappropriate decisions have been reached.

When interpreting evaluation data and making eligibility decisions under Section 504, school systems must draw upon information from a variety of sources. In addition, school systems must establish procedures to document that the evaluation information has been considered in reaching its decisions. The documentation should include such things as meeting notes or evaluation reports or summaries. Regulations further require that school systems inform parents as to the outcome of the Section 504 evaluations of their children. While notification is not required to be in writing, parents can request such written confirmation. Likewise, parents have the right to examine all documents, records, and information relevant to decisions regarding their children's evaluations and service eligibility. Finally, while regulations do not specify timelines for the completion of Section 504 evaluations, the Office of Civil Rights has directed school systems to follow the timelines applicable under state special education rules unless other local procedures have been established.

## 4. PLACEMENT DECISIONS

Section 504 does not specify the membership of the team that will make the final decision on your child's school and classroom placement. In practice, the placement team and the evaluation/eligibility team are often one and the same. Still, at a minimum the placement team is required to be comprised of persons who are knowledgeable about the student, the meaning of the evaluation data, and the placement options available for the student. Parents may be included as members of the placement team at the discretion of the local education agency. Therefore, parents should determine early whether their local school system allows their participation and should seek, when possible, to be included as part of the placement team.

Placement decisions under Section 504 must meet the same least restrictive environment requirements as under IDEA. Likewise, students protected under Section 504 are entitled to certain procedural safeguards before they can be suspended from school beyond ten days or expelled. These safeguards require that the school's placement team determine whether the student's misconduct is due to the student's disability. If it is, the student cannot be suspended for more than ten days or expelled. If the misconduct is not re-lated to the student's disability, the school system may employ its regular disciplinary procedures.**★

There is one exception to the preceding safeguards related to disciplin-ary procedures involving a change of placement. If a student with disabilities is caught bringing a firearm to school, he may immediately receive a 45-day placement in an interim alternative educational setting. As soon as possible after this action is taken, the school district should convene a committee (the IEP or other appropriate committee) to determine whether bringing the fire-arm to school was related to the student's disability. If parents request a due process hearing during this time, the student will remain in the alternative setting pending completion of the committee's work.

## 5. PARENTAL NOTICE AND CONSENT

Similar to IDEA, Section 504 requires school systems to notify parents about the identification, evaluation, and placement of their children. In contrast to IDEA, however, Section 504 does not require that parents provide written consent prior to their children's initial evaluation or their initial placement.

## 6. IMPARTIAL HEARINGS

To resolve disputes arising under Section 504, state education agencies must provide for impartial hearings and reviews with the participation of parents and their attorney or advocate. Many states have authorized state IDEA hear-ing officers to hear and to rule upon Section 504 complaints. In other states, alternative impartial hearing procedures have been established to comply with this requirement.

Parents may use the impartial hearing process to raise any questions they have about whether the school system is appropriately observing their child's protections and procedural rights under Section 504. For example, you may request a review of your child's evaluation process, the eligibility decision, the adequacy of educational accommodations, the placement decision, or the implementation of the individualized plan. In addition, you may use the impartial hearing process to question whether your child is being unfairly discriminated against in the provision of general education programs and/or extracurricular activities.

---

** As this book went to press, the U.S. Congress was considering revision of the discipline and expulsion rules.

As is true under IDEA, requesting a hearing should be one of the last actions you take to secure your child's educational rights under Section 504. If necessary, however, follow the steps described in Chapter 10 for preparing for and participating in a due process hearing. Some changes in these steps may be necessary to adjust for the legal requirements of Section 504 and specific 504 procedures developed by the school system. Nevertheless, these steps should provide you with a sound basis for addressing the legal, factual, and procedural issues that will arise in this hearing.

## ▪ ENFORCING STUDENTS' RIGHTS UNDER ▪ SECTION 504 AND ADA

Students and parents may follow numerous paths to correct errors they believe have occurred in meeting their rights under Section 504 and the ADA. First, parents may contact the Section 504 grievance coordinator within the local school system. The coordinator will then follow existing local procedures designed to resolve informally any conflicts or misunderstandings arising under the implementation of these laws. Second, students or parents can request an impartial hearing at which a hearing officer or other impartial person or panel will render a decision about the existing dispute. Yet a third option is for the student or parent to file a complaint with the Office of Civil Rights (OCR) of the U.S. Department of Education.

### OFFICE OF CIVIL RIGHTS (OCR) COMPLAINTS

Any individual or organization who believes a school system or school official has violated students' or parents' rights under Section 504 or ADA may file a formal complaint with a regional office of OCR. The addresses of these offices may be found in Appendix A. The complaint may reflect alleged violations of the rights of individual students or parents, classes of individuals or parents, or the general practices of a local or state education agency. These complaints must be filed within 180 days of the alleged discriminatory action. OCR will then investigate the circumstances of the complaint and issue a Letter of Finding. The Letter of Finding will either conclude that no violation has occurred, or it will identify specific violations and the corrective actions that the school system must take. Only in extraordinary circumstances will OCR examine alleged violations of individual placement or other educational decisions, and these only when a child is excluded from services or the school system appears to be engaging in an ongoing pattern of discriminatory practices.

## JUDICIAL ACTION

A final alternative for students and parents is to seek enforcement of Section 504 and the ADA through court action. Parents and students who sue under Section 504 and who prevail in their cases are entitled to corrective actions by the school system and to the reimbursement of all court-related expenses. Under some circumstances, students and parents may also receive monetary awards for compensatory damages due to claims of pain and suffering, emotional distress, mental anguish, and medical expenses—though such awards are seldom made by the courts. Finally, when parents take legal action solely under Section 504, they can immediately file suit in court without first having to follow an informal review process or due process procedure.

Because of the time, effort, strain, and costs of judicial action, this path should be your last alternative in trying to enforce your child's and your rights under Section 504 and the ADA. Nevertheless, the seriousness of the discriminatory action, the harm your child may endure, and/or the ineffectiveness of other remedies may all require this final action. It was for these reasons that Congress made this enforcement option available.

## ■ SECTION 504 AND ADA: TWO CRITICAL LAWS ■ COMPLEMENTING SPECIAL EDUCATION

Under the Individuals with Disabilities Education Act (IDEA), students whose disabilities meet certain narrowly specified criteria have been guaranteed a free appropriate public education in the least restrictive environment. Section 504 and the ADA add to these guarantees by ensuring that these students, as well as other students with disabilities not receiving IDEA protections, are not discriminated against in the provision of school programs and services. By understanding the requirements school systems must meet in fulfilling their duties under Section 504 and the ADA, you can ensure that your child obtains the full educational benefits to which he is entitled. And those educational benefits will, in turn, promote the goals of Section 504 and the ADA by allowing your child to participate in, and contribute to, his community as fully as possible.

# 12. MONITORING

## CHECKPOINTS

**Y**ou have traveled a long way since first entering the special education maze. Referral, evaluation, and eligibility determination seem like dim shadows. Even decisions regarding placement and the IEP are less clear than the day they were made. But now your child is in the appropriate classroom, with appropriate services scheduled to be given. The maze is completed!

But wait, not so fast! All that you have done so far has been essential for your journey. But your task is not completed. Placing a child in a class, establishing educational goals and objectives, and scheduling services on an IEP are not the same as achieving those goals and objectives and receiving those services. Your next step involves periodic checking up on your child's progress. For example, you will want to know if she is moving toward those milestones you set as goals and objectives. Is she receiving the related services agreed upon? Is she spending time with other students in the general education classroom and participating in music or art class, going to recess, and eating lunch with friends in the cafeteria?

You have completed your trip through the maze only when your child begins to realize her potential as a result of the education she receives. This trip is finished only when you monitor your child's individualized plan and the educational and developmental growth spelled out in that document. You may have a very young child and have developed an Individualized Family Service Plan under Part H; or your child may have an individualized plan under Section 504; or your child may have an Individualized Education Program *and* an Individualized Transition Plan. No matter which type of plan you and your child are a part of, the principles and techniques described in this chapter will guide you in ensuring the program you helped develop is implemented as planned. This chapter gives suggestions for monitoring your child's specialized (or educational) program by using the Individualized Education Program (IEP) as the example.

## ▪ WHY MONITOR? ▪

But why must you monitor your child's program and progress? Can't you trust the school systems to live up to what they say will be done? Doesn't there come a time when you have to turn the educational reins over to the "experts"? And isn't now that time?

Unfortunately the school's attempts to carry out the IEP may fall short for many reasons: lack of funds to hire occupational therapists, a teacher falling ill for several months, or a sudden increase in enrollment leaving less time to work with your child. These and other factors may result in your child's IEP not being implemented. But they are not legitimate reasons for failing to carry out the goals, objectives, and related services designated in the IEP. If you know the IEP is not being carried out, you may request a meeting with your child's teachers to get it back on track. Likewise, if the IEP you have agreed to is being carried out to the letter but is ineffective, you may also ask for changes. But if you have not monitored the IEP, you may find yourself in the position of Mr. and Mrs. Green.

> The Greens' son, John, had a major speech disability. The IEP for John, therefore, included individual speech therapy, twice a week, for thirty minutes each period. As the year progressed, the Greens saw little advancement in their son's speech skills. Still, they kept hoping progress would come, in time. At the end of the school year, the Greens met with John's teacher, Ms. Prizer. During their conference, Ms. Prizer proudly showed Mr. and Mrs. Green John's language board. The board contained letters of the alphabet, simple signs for frequently used words—I, go, open, close—and other communication symbols. Ms. Prizer explained that John would carry this small board with him throughout the day. When he wanted to communicate with someone, he would point to the appropriate symbols on his board. The Greens were impressed with this innovation, although somewhat surprised they had not learned of it before the end of school. When they asked Ms. Prizer how the board was used with John's speech therapy, they learned of yet another innovation in their son's IEP. "Oh," said Ms. Prizer, "John has not had speech therapy for seven months.

When he showed no progress after two months of therapy, we decided to use the language board as an alternative to speech therapy
to improve his communication skills."

Maybe the language board was more useful than speech therapy, but that
is not the point. No change in your child's IEP should be made without school
personnel notifying you. Unless you monitor your child's IEP, you won't know
whether innovations are being made in her program. Yes, once the IEP is written you can turn the educational reins over to the "experts." But you should
continue to monitor your child's educational and developmental progress.

## ■ MONITORING PRACTICES AND TECHNIQUES ■

Most parents approach the topic of monitoring the IEP with apprehension.
They wonder, "Who am I to question what the teachers are doing?" "How
will I know whether the IEP is being implemented?" "What do I do if the IEP
is not being followed?" Combine this uncertainty with the normal tendency
to trust "authorities," and no wonder parents are hesitant to second-guess
school administrators and teachers.

What can you do to overcome these understandably common fears? Your
first concern should be to focus on selected aspects of the IEP to determine:

1. Is the educational plan being carried out?
   a. Is the classroom instruction following the IEP?
   b. Are the required related services being provided?
2. Is the plan working well for your child?
   a. Is the classroom setting truly appropriate for your
      child's needs?
   b Is your child making educational and/or developmental
      progress in school?

Having identified the questions to ask, your second concern becomes finding
the answers to those questions. Parents have found many techniques to be
helpful when monitoring their child's IEP. The most frequently used methods
include the following:

**Holding Conferences.** Have individual meetings with your child's teachers, school administrators, tutors, therapists, and other professionals on a
regular basis, or whenever there is an issue to be discussed. Keep a written
record of the dates of meetings, topics discussed, and outcomes.

**Making Classroom Observations.** Either visit the classroom with the specific intent of observing some aspect of your child's learning activities, or
volunteer in the class and at the school and use those opportunities to ob-

serve your child and her program. Keep a written record of when you make each observation and a detailed description of what you observe.

**Exchanging a Notebook**. Share comments, suggestions, observations, and the like with your child's teacher via a notebook which your child carries to and from school. Also included can be a checklist of important behavioral goals and objectives from the IEP.

**Joining Groups.** Participate in your local Parent-Teacher Association and in local parent groups such as the Learning Disabilities Association (LDA) and The Arc (formerly the Association of Retarded Citizens). These groups often provide excellent, up-to-date information on programs and school services relevant to your child's IEP.

**Talking with Your Child.** Ask your child how school is going, what activities she enjoys most, and how much time she spends in speech or math. Keep written notes detailing your child's responses. Look over her homework, what she has to do and has done. Help her with homework. Note the length of time spent on homework and how much help you provided.

These are just a few of the techniques you might use to assess your child's program and progress during the school year. While the list is not complete, it provides a starting point from which you can begin to develop your own monitoring plan.

## ▪ You and Your Child's Teacher ▪

The single most important source of information on your child's progress is her teacher. The teacher talks with you after school, at the IEP meeting, and at regularly scheduled conferences. The teacher completes your child's report card and fills out the notebook you send back and forth. The teacher talks with the school psychologist, the physical therapist, and administrators about your child's needs and progress, and then the teacher talks to you.

The free flow of information between you and the teacher will depend mainly upon your relationship with one another. If the teacher perceives you as a concerned parent who also understands the needs and problems of teachers, and if you believe the teacher can teach your child effectively, you will probably receive plenty of up-to-date, specific information about your child's progress. But how do you as a parent develop this cooperative relationship with your child's teacher? You may wish to try some of the following suggestions:

1. Try to develop a personal relationship with your child's teacher. Some families feel comfortable inviting their child's teacher to dinner; others find regular telephone conversations helpful.

2. Give the teachers and specialists sufficient time to get to know your child before asking their opinions about her progress, problems, the appropriateness of her program, and so forth.

3. Let the teachers and specialists know you understand the difficulties they frequently face in doing their jobs—be empathetic to their needs, too!

4. Prepare for conferences in advance by developing and bringing with you a list of questions, concerns, and comments. This saves everybody time and ensures that nothing important will be overlooked.

5. Let teachers and specialists know what is important to you in the education and development of your child.

6. Discuss and share your plan for monitoring your child's IEP, and follow through with that plan.

7. Discuss problems you believe have arisen in implementing the IEP with the teachers and specialists involved. Don't begin by going right to the school administrators.

8. Consider ways you might volunteer time or materials for the classroom.

Each of the preceding activities offers an excellent occasion for you to build bridges of trust and openness with teachers and other specialists working with your child. As these relationships are developed and strengthened, you will experience more and more confidence in your ability to know and understand your child's progress and the extent to which her IEP is actually being implemented.

# ■ OBSERVING IN THE CLASSROOM ■

Besides communicating with the teacher, another useful way to monitor your child's educational progress is through classroom observation. Schools vary in their policies of allowing parents to observe classroom activities. How receptive teachers are to parent classroom visits also differs (another good reason for developing an open relationship with your child's teacher). In all cases, however, before you visit your child's classroom, check first with the teacher and then the school principal to determine your school's specific policy.

Once you know the school policy on classroom visits, you are ready to prepare yourself for this monitoring activity. Following are several suggestions designed to increase the effectiveness of your classroom visit.

1. Give the teacher sufficient prior notice of your visit.

2. Before visiting the class, obtain general information about the classroom. (When does math come? When is recess scheduled? What books are being used?)

3. Decide what you want to observe (e.g., reading group, playground time, math class) and then let the teacher know your plans.

4. Tell the teacher how long you plan to spend in the classroom.

5. Respect the teacher's routines and fit your observations within them when visiting the class.

6. Observe only your own child or interactions involving your child and other children or adults.

7. Keep your conversations with professionals or other adults to a minimum during your observation time.

8. After the classroom visit, make some notes describing your observations, impressions, and/or concerns.

9. Follow up your observation with a brief conference (or phone call or note) thanking the teacher for the opportunity to observe and sharing your findings, thoughts, and questions with the teacher.

10. Tell the teachers and specialists what you like about their teaching style—they'll be pleasantly surprised you noticed.

Whenever you go for a classroom visit, remember that many people, teachers included, can be uncomfortable when they are being observed. The tension created by not knowing why you have come to observe can cause unnecessary anxiety, and even real misunderstanding, between you and the teacher. Notifying the teacher of your plan to observe your child, explaining the purpose of your visit, and following up after the observation can relieve much potential tension. These steps should smooth the way for an informative classroom observation and an open relationship with your child's teacher. You might also want to explain to your child the reasons for your visit in terms that express your interest in her school activities, teachers, and classmates.

# ■ BEING AN INFORMED CONSUMER ■

Besides making classroom visits and communicating with your child's teacher, another helpful monitoring strategy is to become an informed consumer. Although you are not expected to be a special education teacher, physical therapist, or other special education professional, you can still learn many basic ideas important for monitoring your child's education. For example, you can learn about current teaching methods and therapeutic techniques as they relate to your child's disabilities. This information can be obtained in many ways: from parent groups and associations that conduct workshops, including your state's Parent Information and Training Center (See Appendix A); from special lectures or presentations; from individual professionals who are willing to share their knowledge with you; from the local PTA; from continuing education classes at local community colleges and universities; and from books, pamphlets, and magazines. In these and many other ways, you can become a knowledgeable consumer of the special education services in your local school system. And as an informed consumer you will also become an effective monitor of your child's educational program and progress.

## ■ SUMMING UP ■

Monitoring your child's educational program is hard work. Only time, energy, and careful thought can make it pay off. The jargon—"educationese"—found in many IEPs is often impossible to decipher. Educators know what they mean by "voice quality" or "voice intensity," for example, but parents may not. Make certain, therefore, to ask questions at the time of the IEP conference so you do know what the IEP means as well as what it says. This is basic to effective monitoring.

Not knowing whether the goals and objectives are appropriate can cause difficulties also. Your own sense of your child's educational needs helps you here. Completing the Strengthening Exercises described in Chapter 2 will give you added confidence in evaluating the annual goals and short-term objectives suggested for your child's IEP. Monitoring by checking up on the dates of the short-term objectives can help you further in assessing the continuing appropriateness of your child's goals and objectives. Are the objectives being met on schedule? ahead of schedule? or not at all? Answers to these questions will lead you to others. For example, if the results are positive or negative, what accounts for those results? Is it the program, the teacher, or the classroom setting? The answers to all these questions may require some changes in your child's IEP.

## ■ MAKING CHANGES ■

What happens when your monitoring activities convince you change is necessary? Where do you start the change process?

Elements of your child's IEP can be changed at any time through mutual agreement of the IEP team members. But once you have approved an IEP, you should wait a reasonable time before deciding the program is not working or needs changing.

What is a reasonable time? In part, this depends upon your child's age, rate of development, and the educational skills being taught. If your child naturally develops slowly or the educational skill requires significant time to acquire, three to five months may be necessary before noticeable progress occurs. If development is rapid or the skill more readily learned, you may feel that changes should begin within one to three months. In either case, a useful approach would be to wait until the time specified in your child's IEP for assessing achievement of the initial short-term objectives. If these objectives are clearly not being met, a change in program, services, teachers, or some combination of the three may be in order.

**Advocacy Groups**

The preceding diagram of circles suggests that the best place to begin your efforts to change your child's IEP is with her teacher or other specialists. If problems are resolved at this initial level, changes will often be immediate and on target. At this first level of change, the process for correcting problems is the least complicated—although it may not seem so. If your efforts to alter the IEP are unsuccessful at this level, you move out one circle toward the perimeter and seek change at the administrative level.

Your first attempts to work with school administrators in changing your child's IEP should be made informally. An informal request for an IEP change sent to the teacher or principal will often be all that is needed. Your request should be accompanied by a written explanation and monitoring data supporting reasons for your request. If this is not sufficient, you can then begin the administrative review or conciliatory conference procedures available in most school systems. Many states also have a formal mediation system that can assist families and schools in resolving disagreements. Chapter 8 explains the mediation process.

If you cannot obtain satisfactory results through the administrative process, your next step is to request a due process hearing. As pointed out in Chapter 10, you must consider taking this step very carefully. In some instances, however, you may have no alternative. Therefore, even though several months may pass before a final ruling is made to change your child's IEP, the due process hearing remains a viable method for achieving potential change. Of course, if the due process proceedings all seem futile or their results seem biased and inaccurate, you can also seek changes through court action. Considering the time and cost involved in this action, however, its use should be reserved only for major IEP disagreements.

Where, then, does the last circle on the perimeter—political and legal advocacy—enter the IEP change process? This outer circle is often activated to force school systems to do something they currently are not doing, such as providing physical therapy or psychological counseling services. Or political and legal advocacy may also be employed to force school systems to do better and more extensively things they are doing on a limited scale—for example, providing vocational training or speech therapy. In both instances, parents work singly and jointly to persuade school administrators, school boards, city councils, and state legislators to appropriate additional funds for these activities. Or parents sue in court to force school jurisdictions, and indirectly, legislative bodies, to abide by the law and to provide appropriate services. Ideally, both political and legal advocacy can produce the same results—children receive the programs and services in the kinds and amounts appropriate to meet their educational needs.

Although both political and legal advocacy and due process hearings can be highly effective in obtaining educational change, remember: the further you move from the center of the circle, the less the focus is on your child's individual educational needs. Changes made by teachers are usually completed rapidly, with up-to-date information, and in an understanding environment. When IEP changes are generated at points further from your child, the decisions may be slow in coming, out of date, and made out of context. Again, this underscores the need for close relationships with your child's teachers. Begin and end with a teacher whenever you can. You will be miles ahead.

# ■ THE SCHOOL CHECKS UP: MONITORING ■ BY THE SCHOOL

The school system must conduct a formal review of your child's program as it is written in her IEP at least once a year.* This process is referred to as the annual review. The annual review is an opportunity for you, your child's teachers, and other school professionals to look at the past year's IEP goals and objectives and evaluate how well they have been met. The annual review is a time not only to look at past progress but also to consider next year's IEP goals and objectives.

Sometimes teachers or other school personnel may decide before the annual review that your child's progress is not satisfactory. If so, they usually will notify you, seeking additional information or even suggesting a conference. In some instances they may even request formal evaluations of your child. If this happens, the material you read on evaluation procedures in Chapter 3 will once again become relevant to negotiating the special education maze.

As discussed in Chapter 3, IDEA requires the school system to conduct a complete evaluation of your school-aged child once every three years. This is called the *triennial evaluation*. The school system may choose, for legitimate reasons, to reevaluate your child more frequently than required, but in general schools have too few resources to evaluate your child very often.

There are several practical implications for monitoring the triennial evaluation to keep in mind. First, in the three years that elapse between formal evaluations, only the teacher, other professionals working with your child, and you will be monitoring your child's progress. Since even conscientious teachers and other school professionals have limited time to provide services, they often devote little effort to monitoring the results of their work. Therefore, if you don't monitor the IEP carefully, three years could go by before you discover that little or no progress has occurred. Your child cannot afford that time.

There is one other important implication of the requirement for a triennial evaluation that you should not overlook. Every three years you will be faced with a new eligibility determination decision. Pressures on school systems are growing to cut the costs of special education. In the face of these pressures, you must be prepared to present a clear, convincing case as to what, for your child, is an appropriate education in the least restrictive environment. By monitoring your child's IEP carefully and consistently and by following the steps outlined earlier in this book, you should be well on the road to presenting that compelling case for your child each time the triennial evaluation rolls around.

---

* For specific information about monitoring the Individualized Family Service Plan, see Chapter 8.

# 13. A Review of the Special Education Maze

## Does the Maze Ever End?

Over the years parents have often been confused, frustrated, and generally perplexed in their attempts to understand how school officials make decisions about the education of their children. As parents talk with teachers and administrators and hear of evaluation and eligibility procedures, IEPs, learning disabilities, and due process hearings, they often feel that schools have built a complex special education maze through which only educators can find the way. Parents frequently have not known how to take the first step toward negotiating this maze.

This book has been written for parents—and their children. In the preceding pages you were introduced to the corridors of the special education maze—the cyclical process of referral, evaluation, eligibility, IEP, placement, monitoring, and, when necessary, due process procedures. Understanding this process gives you insight into the entry points for the maze, the rules and regulations for traveling through the maze, and potential strategies for negotiating the maze. The end result of your journey, it is hoped, will be that your child receives a free, appropriate public education in the least restrictive environment.

Federal and state laws have created the legal basis for ensuring that children with disabilities receive a free, appropriate public education. Local school systems and their teachers and administrators have the potential knowledge, dedication, and resources to carry out these laws. You, as parents, however, possess the one additional ingredient needed to blend these laws and resources together to produce an effective education for your child. This ingredient is your unique knowledge of your child, what he knows, and how he learns. If this knowledge is not included in educational planning and programming for your child, the program ultimately developed may be inappropriate and, possibly, ineffective. Your child cannot afford to lose days, months, and years in the wrong program. You do not want this time to be lost, or you would not be reading this book.

Emphasis throughout this book is placed upon the importance of acquiring the skills, knowledge, and values essential for becoming effective educational advocates for your child.

Educational advocacy is a means for parents to participate intelligently and collaboratively in decisions affecting the education of their children with disabilities. Educational advocacy offers you an approach for ensuring that your unique knowledge of your child is reflected in the educational programs and the educational environment he encounters. Educational advocacy provides you with a plan of action for successfully negotiating the special education maze.

## ▪ A NEW EXPERIENCE WITH EACH ▪ TRIP THROUGH THE MAZE

The special education planning and programming cycle described in Chapter 1 is a recurring one. Each year the educational goals, objectives, and services outlined in your child's IEP are reexamined and revised as needed. Each time you travel through the special education maze, whether it is for the annual review or the more extensive triennial evaluation, changes will have occurred. You will find new school professionals working with your child; shifts in the laws, regulations, and policies pertaining to special education; and different strategies used by school officials to implement the rules of the maze. The fact that each trip through the maze is a new experience has significant implications for parent educational advocates.

First, each time the cycle begins, you must gather new data about your child; analyze the data; organize it for purposes of making evaluation, eligibility, IEP, and/or placement decisions; and prepare for and participate in the meetings where these decisions are made. All of this, of course, will be more easily accomplished when you have carefully monitored your child's program.

Second, since laws, regulations, policies, and practices change rapidly in the special education field, you should check annually with your state and local education departments for any changes in these procedures that may have occurred since you last traveled the maze. Following this suggestion will ensure that you do not waste valuable time using outmoded procedures, and, more importantly, that you do not overlook any new rights or entitlements your child has been given over the years.

Third, because school personnel come and go as frequently as rules and regulations change, you should also continually update the key people chart found earlier in this book. By asking around, you should be able to learn something about the educational background and experience of these new people. And, by keeping your information about the educators in the special education maze up-to-date, you can help to foster the confidence and trust needed for successful collaboration.

Fourth, each year brings new problems and opportunities to local school systems. These problems and opportunities often are linked to changes in funding which may have either a positive or negative impact on educational programs. On the negative side, you might find fewer services, higher student/teacher ratios, and longer bus rides. On the positive side, some school systems are recognizing the value of strengthening the parent/professional partnership. One way they are doing this is by establishing parent resource centers in their school systems. Such centers offer training courses in educational advocacy for parents and provide information and referral to school and community services. Both positive and negative changes within local school systems will sometimes alter the ways in which school professionals view their duties for educating children with disabilities in accordance with federal and state law. By knowing the particular problems and opportunities confronting your school system, you will be better prepared to face any changes in strategy school officials may seek to implement.

Finally, since each trip through the maze is a new one, you will have to formulate new strategies and tactics to be sure they meet the changed conditions. Although you may have succeeded in obtaining an appropriate education for your child on one trip through the maze, past success does not promise continued success. Only thoughtful, careful, hard work can prepare you to be an effective educational advocate for your child. There is no substitute for diligent preparation for negotiating the maze.

## ■ CHANGING THE MAZE AND THE ■ RULES OF THE MAZE

You may find that no matter how skilled you become in negotiating the special education maze, your child's program never seems appropriate to meet his needs. Classes may be too large, related services unavailable, specialized instruction nonexistent, and transportation inconvenient. When these problems arise and due process procedures, short of court action, fail to correct them, educational advocacy has reached its limits of effectiveness. Legal and political advocacy must then be employed to bring about necessary changes.

Legal advocacy is best used when school officials interpret the law one way and you intrepret it another. Although hearing officers in due process hearings may agree with the interpretations of school officials, their word is not final. Only the courts can definitively answer questions about the interpretation of laws. Courts clarify the meaning of federal and state laws; courts rule authoritatively on whether state and local education policies and regulations conform with federal and state laws. When you feel that state laws conflict with federal laws and school officials will not change their procedures to meet your objections, the courts offer one alternative for changing both the system itself and the policies and regulations governing it.

Yet another option for altering the special education system is political advocacy. In this type of advocacy, groups lobby legislative, executive, and administrative bodies in an attempt to change specific government budgets, policies, and procedures. The Council for Exceptional Children, The Arc, The National Parent Network on Disabilities, and United Cerebral Palsy are just some examples of the many groups that engage in political advocacy. The distinguishing feature of political advocacy is its emphasis upon changing specific elements of the special education maze—for example, procedures for evaluation, criteria for eligibility, budgets appropriated for special education, and certain rules for special education, such as the rights of parents to participate in various meetings. In contrast to educational advocacy, where the advocate is concerned only with the welfare of one child, political advocacy seeks changes either in the overall process or its encompassing rules and regulations in order to benefit all children with disabilities.

Political advocacy may be essential when the process itself is being revamped or when the rules and regulations are viewed by some as inherently unjust or impractical. In these situations educational advocacy will prove insufficient and nothing short of political advocacy will assure a free, appropriate public education for children with disabilities.

In 1997, for example, Congress undertook the re-authorization of IDEA, considering major changes in requirements of the law. Many parent groups as well as special and general education professional associations became involved in providing information and suggestions as to how the law could be improved. As of the publication date of this book, final changes have not been enacted.

Legal and political advocacy have their places, but their effects are sometimes not as immediate as educational advocacy. In the short run, your child needs immediate services and educational programs that meet his unique needs.

Educational advocacy, as outlined in this book, is designed to assist you in meeting these short-run educational needs. As parents gain skill and experience in using legal, political, and educational advocacy, they will learn the situations in which each is most effectively employed—and will use them accordingly. But in the last analysis, when the special education system and accompanying regulations have been changed by legal and political advocacy, success in negotiating the newly designed system will ultimately depend upon parents' abilities to serve as educational advocates for their own children.

## ■ *THROUGH THE MAZE WITH OTHERS* ■

At many points in the special education planning cycle you have been encouraged to ask a friend to assist and accompany you in advocating for your child. This was true in evaluation, eligibility, IEP/placement, and due process proceedings. The purpose of this suggestion is at least twofold. First, another person can enhance your effectiveness as an educational advocate by serving as a source of ideas and suggestions and as a second pair of eyes and ears. Second, another person can provide the personal and emotional support most parents need to cope with the stress of traveling through the special education maze.

While the help and assistance of one or two friends can make you a more effective educational advocate, the combined efforts and support of numerous other parents can increase your effectiveness even further. By forming a group of parents committed to educational advocacy for their children, you will immediately increase your collective knowledge of the local school maze and decrease the debilitating feeling of isolation so often caused by coping alone with the intricacies and frustrations of the maze.

How do you start your own groups of educational advocates? One good place to begin is by having a number of concerned parents study this book together. You may want to enlist the assistance of special education teachers, school psychologists, or other professionals who work with children with disabilities, to provide the group with expertise to explore selected topics in more depth—for example, evaluation, eligibility, IEPs, or due process procedures. But remember, this book was meant for you—the parent. The intent of the group study is to assist you as an educational advocate for your child. Any professional assistance you get should be oriented toward helping you incorporate your unique insights of your child into his special educational plans and programs.

Another step you can take is to contact the Parent Training and Information Center (PTI) in your state. These centers are funded by the U.S. Department of Education to provide training and information to parents of children with disabilities. Your state PTI can assist you with strategies for: participating in the educational decision-making process; communicating with teachers and other professionals involved in your child's education, and obtaining appropriate programs, resources, and services for your child. Appendix A tells you how to get in touch with your state's PTI.

The authors of this book founded the Parent Educational Advocacy Training Center (PEATC) in Alexandria, Virginia, a training and information center funded in part by the U.S. Department of Education. The experience of PEATC has shown just how effective parent groups in educational advocacy can become. Since 1978, PEATC has trained—directly and indirectly—thousands of parents to serve as educational advocates for their children. These parents come together for workshops focused upon the ideas discussed in this book. From these workshops, parents acquire insights into the special education process in their local school jurisdictions, skills in educational advocacy to work within that process, and a sense of identity and solidarity with other parents of children with disabilities.

By attending the course, parents make contact with other parents whom they can call upon for insights, knowledge, and the psychological and moral support needed to sustain them on their journeys through the maze. As these parents have gained proficiency as educational advocates, they have often reached out to help other parents who have not attended an educational advocacy course. This mutual support and assistance is essential if parents are to ensure the responsiveness of the system to their children.

By learning the basics of educational advocacy and speaking up for the rights of your child, you can help forge a strong alliance between parents and school professionals. By banding together and speaking up for the rights of children with disabilities everywhere, parents throughout the United States can help make the promise of a free, appropriate public education for all children with disabilities a reality.

# Glossary

This glossary includes special education terms mentioned in the text, as well as words parents may find used in the school setting. It also defines the disabilities that qualify a child for special education services, but does not contain any other terms related to specific disabilities.

**Accommodation:** *See* **Reasonable Accommodation**.

**Achievement Test:** A test that measures a student's level of development in academic areas such as math, reading, and spelling.

**Activity Center:** A day program where staff members assist adults with disabilities with activities emphasizing community skill training (e.g., learning to use public transportation) and vocational skill development.

**Adaptive Behavior:** The extent to which an individual is able to adjust to and to apply skills to new environments, tasks, objects, and people.

**Adaptive Physical Education:** A physical education program that has been modified to meet the specific needs of a student with disabilities; e.g., inclusion of activities to develop upper body strength in a student with limited arm movement.

**Administrative Review:** A review process whereby disagreements between parents and school systems may be resolved by a committee of school system individuals not directly involved with the case. Also called a conciliatory conference.

**Adult Day Programs:** Programs in which adults with disabilities receive training in daily living skills, social skills, recreational skills, and "pre-vocational" skills.

**Advocacy:** Speaking or acting on behalf of another individual or group to bring about change.

**Advocate:** A person who speaks or acts knowledgeably on behalf of another individual or group to bring about change.

**Aged Out (Aging Out):** Refers to students with special needs who have reached the maximum age limit mandated in their state for special education and related services.

**Americans with Disabilities Act (ADA):** An anti-discrimination law giving

individuals with disabilities civil rights protection similar to those rights given to all people on the basis of race, sex, national origin, or religion.

**Annual Goal:** Statement describing the anticipated growth of a student's skill and knowledge written into a student's yearly Individualized Education Program.

**Annual Review:** A meeting held at least once a year to look at, talk about, and study a student's Individualized Education Program (IEP). The purpose of the review is to make decisions about changes in the IEP, review the placement, and develop a new IEP for the year ahead.

**Appropriate:** In free, appropriate public education provided by the Individuals with Disabilities Education Act (IDEA), "appropriate" refers to an educational plan that meets the individual needs of a student with disabilities.

**Aptitude Test:** A test that measures an individual's potential in a specific skill area, such as clerical speed, numerical ability, or abstract thinking.

**Assessment:** *See* **Evaluation.**

**Assistive Technology:** Any item, piece of equipment, or product system that is used to increase, maintain, or improve the functional capabilities of children with disabilities; e.g., augmentative communication boards, computer input devices, special switches.

**At-Risk:** Term used to describe children who are considered likely to have difficulties because of home life circumstances, medical difficulties at birth, or other factors, and who may need early intervention services to prevent future difficulties.

**Audiologist**: A professional non-medical specialist who measures hearing levels and evaluates hearing loss.

**Auditory Discrimination:** The ability to identify and distinguish among different speech sounds; e.g., the difference between the sound of "a" in *say* and in *sad.*

**Autism:** A developmental disability significantly affecting verbal and nonverbal communication and social interaction, generally evident before age 3.

**Behavior Disorders (BD):** Disorders characterized by disruptive behavior in school, home, and other settings. They can include attention deficit hyperactivity disorder (ADHD), conduct disorder, difficulty learning, and inability to establish satisfactory relationships with others. Such behavior is considered inappropriate, excessive, chronic, and abnormal.

**Behavioral Observation**: A systematic way of observing, recording, and interpreting the behavior of a student as he/she works on the job in order to gain a broad picture of the student's interests and abilities. Part of a vocational assessment.

**Blind (Blindness):** Complete loss of sight. Educationally, individuals who are severely visually impaired, or have no vision and must learn to read by braille, are considered blind. See also **Legally Blind.**

**Buckley Amendment:** More commonly known name for the Family Educational Rights and Privacy Act of 1974. The law gives parents and students (over age 18) the right to see, correct, and control access to school records.

**Career Education:** A progression of activities intended to help students acquire the knowledge, skills, and attitudes that make work a meaningful part of life. Career education has four stages: 1) awareness/orientation, 2) exploration, 3) preparation, including vocational education, and 4) job placement/follow-up.

**Carl D. Perkins Vocational and Applied Technology Education Act (1990):** A federal law stipulating that students with disabilities be guaranteed the opportunity to participate in federally funded vocational programs that are equal to those afforded to the general student population.

**Case Manager:** *See* **Service Coordinator.**

**Child Find:** A state and local program mandated by the Individuals with Disabilities Education Act (IDEA) to identify individuals with disabilities between the ages of birth and twenty-one and to direct them to appropriate early intervention or educational programs.

**Child Study Team or Screening Committee:** A local school-based committee, whose members determine if a student should be evaluated for special education eligibility.

**Cognition:** A term that describes the process people use for remembering, reasoning, understanding, and judgement.

**Communication Disorder:** A general term for any language and/or speech impairment.

**Community Participation:** Activities by a person with disabilities within the community which contribute to the well-being and improvement of that community, such as volunteering at the hospital, planting trees, serving on the board of a nonprofit agency.

**Competitive Employment:** Everyday jobs with wages at the going rate in the open labor market. Jobs can be either on a part-time or full-time basis.

**Compliance File:** School records containing all reports of meetings, correspondence, and other contacts between parents and school officials.

**Conciliatory Conference:** *See* **Administrative Review**.

**Confidential File:** A file having restricted access and containing records of a child's evaluation and other materials related to special education (medical reports, independent evaluations, reports of eligibility meetings, etc.).

**Confidentiality:** The limiting of access to a child or family's records to personnel having direct involvement with the child.

**Congenital:** A term referring to a condition present or existing at birth.

**Consent:** Parental permission, usually given by signing a letter or form, agreeing to let the schools take an action which affects a child's education. Consent is required before a child can be evaluated or receive special education services under IDEA.

**Contract Services:** Services provided to students with disabilities by private service providers (private schools, institutions, therapists, etc.) when the school system is unable to provide the needed service.

**Cumulative File:** A file containing report cards, standardized achievement test scores, teacher reports, and other records of a student's school progress.

**Deaf (Deafness):** A hearing impairment so severe that an individual cannot process sounds even with amplification such as hearing aids.

**Deaf-Blind:** The combination of visual and hearing impairments causing such severe communication and other developmental and educational problems that a child cannot adequately be served in a special education program solely for deaf or blind children.

**Developmental:** Having to do with the steps or stages in growth and development before the age of 18.

**Developmental Delay:** Term used to describe slower than normal development of an infant or child in one or more areas.

**Developmental Disability (DD):** Any severe disability, mental and/or physical, which is present before an individual becomes eighteen years old, which substantially limits his activities, is likely to continue indefinitely, and requires life-long care, treatment, or other services. Examples of developmental disabilities include Down syndrome, autism, and cerebral palsy.

**Disability:** A problem or condition which makes it hard for a student to learn or do things in the same ways as most other students. A disability may be short term or permanent.

**Due Process:** A system of procedures ensuring that an individual will be notified of, and have opportunity to contest, decisions made about him. As it pertains to early intervention (Part H) and special education (Part B) of IDEA, due process refers to the legal right to appeal any decision regarding any portion of the process (evaluation, eligibility, IEP or IFSP, placement, etc.).

**Due Process Hearing:** A formal session conducted by an impartial hearing officer to resolve special education disagreements between parents and school systems.

**Early Intervention:** Providing services and programs to infants and toddlers (under age three) with disabilities in order to minimize or eliminate the disability as they mature.

**Education of the Handicapped Act (EHA):** *See* **Individuals with Disabilities Education Act (IDEA).**

**Educational Advocate:** An individual who speaks or acts knowledgeably for the educational needs of another.

**Educational Diagnostician:** A professional who is certified to conduct educational assessments and to design instructional programs for students.

**Eligibility:** The determination of whether or not a child qualifies to receive early intervention or special education services based on meeting established criteria.

**Emotional Disorders (ED):** Disorders characterized by their effect on an individual's emotional state. They may cause anxiety, such as separation anxiety, phobias, and post traumatic stress disorder. Other emotional disorders are affective or mood disorders, such as childhood depression, or bi-polar disorder.

**Employability Skills:** Personal habits and traits such as cleanliness, dependability, and punctuality that are necessary for successful employment; sometimes called "work adjustment skills."

**Evaluation:** The process of collecting information about a student's learning needs through a series of individual tests, observations, and talks with the student, the family, and others. Also, the process of obtaining detailed information about an infant or toddler's developmental levels and needs for services. May also be called **Assessment.**

**Expressive Language:** The ability to communicate through speech, writing, augmentative communication, or gestures.

**Extended School Year:** Special education provided during summer months to students found to require year-round services to receive an appropriate education.

**Family Care**: Care provided by individuals who are licensed by the state to provide family-like settings for adults with disabilities.

**Fine Motor Skills:** Body movements which use small muscles; for example: picking up a small object, writing, or eating.

**Free Appropriate Public Education (FAPE):** The words used in the federal law, the Individuals with Disabilities Education Act (IDEA), to describe a student's right to a special education program that will meet his or her individual special learning needs, at no cost to the family.

**Functional Vocational Evaluation.** *See* **Vocational Assessment.**

**General Education Diploma (GED):** A method for obtaining a diploma for adults who did not complete high school. GED tests, which measure achievement in writing skills, social studies, science, literature, and mathematics, enable individuals to demonstrate that they have acquired a level of learning comparable to that of traditional high school graduates.

**Goal:** *See* **Annual Goal**.

**Gross Motor Skills:** Body movements which use large muscles; for example: sitting, walking, or climbing.

**Habilitation:** The process of helping an individual develop specific skills and abilities (e.g., dressing, eating, maneuvering a wheelchair) in order to become as independent and productive as possible.

**Handicapped Children's Protection Act:** The law providing for the reimbursement of reasonable attorneys' fees to parents who win their cases in administrative proceedings under IDEA.

**Hard-of-Hearing:** Impaired hearing which can be corrected sufficiently with a hearing aid to enable an individual to hear and process sounds. Also used to describe hearing loss occurring after an individual has developed some spoken language.

**Hearing Impaired:** This term includes both individuals who are deaf and who are hard-of-hearing. The difference between deafness and hard-of-hearing is defined by amount of hearing loss.

**Homebased Services**: Early intervention services provided to a child and family in their own home.

**Homebound Instruction:** Educational instruction given in a student's home when he is unable to attend school for medical or other reasons.

**IEP:** *See* **Individualized Education Program**.

**IFSP:** *See* **Individualized Family Service Plan**.

**I.Q.:** See **Intelligence Quotient**.

**Impartial Hearing Officer:** Individual presiding over a due process hearing, appointed by the state education agency, and not connected in any way with either party in a dispute.

**Inclusion:** Ensuring that necessary supports and services are provided so that children with disabilities can participate with children who do not have disabilities in school, community, and recreation activities.

**Independent Educational Evaluation:** An evaluation/assessment of a student conducted by one or more professionals not employed by the school system. The person(s) doing the evaluation must be fully trained and qualified to do the kind of testing required.

**Independent Living Skills:** Basic skills needed by people with disabilities to function on their own, with as little help as possible. Skills include self-help (e.g., bathing, dressing), housekeeping, community living (e.g., shopping, using public transportation), etc.

**Individualized Determination Plan:** A written plan for each student who receives services, modifications, and accommodations under Section 504 of the Rehabilitation Act of 1973. In some schools, it is referred to as a "504 Plan."

**Individualized Education Program (IEP):** A written plan for each student in special education describing the student's present levels of performance, annual goals including short-term objectives, specific special education and related services, dates for beginning and duration of services, and how the IEP will be evaluated.

**Individualized Family Service Plan (IFSP):** A written statement for each infant or toddler receiving early intervention services that includes goals and outcomes for the child and family. It also includes a plan for making the transition to services for children over age 2.

**Individuals with Disabilities Education Act (IDEA):** The authorizing federal legislation which mandates a free, appropriate public education for all children with disabilities. Formerly known as the Education for All Handicapped Children Act. **Part B** of the act refers to special education services for children age three through twenty-one. **Part H** refers to the early intervention program for infants and toddlers with disabilities from birth through age two and their families.

**Infant Stimulation:** A program designed to provide specific activities that encourage growth in developmental areas such as movement, speech and language, etc., in infants with developmental delays.

**Intelligence Quotient (I.Q.):** A measurement of thinking (cognitive) ability that compares an individual with others in his age group.

**Interagency Coordinating Council (ICC):** Federal, state, or local group consisting of parents, advocates and professionals who serve in an advisory capacity to plan and implement early intervention services for infants and toddlers with disabilities and their families.

**Intermediate Care Facility:** Licensed facilities operating under strict regulations and providing intensive support for people with disabilities in the areas of personal care, communication, behavior management, etc.

**Itinerant Teacher:** A teacher who provides services to students in a variety of locations.

**Job Coach:** A service agency professional who works with an individual with disabilities at the job site, providing support by helping the employee to improve job skills, interpersonal relations, or any other job-related needs.

**Lead Agency:** State agency which has been designated by the governor to administer and implement a statewide comprehensive, coordinated, multidisciplinary, interagency service delivery system for infants and toddlers with disabilities and their families.

**Learning Disability:** A disorder in one or more of the processes involved in understanding or using language, spoken or written, resulting in difficulty with listening, thinking, speaking, writing, spelling, or doing mathematical calculations. This term does not include children with learning problems related to other disabilities such as mental retardation.

**Learning Style:** The unique way that an individual learns best, for example, by playing games, imitating, reading a book, listening to a lecture, or handling materials. Most children learn through a combination of processes.

**Least Restrictive Environment (LRE):** Placement of a student with disabilities in a setting that allows maximum contact with students who do not have disabilities, while appropriately meeting the student's special education needs.

**Legally Blind:** An individual is considered to be legally blind if his vision, even with corrective lenses, is 20/200 or less, which means being able to see at 20 feet what a person with normal vision sees at 200 feet.

**Mainstreaming:** The concept that students with disabilities should be educated with nondisabled students to the maximum extent possible.

**Major Life Activity:** Such activities as caring for one's self, performing manual tasks, walking, seeing, hearing, speaking, learning and working.

**Mediation:** A formal intervention between parents and personnel of early intervention or school systems to achieve reconciliation, settlement, or compromise.

**Medicaid:** A federal/state program that provides medical services primarily to individuals with low incomes.

**Mental Retardation:** A broad term describing delayed intellectual development resulting in delays in other areas such as academic learning, communication, social skills, rate of maturation, and physical coordination.

**Minimum Competency:** In order to receive a regular high school diploma, many states require students to pass a minimum competency test, demonstrating their academic skills to be at a state-defined level of achievement.

**Multidisciplinary Evaluation:** The testing of a child by a group of professionals, including psychologists, teachers, social workers, speech therapists, nurses, etc.

**Multiple Disabilities:** An educational label given to students having a combination of impairments such as mental retardation and blindness or orthopedic impairments and deafness which cause such educational problems that they cannot be accommodated in programs for any one impairment. This term does not include deaf-blind children.

**Natural Homes:** Places that are generally thought of as dwellings for people, such as apartments, houses, townhouses, trailers, etc.

**Non-Categorical:** Term relating to programs based on instructional needs rather than on categories of disabilities. Many states have only non-categorical programs; e.g., Maryland, Massachusetts, Minnesota, and others.

**Nondiscriminatory Evaluation:** An evaluation in which the materials and procedures used are not racially or culturally biased. In addition, an individual's disability must be accommodated such as by allowing more time, using a computer, etc.

**Objective:** An objective is a short-term step taken to reach an annual goal. IEP objectives are the steps between a student's present level of performance and an annual goal.

**Occupational Therapy (OT):** Activities focusing on fine motor skills and perceptual abilities that assist in improving physical, social, psychological, and/or intellectual development; e.g., rolling a ball, finger painting, sorting objects.

**On-the-Job-Training (OJT):** Short-term training that enables a person to work on a job site while learning the job duties.

**Orthopedic Impairment:** A physical disability severe enough to affect a child's educational performance. Orthopedic impairments can be congenital, or caused by disease or injury.

**Other Health Impairment (OHI):** Term used in IDEA to describe conditions that adversely affect a child's educational performance and are not covered by other disability definitions (e.g., Learning Disabilities, Mental Retardation, etc.). This term is frequently used for various medical conditions such as a heart condition, diabetes, cystic fibrosis, leukemia, etc.

**P.L. 101-476, P.L. 94-142, and P.L. 99-457:** *See* **Individuals with Disabilities Education Act.**

**Part B or Part H:** *See* **Individuals with Disabilities Education Act.**

**Physical Therapy (PT):** Activities or routines designed to increase gross motor skills.

**Placement:** The setting in which a child with disabilities is educated. Placement includes the school, the classroom, related services, community-based services, and the amount of time a student will spend with peers and others who do not have disabilities.

**Postsecondary Education:** Education programs for students who have completed high school, such as community and junior colleges, four-year colleges, and universities.

**Psychiatrist:** A medical doctor with advanced training who specializes in the diagnosis and treatment of emotional, behavioral, and mental disorders.

**Psychological Evaluation:** The portion of a child's overall evaluation/assessment for special education that tests his or her general aptitudes and abilities, eye-hand coordination, social skills, emotional development, and thinking skills.

**Psychologist:** A professional, not a medical doctor, with advanced training in the study of mental processes and human behavior. A school psychologist conducts various evaluations, especially aptitude and ability tests, and may work with students, classroom teachers, parents, and school administrators on behavior assessments and behavior management programs.

**Reasonable Accommodation:** The modification of programs in ways that permit students with disabilities to participate in educational programs that receive federal funding. The concept also applies to the modification of job requirements and equipment for workers with disabilities.

**Receptive Language:** The process of receiving and understanding written, gestured, or spoken language.

**Reevaluation:** *See* **Triennial Evaluation**.

**Referral:** A formal notification to the early intervention system or local school that a child is experiencing difficulties which may require a full evaluation for early intervention or special education. A referral may be made by a family, teacher, or other professional.

**Rehabilitation Act Amendments of 1992:** Federal legislation that requires state vocational rehabilitation agencies to work cooperatively with local agencies, including schools, to create a unified system to serve people with disabilities.

**Rehabilitation Act of 1973 (Section 504):** A nondiscrimination statute. Section 504 of the Act stipulates that individuals with disabilities may not be excluded from participating in programs and services receiving federal funds. It also prohibits job discrimination against people with disabilities in any program receiving federal financial assistance.

**Related Services:** Those services a student must receive to benefit from special education; for example, transportation, counseling, speech therapy, crisis intervention, etc.

**Residential Services:** The placement of a student in a setting that provides educational instruction and 24-hour care.

**Resource Room:** A setting in a school where a student receives instruction for a part of the school day from a special education teacher.

**School-Based Screening Committee:** *See* **Screening Committee**.

**Screening:** A brief examination of a child designed to pick up potential difficulties and to identify children who need further evaluation and diagnosis.

**Screening Committee:** A local school-based committee, whose members determine if a student should be fully evaluated for special education eligibility.

**Section 504:** *See* **Rehabilitation Act of 1973**.

**Self-Advocacy:** The abilities required to take primary responsibility for one's life and to make choices regarding one's actions free from undue interference. Also called **self-determination**.

**Self-Contained Classroom:** A classroom in which a group of students with disabilities receive their entire instructional program with little or no interaction with nondisabled students.

**Self-Determination:** *See* **Self-Advocacy**.

**Service Coordinator:** Someone who acts as a coordinator of a child's and family's services and works in partnership with the family and other service providers.

**Sheltered Workshop:** A work setting in which employees with disabilities do contract work, usually on a piece-rate basis, such as preparing bulk mailings or refinishing furniture.

**Social Worker:** A professional who may provide services to the family including: arranging or attending parent-student conferences; providing family counseling, family education, information, and referral; writing a social-developmental history; and/or conducting a behavioral assessment. Social workers sometimes conduct parent education in the school and community.

**Sociocultural Report:** The portion of a child's overall evaluation/assessment for special education that describes a child's background and behavior at home and at school. It is usually completed by a social worker.

**Special Education:** Specially designed instruction to meet the unique needs of a child with a disability, as defined in the Individuals with Disabilities Education Act.

**Special Education File:** *See* **Confidential File**.

**Special Needs:** A term to describe a child who has disabilities, chronic illness, or is at risk for developing disabilities and who needs educational services or other special treatment in order to progress.

**Specialized Nursing Homes:** Licensed facilities operating under strict regulations and providing intensive support for people with disabilities in the areas of personal care, communication, behavior management, etc.

**Specific Learning Disability (SLD):** *See* **Learning Disability**.

**Speech Impaired:** A communication disorder involving poor or abnormal production of the sounds of language.

**Speech-Language Pathologist:** A professional who evaluates and develops programs for individuals with speech or language problems.

**Speech Therapy:** Activities or routines designed to improve and increase communication skills.

**Standardized Tests:** In a vocational assessment, standardized tests are used to predict how a student is likely to perform in jobs calling for certain interests and skills.

**Substantially Limits** (a major life activity): Refers to a disability that restricts the conditions, manner, or duration under which activities can be performed in comparison to most people, as defined by the Americans with Disabilities Act.

**Supervised Living Arrangements:** Homes or apartments for persons with disabilities that are managed by public or private agencies. Paid staff supervise the residents and assist them with budgeting, food preparation, transportation, etc.

**Supplemental Security Income (SSI):** A federal program administered through the Social Security Administration that provides payments to individuals who are elderly and/or have disabilities. Children may be eligible for SSI if they have disabilities and are from families with low income. In addition, children who are hospitalized for 30 days or more and have a disability expected to last 12 months or more may receive SSI.

**Supported Employment:** Paid employment for workers with disabilities in settings with people who are nondisabled. A job coach provides support by helping the employee to improve job skills, interpersonal relations, or any other job-related needs.

**Trade and Technical Schools:** Schools which prepare students for employment in recognized occupations such as secretary, air conditioning technician, beautician, electrician, welder, carpenter, etc.

**Transition:** The process of moving from one situation to another. Frequently used to mean moving from preschool programs into elementary school or from school to work and the community.

**Transition Coordinator:** School personnel chosen to manage transition services for students with disabilities.

**Transition Planning:** Careful preparation by the student, parents, educators, and other service providers, for the time when the student leaves high school. The plan is written in the Individualized Transition Plan.

**Transition Planning Team:** The people who are involved in transition planning for a student, including the student, parents, school personnel (teachers, guidance counselor, vocational coordinator, school administrator), and adult service agency representatives (vocational rehabilitation counselor, independence living center staff).

**Transition Services:** A coordinated set of activities for a student that promotes movement from school to post-school activities, including postsecondary education, vocational training, integrated employment, continuing and adult education, adult services, independent living, or community participation.

**Transitional Employment:** A relatively short-term program designed to help an individual obtain a job, or to develop the work habits and learn the skills needed for a particular job.

**Traumatic Brain Injury:** An acquired injury to the brain caused by an external physical force causing a disability which affects a child's educational performance; e.g., cognition, memory, language, motor abilities.

**Triennial Review:** Every three years, a student in special education must be given a completely new evaluation/assessment to determine the student's progress and to make a new determination of eligibility for continued special education services.

**Visual-Motor Integration:** The extent to which an individual can coordinate vision with body movement or parts of the body; e.g., being able to copy words from the blackboard.

**Visually Impaired:** Having a mild to severe vision disorder, which adversely affects a child's educational performance.

**Vocational Assessment (Evaluation):** A systematic process of evaluating an individual's skills, aptitudes, and interests as they relate to job preparation and choice. Assessments include work sampling, standardized tests, and behavioral observation.

**Vocational Education:** Formal training designed to prepare individuals to work in a certain job or occupational area, such as construction, cosmetology, food service, or electronics. Also called vocational training and vocational program.

**Vocational Rehabilitation:** A comprehensive system that assists individuals with temporary or permanent disabilities in the areas of assessment, counseling, training, physical rehabilitation, and job placement.

**Work Activity Centers:** Programs for adults with disabilities providing training in vocational skills, as well as daily living skills, social skills, and recreational skills.

**Work Adjustment Skills:** *See* **Employability Skills**.

**Work Sampling Test:** The portion of a vocational assessment which tests a student's hands-on performance in certain simulated and actual work environments.

**Work-Study Programs:** Education programs in which the student receives employment training and earns credit toward graduation through employment.

# APPENDIX A
# PARENT PROGRAMS

## PARENT TRAINING AND INFORMATION PROGRAMS (PTIs)

PTIs are funded by the Division of Personnel Preparation, Office of Special Education Programs in the U.S. Department of Education. The Department's goal is to have the services of a PTI available to parents in every state. PTIs help parents to understand their children's specific needs, communicate more effectively with professionals, participate in the educational planning process, and obtain information about relevant programs, services, and resources. To find out about the parent information and training center in your state, contact the following:

*The Technical Assistance to*
  *Parent Projects (TAPP)*
Federation for Children
  with Special Needs
95 Berkeley Street, Suite 104
Boston, MA  02116
(617) 482-2915

*West Regional Center*
Washington PAVE
6316 S. 12th St.
Tacoma, WA 98645
(206) 565-2266

*South Regional Center*
Parents Educating Parents
ARC/Georgia
1851 Ram Runway, Ste. 104
College Park, GA 30337
(404) 761-3150

*Mid West Regional Center*
PACER Center
4826 Chicago Ave. South
Minneapolis, MN 55417
(612) 827-2966

*Northeast Regional Center*
Parent Information Center
P.O. Box 2405
Concord, NH 03302-2405
(603) 224-7005

*Technical Assistance Alliance*
  *for Parent Centers*
PACER Center
4826 Chicago Avenue South
Minneapolis, MN  55417
(612) 827-2966

*West Regional Center*
Matrix Parent Network and
  Resource Center
555 Northgate Drive, Suite A
San Rafael, CA  94903
(415) 499-3877

*South Regional Center*
Partners Resource Network, Inc.
1090 Longfellow Drive, Suite B
Beaumont, TX  77706-4819
(409) 898-4684

*Mid West Regional Center*
OCECD
165 West Center Street, Suite 302
Marion, OH  43302-3741
(614) 382-5452

## Parent to Parent Programs

Parent to Parent programs offer support to parents—from other parents of children with special needs or disabilities. Programs typically include veteran parents who are specially trained to provide support to newly referred parents. Many programs also include support groups and activities for family members. The Beach Center in Lawrence, Kansas, has been conducting research on parent to parent programs and has the most extensive list of parent to parent programs. If you are unable to locate a program through local resources in your area, contact:

> The Beach Center on Families and Disabilities
> University of Kansas
> 3111 Haworth Hall
> Lawrence, KS 66045
> (913) 864-7600

## National Information Center for Children and Youth with Disabilities (NICHCY)

NICHCY is a clearinghouse of information on children and young people with special needs. It has a variety of information for parents, including information about specific disabilities, "state sheets" listing points of contact for organizations and agencies in each state, and briefing papers summarizing key topics regarding the education of children with disabilities.

> NICHCY
> P.O. Box 1492
> Washington, D.C. 20013-1492
> (800) 695-0285

# APPENDIX B
# STATE OFFICES

For each state, contact information for the following offices is listed:
1. Referral and information about Early Intervention Services
2. Director of Special Education
3. Protection and Advocacy (P&A)
4. Client Assistance Program (CAP) for Vocational Rehabilitation

## ALABAMA
Early Intervention–800/543-3098

Director of Special Education
Alabama Department of Education
Division of Special Education Services
P.O. Box 302101
Montgomery, AL 36130-2101
334/242-8114

Program Director
Alabama Disabilities Advocacy Program
P.O. Drawer 870395
Tuscaloosa, AL 35487-0395
205/348-4928
800/826-1675

Director
Rehabilitation and Crippled Children Service
2129 E. South Blvd.
P.O. Box 11586
Montgomery, AL 36116
205/281-8780

## ALASKA
Early Intervention–800/478-2221

Director of Special Education
Office of Special Services
Alaska Department of Education
Office of Special and Supplemental Services
801 West 10th St., Suite 200
Juneau, AK 99801-1894
907/465-2971

Director
Disability Law Center of Alaska
615 E. 82nd Avenue, Suite 101
Anchorage, AK 99518
907/344-1002
800/478-1234

Director
ASIST
2900 Boniface Parkway, #100
Anchorage, AK 99504-3195
907/333-2211

## AMERICAN SAMOA
Early Intervention–800/633-4929

Director of Special Education
Special Education
Department of Education
Pago Pago, American Samoa 96799
684/633-1323

P&A and CAP
Client Assistance Program
P.O. Box 3937
Pago Pago, American Samoa 96799
684/633-2441

## ARIZONA
Early Intervention–800/232-1676

Director of Special Education
Special Education Section
Department of Education

1535 W. Jefferson
Phoenix, AZ 85007-3280
602/542-3084

P&A and CAP
Arizona Center for Law in the Public Interest
3724 N. 3rd Street, Suite 300
Phoenix, AZ 85012
602/274-6287

## ARKANSAS
Early Intervention–800/752-2160

Director of Special Education
Special Education Section
Arkansas Department of Education
Education Bldg., Room 105-C
#4 State Capitol Mall
Little Rock, AR 72201-1071
501/682-4221

P&A and CAP
Executive Director
Advocacy Services, Inc.
1100 N. University
Suite 201, Evergreen Place
Little Rock, AR 72207
501/324-9215
800/482-1174

## CALIFORNIA
Early Intervention–800/515-2229

Director of Special Education
California Department of Education
515 L Street, Suite 270
Sacramento, CA 95814
916/445-4602

Executive Director
Protection & Advocacy, Inc.
100 Howe Avenue, Suite 185N
Sacramento, CA 95825
916/488-9950
800/952-5746

Client Assistance Program
830 K St. Mall
Sacramento, CA 95814
916/322-5066

## COLORADO
Early Intervention–800/288-3444

Director of Special Education
Special Education Services Unit
Colorado Department of Education
201 E. Colfax
Denver, CO 80203
303/866-6695

P&A and CAP
Executive Director
The Legal Center
455 Sherman Street, Suite 130
Denver, CO 80203
303/722-0300

## CONNECTICUT
Early Intervention–800/505-7000

Bureau Chief
Bureau of Special Education and
Pupil Personnel Services
Connecticut Department of Education
25 Industrial Park Rd.
Middletown, CT 06457
860/638-4265

Executive Director
Office of Protection & Advocacy for Persons
with Disabilities
60 Weston Street
Hartford, CT 06120-1551
203/297-4300
800/842-7303

## DELAWARE
Early Intervention–302/577-4643

Director of Special Education
Exceptional Children/Special Programs Division
Department of Public Instruction
P.O. Box 1402
Dover, DE 19903-1402
302/739-5471

Administrator
Disabilities Law Program
144 E. Market St.
Georgetown, DE 19947
302/856-0038

Director
Client Assistance Program
United Cerebral Palsy, Inc.
254 Camden-Wyoming Ave.
Camden, DE 19934
302/698-9336

Department of Defense/Dependents Services
Department of Defense
Office of Dependents' Education
4040 Fairfax Drive
Arlington, VA 22203
703/696-4493

## DISTRICT OF COLUMBIA
Early Intervention–202/727-8300

Director of Special Education
Goding School
10th and F St. NE
Washington, DC 20002
202/724-4800

Executive Director
Information, Protection, and Advocacy
Center for Handicapped Individuals, Inc.
4455 Connecticut Ave., NW, Suite B-100
Washington DC 20008
202/966-8081

Administrator
Client Assistance Program
D.C. Rehabilitation Services Administration
Commission on Social Services
Department of Human Services
605 G St., NW, Room 1101
Washington, DC 20001
202/727-0977

## FLORIDA
Early Intervention–800/654-4440

Director of Special Education
Bureau of Student Services/Exceptional
    Education
Florida Education Center
325 Gaines Street, Suite 614
Tallahassee, FL 32399-0400
904/488-1570

P&A and CAP
Executive Director
Advocacy Center for Persons with
    Disabilities, Inc.

2671 Executive Center, Circle West
Webster Bldg., Suite 100
Tallahassee, FL 32301-5024
904/488-9070
800/342-0823

## GEORGIA
Early Intervention–800/229-2038

Director of Special Education
Division for Exceptional Children
Georgia Department of Education
1952 Twin Towers East
205 Butler Street
Atlanta, GA 30334-5040
404/656-3963

Executive Director
Georgia Advocacy Office, Inc.
999 Peachtree Street NW, Suite 870
Atlanta, GA 30309
404/885-1234
800/282-4538

Director
Division of Rehabilitation Services
2 Peachtree St., NW, 23rd floor
Atlanta, GA 30303
404/657-3009

## GUAM
Early Intervention–671/475-0549

Director of Special Education
Department of Education
P.O. Box DE
Agana, Guam 96910
671/647-4400

Administrator
The Advocacy Office
Micronesia Mall, Office A
West Marine Drive
Dededo, Guam 96912
671/632-7233

Director
Client Assistance Program
Parent Agencies Network
P.O. Box 23474
GMF, Guam 96921
671/649-1948

# HAWAII

Early Intervention–800/235-5477
   808/955-7273 (Oahu only);

Director of Special Education
Special Needs Branch
Hawaii Department of Education
Special Education Section
3430 Leahi Avenue
Honolulu, HI 96815
808/733-4990

P&A and CAP
Executive Director
Protection & Advocacy Agency of Hawaii
1580 Makaloa St., Suite 1060
Honolulu, HI 96814
808/949-2922

# IDAHO

Early Intervention–800/962-2588

Supervisor
Special Education Section
Idaho Department of Education
P.O. Box 83720
Boise, ID 83720-0027
208/334-3940

P&A and CAP
Idaho's Coalition of Advocates for
   the Disabled, Inc.
447 Emerald, Suite B100
Boise, ID 83706
208/336-5353

# ILLINOIS

Early Intervention–800/323-4679

Director of Special Education
Center on Policy, Planning, Resource
Illinois State Board of Education
Mail Code E-216
100 North First Street
Springfield, IL 62777-0001
217/782-6601

Director
Equip for Quality, Inc.
11 E. Adams, Suite 1200
Chicago, IL 60603
312/341-0022

Director
Illinois Client Assistance Program
100 N. First Street, 1st floor W
Springfield, IL 62702
217/782-5374

# INDIANA

Early Intervention–800/964-4746

Director of Special Education
Division of Special Education
Indiana Department of Education
229 State House
Indianapolis, IN 46204-2798
317/232-0570

P&A and CAP
Indiana Advocacy Services
850 North Meridian, Suite 2-C
Indianapolis, IN 46204
317/232-1150
800/622-4845

# IOWA

Early Intervention–800/779-2001

Chief
Bureau of Special Education
Iowa Department of Public Instruction
Grimes State Office Building
Des Moines, IA 50319-0146
515/281-3176

Director
Iowa Protection & Advocacy Services, Inc.
3015 Merle Hay Rd., Suite 6
Des Moines, IA 50310
515/278-2502
800/779-2502

Administrator
Client Assistance Program
Lucas State Office Bldg.
Des Moines, IA 50319
515/281-3957

# KANSAS

Early Intervention–800/332-6262

Director of Special Education
Student Support Services
Kansas Department of Education

120 S.E. Tenth Street
Topeka, KS 66612-1182
913/296-0946

Executive Director
Kansas Advocacy & Protection Services
2601 Anderson Avenue, Suite 200
Manhattan, KS 66502
913/776-1541
800/432-8276

Client Assistance Program
Biddle Bldg., 2nd Floor
2700 West 6th Street
Topeka, KS 66606
913/296-1491

## KENTUCKY
Early Intervention–800/442-0087

Director of Special Education
Kentucky Department of Education
Division of Exceptional Children's Services
500 Mero Street
Room 805
Frankfort, KY 40601
502/564-4970

Director
Office for Public Advocacy
Division for Protection and Advocacy
100 Fair Oaks Lane, 3rd Floor
Frankfort, KY 40601
502/564-2967
800/372-2988

Administrator
Client Assistance Program
Capitol Plaza Tower
Frankfort, KY 40601
502/564-8035

## LOUISIANA
Early Intervention–800/922-3425

Director of Special Education
Louisiana Department of Education
Special Education Services
P.O. Box 94064, 9th Floor
Baton Rouge, LA 70804-9064
504/342-3633

P&A and CAP
Executive Director
Advocate Center for the Elderly & Disabled
210 O'Keefe, Suite 700
New Orleans, LA 70112
504/522-2337
800-662-7705

## MAINE
Early Intervention–207/278-3272

Director of Special Education
Division of Special Services
Maine Department of Educational and Cultural Services
23 State House Station
Augusta, ME 04333
207/287-5950

Director
Maine Advocacy Services
32 Winthrop Street
P.O. Box 2007
Augusta, ME 04338-2007
207/626-2774
800/452-1948

CARES, Inc.
4-C Winter Street
Augusta, ME 04330
207/622-7055

## MARYLAND
Early Intervention–800/535-0182

Director of Special Education
Division of Special Education
Maryland State Department of Education
200 W. Baltimore Street
Baltimore, MD 21201-2595
410/767-0238

Director
Maryland Disability Law Center
2510 St. Paul St.
Baltimore, MD 21218
410/235-4700
800/233-7201

Client Assistance Program
Division of Vocational Rehabilitation
2301 Argonne Drive
Baltimore, MD 21218-1696
410/554-3224

## MASSACHUSETTS
Early Intervention–800/462-5015

Administrator
Program Quality Assurance
Massachusetts Department of Education
350 Main Street
Malden, MA  02148-5023
617/388-3300

Executive Director
Disability Law Center of Massachusetts
11 Beacon Street, Suite 925
Boston, MA 02108
617/723-8455

MA Office of Disability
Client Assistance Program
One Ashburton Place, Room 1305
Boston, MA 02108
617/7440

## MICHIGAN
Early Intervention–800/327-5966

Director of Special Education
Special Education Services
Michigan Department of Education
P.O. Box 30008
Lansing, MI 48909-7508
517/373-9433

Executive Director
Michigan Protection & Advocacy
      Service, Inc.
106 W. Allegan, Suite 210
Lansing, MI 48933
517/487-1755

State Director
Client Assistance Program
P.O. Box 30018
Lansing, MI 48909
517/373-8193

## MINNESOTA
Early Intervention–800/728-5420

Director of Special Education
Department of Children, Families,
      and Learning
811 Capitol Square Bldg.
550 Cedar Street

St. Paul, MN 55101-2233
612/296-1793

Protection and Advocacy and CAP
Minnesota Disability Law Center
430 First Avenue N, Suite 300
Minneapolis, MN 55401-1780
612/334-5785

## MISSISSIPPI
Early Intervention–800/451-3903

Director of Special Education
Office of Education
State Department of Education
P.O. Box 771
Jackson, MS 39205-0771
601/359-3498

Executive Director
Mississippi Protection & Advocacy
      System for DD, Inc.
5330 Executive Place, Suite A
Jackson, MS 39206
601/981-8207

Client Assistance Program
Easter Seal Society
3226 N. State Street
Jackson, MS 39216
601/362-2585
601/982-7051

## MISSOURI
Early Intervention–800/873-6623

Director of Special Education
Special Education Programs
Department of Elementary and Secondary
Education
P.O. Box 480
Jefferson City, MO 65102-0480
314/751-2965

Protection and Advocacy and CAP
Missouri Protection & Advocacy Services
925 S. Country Club Drive, Unit B-1
Jefferson City, MO 65109
314/893-3333

## MONTANA
Early Intervention–800/222-7585

Director
Office of Public Instruction
Division of Special Education
P.O. Box 202501
State Capitol
Helena, MT 59620-2501
406/444-4429

Protection and Advocacy and CAP
Executive Director
Montana Advocacy Program
316 N. Park, Room 211
P.O. Box 1680
Helena, MT 59623
406/444-3889
800/245-4743

## NATIVE AMERICAN INDIAN AFFAIRS
Early Intervention–202/208-6675

Branch of Exceptional Education/BIA
Mail Stop #3530
1951 Constitution Ave., NW
Washington, DC 20245
202/208-6675

Protection and Advocacy
DNA People's Legal Service, Inc.
P.O. Box 306
Window Rock, AZ 86515
602/871-4151

## NEBRASKA
Early Intervention–800/742-7594

Director of Special Education
Office of Special Education
Nebraska Department of Education
301 Centennial Mall S.
Box 94987
Lincoln, NE 68509-4987
402/471-2471

Executive Director
Nebraska Advocacy Services, Inc.
522 Lincoln Center Bldg.
215 Centennial Mall South
Lincoln, NE 68508
402/474-3183

Client Assistance Program
Division of Rehabilitative Services
State Department of Education
301 Centennial Mall South, 6th Floor
Lincoln, NE 68509
402/471-3656

## NEVADA
Early Intervention–800/522-0066

Director of Special Education
Special Education Branch
Nevada Department of Education
400 W. King Street
Capitol Complex
Carson City, NV 89710-0004
702/687-3140

Director
Office of Protection & Advocacy, Inc.
Financial Plaza
1135 Terminal Way, Suite 105
Reno, NV 89502
702/688-1233
800/922-5715

Client Assistance Program
1755 East Plumb Lane, #128
Reno, NV 89502
702/688-1440
800/633-9879

## NEW HAMPSHIRE
Early Intervention–800/298-4321

Director of Special Education
Special Education Bureau
New Hampshire Department of Education
101 Pleasant Street
Concord, NH 03301-3860
603/271-6693

Executive Director
Disabilities Rights Center, Inc.
P.O. Box 3660
18 Low Avenue
Concord, NH 03302-3660
603/228-0432

Director Client Assistance Program
Governors Commission for the Handicapped
57 Regional Drive
Concord, NH 03301-0686
603/271-2773

## NEW JERSEY
Early Intervention–800/792-8858

Director of Special Education
Office of Special Education
New Jersey Department of Education
P.O. Box CN 500
225 W. State St.
Trenton, NJ 08625-0050
609/633-6833

Protection and Advocacy and CAP
NJ Department of Protection and Advocate
210 S. Broad, 3rd Floor
Trenton, NJ 08608
609/292-9742
800/792-8600

## NEW MEXICO
Early Intervention–800/552-8195

Director of Special Education
State Department of Education
300 Don Gasper Ave.
Santa Fe, NM 87501-2786
505/827-6541

Protection and Advocacy and CAP
Protection & Advocacy System
1720 Louisiana Blvd. NE, Suite 204
Albuquerque, NM 87110
505/256-3100
800/432-4682

## NEW YORK
Early Intervention–800/522-4369

Assistant Commissioner
Office for Special Education
New York State Education Department
1 Commerce Plaza, Room 1624
Albany, NY 12234-0001
518/474-5548

Protection and Advocacy and CAP
Commissioner
New York Commission on Quality of
Care for the Mentally Disabled
99 Washington Ave., Suite 1002
Albany, NY 12210
518/473-7378

## NORTH CAROLINA
Early Intervention–800/852-0042

Director of Special Education
Division of Exceptional Children's Services
North Carolina Department of Public
Instruction
301 N. Wilmington Street
Raleigh, NC 27601-2825
919/715-1565

Director
Governor's Advocacy Council for
Persons with Disabilities
2113 Cameron Street, Suite 218
Raleigh, NC 27605-1344
919/733-9250
800/821-6922

Director
Client Assistance Program
Division of Vocational Rehabilitation
Services
P.O. Box 26053
Raleigh, NC 27611
919/733-3364

## NORTH DAKOTA
Early Intervention–800/472-8529

Director of Special Education
Special Education
Department of Public Instruction
600 E Blvd.
Bismarck, ND 58505-0440
701/328-2277

Director
Protection & Advocacy
400 E. Broadway, Suite 616
Bismarck, ND 58501-4038
701/328-2972
800/472-2670

Associate Director
Client Assistance Program
400 E. Broadway, Suite 303
Bismarck, ND 58501-4038
701/328-3970

# NORTHERN MARIANA ISLANDS

Director
Special Education Programs
CNMI Public School System
P.O. Box 1370
Saipan, MP 96950
670/322-9956

Protection and Advocacy and CAP
Karidat
P.O. Box 745
Saipan, MP 96950
670/234-6981

# OHIO

Early Intervention–800/374-2806

Director of Special Education
Ohio Department of Education
Division of Special Education
933 High Street
Worthington, OH 43085-4087
614/466-4859

Executive Director
Ohio Legal Rights Service
8 E. Long St., 6th Floor
Columbus, OH 43215
614/466-7264
800/282-9181

Client Assistance Program
Governor's Office of Advocacy for People
with Disabilities
30 E. Broad Street, Suite 1201
Columbus, OH 43215
614/466-9956

# OKLAHOMA

Early Intervention–800/426-2747

Executive Director
Special Education Section
State Department of Education
2500 N. Lincoln Blvd., Suite 411
Oklahoma City, OK 73105-4599
405/521-4859

Director
Oklahoma Disability Law Center, Inc.
4150 S. 100 East Avenue
210 Cherokee Bldg.,
Tulsa, OK 74146-3661
918/664-5883

Client Assistance Program
Oklahoma Office of Hndcp. Concerns
4300 N. Lincoln Blvd., Suite 200
Oklahoma City, OK 73105
405/521-3756

# OREGON

Early Intervention–800/322-2588

Director of Special Education
Special Education and Student Services
        Division
Oregon Department of Education
700 Pringle Pkwy. SE
Salem, OR 97310-0290
503/378-3598

Executive Director
Oregon Advocacy Center
620 S.W. 5th Avenue, 5th Floor
Portland, OR 97204
503/243-2081

Oregon Advocacy Center
1257 Ferry Street S.E.
Salem, OR 97310
503/378-3142

# PALAU

Early Intervention–670/664-3754

Special Education Coordinator
P.O. Box 278
Koror Palau, 96940
680/488-2568

# PENNSYLVANIA

Early Intervention–800/692-7288

Director of Special Education
Bureau of Special Education
Pennsylvania Department of Education
333 Market Street
Harrisburg, PA 17126-0333
717/783-6913

Pennsylvania Protection & Advocacy, Inc.
116 Pine St.
Harrisburg, PA 17101
717/236-8110
800/692-7443

Client Assistance Program (SEPLS)
1617 JFK Blvd., Suite 800
Philadelphia, PA 19103
215/557-7112

Client Assistance Program (Western PA)
211 N. Whitfield Street, Suite 215
Pittsburgh, PA 15206
412/363-7223

## PUERTO RICO
Early Intervention–800/981-8492

Assistant Secretary of Special Education
Department of Education
P.O. Box 190759
San Juan, PR 00919-0759
809/759-2000

Director
Planning Research and Special Projects
Ombudsman for the Disabled
Governor's Office
P.O. Box 5163
Hato Rey, PR 00936
809/766-2338

Assistant Secretary for Vocational Rehabilitation
Department of Social Services
P.O. Box 118
Hato Rey, PR 00919
809/725-1792

## RHODE ISLAND
Early Intervention–800/464-3399

Director of Special Education
Roger Williams Bldg., Room 209
22 Hayes Street
Providence, RI 02908-5025
401/277-3505

Protection and Advocacy and CAP
Executive Director
Rhode Island Protection & Advocacy System
151 Broadway, 3rd Floor
Providence, RI 02903
401/831-3150

## SOUTH CAROLINA
Early Intervention–800/922-1107

Director
Office of Programs for Exceptional Children
State Department of Education
Room 808
Rutledge Bldg. 1429 Senate
Columbia, SC 29201
803/739-8806

Executive Director
South Carolina Protection & Advocacy System for the Handicapped, Inc.
3710 Landmark Drive, Suite 208
Columbia, SC 29204
803/782-0639
800/922-5225

Office of the Governor
Division of Ombudsman and Citizen Services
P.O. Box 11369
Columbia, SC 29211
803/734-0457

## SOUTH DAKOTA
Early Intervention–800/529-5000

Director
Office of Special Education
Department of Education and Cultural Affairs
700 Governors Drive
Pierre, SD 57501-2291
605/773-3678

Protection and Advocacy and CAP
Executive Director
South Dakota Advocacy Services
221 S. Central Ave.
Pierre, SD 57501
605/224-8294
800/742-8108

## TENNESSEE
Early Intervention–800/852-7157

Assistant Commissioner
Division of Special Education
Tennessee Department of Education
Gateway Plaza, 8th Floor
710 James Robertson Pkwy.

Nashville, TN 37243-0380
615/741-2851

Protection and Advocacy and CAP
Director
Tennessee Protection and Advocacy, Inc.
P.O. Box 121257
Nashville, TN 37212
615/298-1080
800/342-1660

## TEXAS

Early Intervention—512/502-4920

Director of Special Education
Special Education Unit
Texas Education Agency
WB Travis Bldg. Room 5-120
1701 N. Congress Ave.
Austin, TX 78701-2486
512/463-9414

Protection and Advocacy and CAP
Executive Director
Advocacy, Inc.
7800 Shoal Creek Blvd., Suite 171-E
Austin, TX 78757
512/454-4816
800/252-9108

## UTAH

Early Intervention—800/333-8824

Director
Special Education Services Unit
Utah State Office of Education
250 E. 500 South
Salt Lake City, UT 84111-3204
801/538-7587

Protection and Advocacy and CAP
Executive Director
Legal Center for People with Disabilities
455 East 400 South, Suite 201
Salt Lake City, UT 84111
801/363-1347
800/662-9080

## VERMONT

Early Intervention—800/727-3687

Director
Division of Special Education
Vermont Department of Education
State Office Bldg.
120 State Street
Montpelier, VT 05602-3403
802/828-3141

Director
Vermont DD Law Project
264 Winoosk Avenue
P.O. Box 1367
Burlington, VT 05401
802/863-2881

Client Assistance Program
Ladd Hall
103 South Main Street
Waterbury, VT 05676

## VIRGIN ISLANDS

Early Intervention—809/773-8804

Director of Special Education
Department of Education
State Office of Special Education
P.O. Box 6640
Charlotte Amalie, St. Thomas
Virgin Islands 00801
809/776-5802

Protection and Advocacy and CAP
Director
Virgin Islands Advocacy Agency
7A Whim Street, Suite 2
Frederiksted, VI 00840
809/772-1200

## VIRGINIA

Early Intervention—800/234-1448

Director of Special Education
Virginia Department of Education
P.O. Box 2120
Richmond, VA 23216-2120
804/225-2402

Protection and Advocacy and CAP
Director
Department of Rights of Virginians
    with Disabilities
James Monroe Bldg.
101 N. 14th St., 17th Floor
Richmond, VA 23219
804/225-2042
800/552-3962

## WASHINGTON
Early Intervention–800/322-2588

Director of Special Education
Special Education Section
Superintendent of Public Instruction
Old Capital Bldg.
Olympia, WA 98502-0001
206/753-6733

Washington Protection & Advocacy System
1401 E. Jefferson Street, Suite 506
Seattle, WA 98122
206/324-1521

Client Assistance Program
P.O. Box 22510
Seattle, WA 98122
206/721-4049

## WEST VIRGINIA
Early Intervention–800/734-2319

Director
Office of Special Education
West Virginia Department of Education
Bldg. #6, Room B-304
1800 Kanawha Blvd.
Charleston, WV 25305
304/558-2696

Executive Director
West Virginia Advocates, Inc.
Litton Building, 4th Floor
1207 Quarrier St.
Charleston, WV 25301
304/346-0847
800/950-5250

## WISCONSIN
Early Intervention–800/642-7837

Assistant Superintendent
Division of Learning Support: Equity
    and Advocacy
Department of Public Instruction
125 S. Webster
P.O. Box 7841
Madison, WI 53707-7841
608/266-1649

Executive Director
Wisconsin Coalition for Advocacy, Inc.
16 N. Carroll Street, Suite 400
Madison, WI 53703
608/267-0214

Governors Commission for People
    with Disabilities
1 W. Wilson Street, Room 558
P.O. Box 7852
608/267-7422
800/362-1290

## WYOMING
Early Intervention–800/438-5791

Federal Programs Unit
State Department of Education
Hathaway Bldg.
2300 Capitol Avenue
Cheyenne, WY 82002-0050
307/777-7417

Executive Director
Protection & Advocacy System, Inc.
2424 Pioneer Ave., No. 101
Cheyenne, WY 82001
307/638-7668
800/624-7648

# Appendix C
# National Organizations Serving Persons with Disabilities

The organizations listed in this appendix offer a range of information and services. Some organizations have regional or local chapters across the United States. Many regularly publish journals or newsletters of interest to parents, professionals, and individuals with disabilities. This list is not intended to be all-inclusive, but rather a place to begin reaching out and gathering information.

## Organizations Serving the General Population

Abledata (Assistive Technology)
8455 Colesville Road, Suite 935
Silver Spring, MD 20910
301/588-9284 (voice/TDD)
800/227-0216 (voice/TDD)

ARCH National Resource Center
    (Respite Care)
800 Eastowne Drive, Suite 105
Chapel Hill, NC 27514
800/773-5433 (voice)

Association for Persons with Severe
    Handicaps (TASH)
29 West Susquehanna Avenue, Suite 210
Baltimore, MD 21204
410/828-8274 (voice)
410/828-1306 (TDD)

Center for Law and Education
Larsen Hall, 6th Floor
14 Appian Way
Cambridge, MA 02138
617/876-6611

Children's Defense Fund
25 E Street, NW
Washington, DC 20001
202/628-8787 (voice)
800/233-1200 (voice)

Clearinghouse on Disability Information
Office of Special Education and
    Rehabilitation Services
U.S. Department of Education
330 C Street, SW
Switzer Building, Room 3132
Washington, DC 20202
202/205-8241 (voice/TDD)

Council for Exceptional Children (CEC)
1920 Association Drive
Reston, VA 22091
703/620-3660 (voice)

Disability Rights Education and Defense
    Fund (DREDF)
2212 Sixth Street
Berkeley, CA 94710
510/644-2555 (voice/TDD)
800/466-4232 (voice/TDD)

ERIC Clearinghouse on Disabilities and
    Gifted Education
Council for Exceptional Children
1920 Association Drive
Reston, VA 22091
703/264-9474 (voice)
800/328-0272 (voice)

Independent Living Research Utilization
    Project (ILRU)
Institute for Rehabilitation and Research
2323 South Shepherd, Suite 1000
Houston, TX 77019
713/520-0232

National Association of Protection and
    Advocacy Systems
900 Second Street, NE, Suite 211
Washington, DC 20002
202/408-9514 (voice)
202/408-9521 (TDD)

National Clearinghouse on
    Postsecondary Education for
    Individuals with Disabilities
HEATH Resource Center
One Dupont Circle, NW, Suite 800
Washington, DC 20036
202/939-9320 (voice/TDD)
800/544-3284 (voice/TDD)

National Easter Seal Society
230 West Monroe
Chicago, IL 60606
312/726-6200 (voice)
312/726-4258 (TDD)

National Information Center for Children
    and Youth with Disabilities (NICHCY)
P.O. Box 1492
Washington, DC 20013
202/884-8200 (voice/TDD)
800/695-0285

National Library Service for the Blind
    and Physically Handicapped
Library of Congress
1291 Taylor Street, NW
Washington, DC 20542
202/707-5100 (voice)
202/707-0744 (TDD)

National Maternal and Child
    Health Clearinghouse
8201 Greensboro Drive, Suite 600
McLean, VA 22102
703/821-8955, ext. 254 (voice)

National Rehabilitation Information
    Center (NARIC)
8455 Colesville Road, Suite 935
Silver Spring, MD 20910
301/588-9284
800/346-2746

National Self-Help Clearinghouse
CUNY Grad School, University Center
25 West 43rd Street, Room 620
New York, NY 10036
212/354-8525 (voice)

Pike Institute on Law and Disability
Boston University School of Law
765 Commonwealth Avenue
Boston, MA 02215
617/353-2904 (voice/TDD)

Sibling Information Network
The A.J. Pappanikou Center
University of Connecticut
249 Glenbrook Rd., U-64
Storrs, CT 06269-2064

Specialized Training of Military Parents
    (STOMP)
c/o Washington PAVE
12208 Pacific Highway, SW
Tacoma, WA 98499
206/588-1741
800/298-3543

Travel Information Service
Moss Rehab Hospital
1200 West Tabor Road
Philadelphia, PA 19141
215/456-9600 (voice)
215/456-9602 (TDD)

World Institute on Disability
510 Sixteenth Street, Suite 100
Oakland, CA 94612
510/763-4100 (voice/TDD)

# Organizations Serving a Specific Population

## Allergies

Asthma and Allergy Foundation of America
1125 Fifteenth Street, NW, Suite 502
Washington, DC 20005
202/466-7643
800/727-8462

National Institute of Allergy and
 Infectious Diseases
Office of Communication
Building 31, Room 7A50
9000 Rockville Pike
Bethesda, MD 20892
301/496-5717 (voice)

## Attention Deficit Disorder

Children and Adults with Attention
 Deficit Disorders (CHADD)
499 NW 70th Avenue, Suite 109
Plantation, FL 33317
305/587-3700
800/233-4050

## Autism

Autism Society of America
7910 Woodmont Avenue, Suite 650
Bethesda, MD 20814
301/657-0881
800/328-8476

## Birth Defects

Association of Birth Defect Children
827 Irma Avenue
Orlando, FL 32803
407/245-7035 (voice)
800/313-2232 (voice)

March of Dimes Birth Defects
 Foundation
1275 Mamaroneck Avenue
White Plains, NY 10605
914/428-7100 (voice)

## Blindness and Visual Impairments

American Council of the Blind
1155 Fifteenth Street, NW, Suite 720
Washington, DC 20005
202/467-5081
800/424-8666

American Foundation for the Blind
11 Penn Plaza
New York NY 10001
212/507-7600
800/232-5463

National Association for Visually
 Handicapped
22 West 21st Street, 6th Floor
New York, NY 10010
212/889-3141

Recording for the Blind and Dyslexic
20 Roszel Road
Princeton, NJ 08540
609/452-0606

## Cerebral Palsy

United Cerebral Palsy Associations
 (UCP)
1660 L Street, NW, Suite 700
Washington, DC 20036
202/776-0406 (voice/TDD)
800/872-5827

## Chronic Illness

Association for the Care of Children's
 Health (ACCH)
7910 Woodmont Avenue, Suite 300
Bethesda, MD 20814
301/654-6549, ext. 306 (voice)

Candlelighters Childhood Cancer
 Foundation
7910 Woodmont Avenue, Suite 460
Bethesda, MD 20814
800/366-2223

Center for Children with Chronic Illness
 and Disability
University of Minnesota
Box 721 UMHC
420 Delaware Street, SE

Minneapolis, MN 55455
612/626-4032 (voice)
612/624-3939 (TDD)

Children's Hospice International
700 Princess Street, Lower Level
Alexandria, VA 22314
703/684-0330
800/242-4453

## Cleft Palate

Cleft Palate Foundation
1218 Grandview Ave.
Pittsburgh, PA 15211
800/242-5338

## Craniofacial Differences

AboutFace
P.O. Box 93
Limekiln, PA 19535
800/225-3223

FACES
The National Association for the
Craniofacially Handicapped
P.O. Box 11082
Chattanooga, TN 37401
800/332-2373

## Deaf and Hearing Impaired

Alexander Graham Bell Association for
the Deaf
3417 Volta Place, NW
Washington, DC 20007
202/337-5220 (voice/TDD)

American Society for Deaf Children
2848 Arden Way, Suite 210
Sacramento, CA 95825
800/942-2732 (voice/TDD)

National Information Center on Deafness
Gallaudet University
800 Florida Avenue, NE
Washington, DC 20002
202/651-5051 (voice)
202/651-5052 (TDD)

Registry of Interpreters for the Deaf
8630 Fenton Street, Suite 324

Silver Spring, MD 20910
301/608-0050 (voice/TDD)

## Deaf/Blind

American Association of the Deaf/Blind
814 Thayer Avenue, Suite 302
Silver Spring, MD 20910
301/588-6545 (TDD)

National Information Clearinghouse on
Children Who Are Deaf-Blind
345 N. Monmouth Avenue
Monmouth, OR 97361
800/438-9376 (voice)
800/854-7013 (TDD)

## Diabetes

American Diabetes Assocation
National Service Center
1660 Duke Street
Alexandria, VA 22314
703/549-1500
800/232-3472

Juvenile Diabetes Foundation
International
432 Park Avenue, S., 16th Floor
New York, NY 10016
212/889-7575
800/533-2873

National Diabetes Information
Clearinghouse
One Information Way
Bethesda, MD 20892
301/654-3327 (voice)

## Down Syndrome

National Down Syndrome Congress
1605 Chantilly Drive, Suite 250
Atlanta, GA 30324
404/633-1555
800/232-6372

National Down Syndrome Society
666 Broadway, 8th Floor
New York, NY 10012
212/460-9330
800/221-4602

## Emotional Disorders

Federation of Families for Children's
    Mental Health
1021 Prince Street
Alexandria, VA 22314
703/684-7710

National Institute of Mental Health
Information Resources and Inquiries
    Branch
5600 Fishers Lane, Room 7C-02
Rockville, MD 20857
301/443-4513 (voice)
301/443-8431 (TDD)

National Mental Health Association
1021 Prince Street
Alexandria, VA 22314
703/684-7722
800/969-6642

## Epilepsy

Epilepsy Foundation of America
4351 Garden City Drive
Landover, MD 20785
301/459-3700
800/332-1000 (voice)
800/332-2070 (TDD)

## Fragile X Syndrome

National Fragile X Foundation
1441 York Street, Suite 303
Denver, CO 80206
303/333-6155
800/688-8765

## Head Injury

National Head Injury Foundation
1776 Massachusetts Avenue, NW, Suite
100
Washington, DC 20036
202/296-6443
800/444-6443

## Learning Disabilities

Learning Disabilities Association of
    America
4156 Library Road
Pittsburgh, PA 15234
412/341-1515

National Center for Learning Disabilities
381 Park Avenue, South, Suite 1420
New York, NY 20016
212/545-7510

Orton Dyslexia Society
Chester Building, Suite 382
8600 LaSalle Road
Baltimore, MD 21286
410/296-0232
800/222-3123

## Mental Retardation

The Arc
National Headquarters
500 East Border Street, Suite 300
P.O. Box 1047
Arlington, TX 76010
817/261-6003
800/433-5255

## Muscular Dystrophy

Muscular Dystrophy Association
3300 East Sunrise Drive
Tucson, AZ 85718
602/529-2000
800/572-1717

## Rare Disorders

National Health Information Clearinghouse
    and National Information Center for
    Orphan Drugs and Rare Diseases
P.O. Box 1133
Washington, DC 20013
800/336-4797

National Organization for Rare Disorders
    (NORD)
100 Route 37
P.O. Box 8923
New Fairfield, CT 06812
203/746-6518
800/999-6673

## Respiratory Diseases

American Lung Association
1740 Broadway
New York, NY 10019
212/315-8700
800/586-4872

Cystic Fibrosis Foundation
6931 Arlington Road
Bethesda, MD 20814
301/951-4422
800/344-4823

## Speech and Language Disorders

American Speech-Language-Hearing
    Association
10801 Rockville Pike
Rockville, MD 20850
301/897-5700 (voice/TDD)
800/638-8255 (voice/TDD)

## Spina Bifida

Spina Bifida Association of America
4590 MacArthur Boulevard
Rockville, MD 20852
301/805-0213
800/621-3141

## Tourette Syndrome

Tourette Syndrome Association
42-40 Bell Boulevard
Bayside, NY 11361
718/224-2999
800/237-0717

## Other Toll-Free Numbers

American Association on Mental
    Retardation
800/424-3688

AMC Cancer Information Center
800/525-3777

American Cleft Palate Education
    Foundation
800/242-5338

American Diabetes Association
800/232-3472

American Foundation for the Blind
800/232-5463

American Kidney Fund
800/638-8299

American Liver Foundation
800/223-0179

American Paralysis Association
800/225-0292

ATT Accessible Products Center
800/1222

Cancer Information Service National Line
800/4-CANCER

Captioned Films for the Deaf
800/237-6213

Chrysler Corporation Assistance Line for
    the Disabled Driver
800/255-9877

Cornelia de Lange Syndrome Foundation
800/223-8355

International Shriners Headquarters
800/237-5055

Job Accommodation Network (JAN)
800/JAN-PCEH

Job Opportunities for the Blind
800/638-7516

Lung Disease
800/222-LUNG

Medicaid Hotline
800/638-6833

National Adoption Center
800/862-3678

National Association for Hearing and
    Speech Action
800/638-8255

National Association for Parents of the
    Visually Impaired
800/562-6265

National Center for Stuttering
800/221-2483

National Child Abuse Hotline
800/4-A-CHILD

National Crisis Center for the Deaf
800/446-9876 (TDD only)

National Hearing Aid Society
800/521-5247

National Information Center for
    Developmental Disabilities
800/922-9234

National Information System for Health
    Related Services
800/922-9234

National Multiple Sclerosis Society
800/344-4867

National Spinal Cord Injury Hotline
800/526-3456

National Tuberous Sclerosis Association
800/225-NTSA

Retinitis Pigmentosa Association
800/344-4877

Sickle Cell Disease Association of
    America
800/421-8453

# Appendix D
# Selected Reading

This bibliography contains further reading on special education and a variety of disability issues. Books about specific disabilities have been deliberately omitted. For materials on specific disabilities, contact disability organizations such as The Arc, the Learning Disabilities Association, or the Tourette Syndrome Association. These organizations, listed in Appendix C, should be able to provide bibliographies of current and comprehensive materials.

Many of the books listed here may be available in your local public library. If you would like to order a copy of any book for yourself, you can find publishers' addresses through a publication called *Books in Print*, which is updated annually and is available at any library or bookstore. *Books in Print* has a subject index that you can use to see what is currently available on any topic.

## GENERAL INTEREST

Accardo, Pasquale J. & Barbara Y. Whitman, Ed. *Dictionary of Developmental Disabilities Terminology*. Baltimore, MD: Brookes Publishing Company, 1996.
This dictionary provides more than 3,000 clear, concise definitions of the most common terms associated with disabilities.

Amado, Angela Novak. *Friendships and Community Connections between People with and without Developmental Disabilities*. Baltimore, MD: Brookes Publishing Company, 1993.
This book highlights practical ways to use natural social connections as the foundation for building successful friendships between persons with disabilities and other community members. It was written for persons with disabilities, their families, service providers, and advocates.

Bailey, Sally Dorothy. *Wings to Fly: Bringing Theatre Arts to Students with Special Needs*. Bethesda, MD: Woodbine House, 1993.
This guide describes proven techniques for use in elementary through high school to teach drama to students with a wide array of special needs. Also included are suggestions for using dramatic techniques such as role play to teach functional and academic skills in the classroom.

Batshaw, Mark L. & Yvonne M. Perret. *Children with Disabilities: A Medical Primer, Third Edition*. Baltimore, MD: Brookes Publishing Company, 1992.
This highly acclaimed reference provides in-depth descriptions of all the major types of disabilities in a style that can be understood by parents and professionals alike. It includes more than 200 detailed illustrations, a helpful glossary, and a thorough resource list.

Buck, Pearl S. *The Child Who Never Grew, Second Edition*. Bethesda, MD: Woodbine House, 1992.
This edition brings back into print a special memoir of one of America's most distinguished writers. New material amplifies the story of her daughter, who had mental retardation, and gives historical perspective.

*The Exceptional Parent*. Published monthly 12 times a year. Editorial Office, 209 Harvard Street, Suite 303, Brookline, MA 02146.
This magazine is an excellent source of up-to-date information for parents of children with disabilities. The annual *Exceptional Parent Resource Guide* features directories of national organizations, associations, products, and services.

Flippo, Karen F., Katherine Inge & J. Michael Barcus, ed. *Assistive Technology: A Resource for School, Work, and Community*. Baltimore, MD: Brookes Publishing Company, 1995.
This comprehensive resource covers both legislative and technological developments in assistive technology. It offers professionals and users information on consumer involvement, assessment, funding, and training.

Kroll, Ken & Erica Levy Klein. *Enabling Romance: A Guide to Love, Sex, and Relationships for the Disabled*. Bethesda, MD: Woodbine House, 1995.
This illustrated guide was written by a husband and wife team and was inspired by their own story. Several chapters are devoted to living and loving with specific physical disabilities, while others address sexual variations and alternatives, safe sex, family planning, and dealing with attendants.

Leff, Patricia T. & Elaine Walitzer. *Building the Healing Partnership: Parents, Professionals & Children with Chronic Illnesses and Disabilities*. Cambridge, MA: Brookline Books, 1992.
This book is intended to help parents and professionals see the "other side" of the health care partnership and to experience the bond of hearing others share their fears and hopes, joy and pain.

Marsh, Jayne D.B., ed. *From the Heart: On Being the Mother of a Child with Special Needs*. Bethesda, MD: Woodbine House, 1995.
In their own words, nine mothers share the successes and struggles, stresses and joys of raising a child with a disability. Issues addressed include family life, school issues, and relationships with professionals, family, and friends.

Meyer, Donald J., Ed. *Uncommon Fathers: Reflections on Raising a Child with a Disability*. Bethesda, MD: Woodbine House, 1995.
Nineteen fathers from many different backgrounds and walks of life describe how raising a child with disabilities has altered their life—both for the better and the worse. Their children range in age from four through early adulthood and

have such special needs as Down syndrome, autism, brain damage, and mental retardation.

Miller, Nancy B., Susie Burmester, Diane G. Callahan, Janet Dieterle & Stephanie Niedermeyer. *Nobody's Perfect: Living and Growing with Children Who Have Special Needs.* Baltimore, MD: Brookes Publishing Company, 1994.
This book offers parents a refreshing perspective, a strong sense of support, and specific guidance as they integrate the challenges of raising a child with special needs into every aspect of their lives. The chapters guide parents through the four stages of adaptation with candid, inspiring, and often humorous reflections of four mothers who are raising children with disabilities.

Perske, Robert. *Circles of Friends: People with Disabilities and Their Friends Enrich the Lives of One Another.* Nashville, TN: Abingdon Press, 1988.
Illustrated by Martha Perske, this book describes "true stories of friendships." Based on a belief that all people should be members of the community, *Circles of Friends* alternates between accounts of friendships and points to consider. Friendship settings range from housing cooperatives to schools to neighborhoods.

Powell, Thomas H. & Peggy Ahrenhold Gallagher. *Brothers and Sisters: A Special Part of Exceptional Families, Second Edition.* Baltimore, MD: Brookes Publishing Company, 1993.
This book mingles reliable research with the perceptive wisdom of siblings of children and adults with developmental disabilities to explore the unique affinity experienced among siblings. Siblings speak openly about the joys and challenges they face daily at home, at school, and in the community. It offers perceptive insights and practical strategies for strengthening both parent-child and sibling-sibling relationships.

Rosenfeld, Lynn Robinson. *Your Child and Health Care: A "Dollars & Sense" Guide for Families with Special Needs.* Baltimore, MD: Brookes Publishing Company, 1994.
This guide is designed to help families of children with disabilities or chronic illnesses plan successful financial strategies. It examines a wide range of public and private services, along with a number of effective ways to gain access to, pay for, and evaluate those services.

Simons, Robin. *After the Tears: Parents Talk about Raising a Child with a Disability.* New York: Harcourt Brace Jovanovich, 1987.
This book tells the stories of parents who have struggled, learned, and grown in the years since their children were born and who wish to encourage other parents in similar circumstances.

Spiegle, Jan A. & Richard A. Van den Pol. *Making Changes: Family Voices on Living with Disabilities.* Cambridge, MA: Brookline Books, 1993.
What is the impact on the everyday lives of people who become disabled through an accident or progressive disease? What is the impact on the family when a child with disabilities is born? The editors have collected reports that illuminate the changing conditions of these people's lives and developed a course to help able bodied persons understand and be more supportive of the efforts of persons with disabilities to live in their community.

Sullivan, Tom. *Special Parent, Special Child*. New York: G.P. Putnam's Sons, 1995.
These are the stories of six families who have children with disabilities. They
describe their trials, triumphs, and hard-won wisdom.

Thompson, Mary. *My Brother, Matthew*. Bethesda, MD: Woodbine House, 1992.
This is a realistic, compassionate tale about how family life focuses on the needs
of a child with disabilities and the effects that can have on the other children in
the family.

Turnbull, Ann P., Joan M. Patterson, Shirley K. Behr, Douglas L. Murphy, Janet G.
Marquis & Martha J. Blue-Banning. *Cognitive Coping, Families, and Disability*.
Baltimore, MD: Brookes Publishing Company, 1993.
Here is one of the first attempts in the field of developmental disabilities to focus
on cognitive coping theory as a means of enhancing family well-being. Through
a participatory process, family members, service providers, theorists, and researchers reveal their personal and professional experience with disability and
cognitive coping.

# EARLY CHILDHOOD/EARLY INTERVENTION

Beckman, Paula J. & Gayle Beckman Boyes. *Deciphering the System: A Guide for Families of Young Children with Disabilities*. Cambridge, MA: Brookline Books, 1993.
This book provides basic information about parents' rights under legislation
affecting young children with disabilities, between birth and five years of age.
Topics include educational assessment, IEP and IFSP meetings, due process, and
obtaining support from other parents. It includes a glossary and resource list.

Bricker, Diane & Juliann J. Woods Cripe. *An Activity-Based Approach to Early Intervention*. Baltimore, MD: Brookes Publishing Company, 1992.
Activity-based intervention shows how to use natural and relevant events to
teach infants and young children effectively and efficiently. This resource
presents a model in early intervention that not only synthesizes strategies found
in behavior analytic and early childhood intervention approaches but is also
consistent with current educational reforms.

Coleman, Jeanine G. *The Early Intervention Dictionary: A Multidisciplinary Guide to
Terminology*. Bethesda, MD: Woodbine House, 1993.
This book defines and clarifies terms used by the many different medical,
therapeutic, and educational professionals who provide early intervention
services to children from birth through age three. It is a valuable training and
reference guide for professionals. Parents will find it helps them to understand
the intervention process and to be knowledgeable advocates for their children.

Johnson, Lawrence J., et al, ed. *Meeting Early Intervention Challenges: Issues from Birth
to Three, Second Edition*. Baltimore, MD: Brookes Publishing Company, 1994.
Prominent leaders in the field of early intervention detail critical, new approaches to service delivery and provide concrete strategies for personnel
development and policy application. Complete with reliable research data and

fundamental guidelines, this resource will be of vital interest to early interventionists, early childhood educators, service providers, and advocates.

Pueschel, Siegfried M., Patricia S. Scola, Leslie E. Weidenman & James C. Bernier. *The Special Child: A Source Book for Parents of Children with Developmental Disabilities, Second Edition.* Baltimore, MD: Brookes Publishing Company, 1994.
This home reference provides easy-to-understand descriptions and explanations plus prognoses and treatments. Sensitively written and highly readable, this source book helps dispel many of the misconceptions about disabilities. Included are answers to questions about the roles of professionals, diagnostic tests, medical treatments, educational strategies, legal issues, and counseling.

Rosenkoetter, Sharon E., Ann H. Hains & Susan A. Fowler. *Bridging Early Services for Children with Special Needs and Their Families: A Practical Guide for Transition Planning.* Baltimore, MD: Brookes Publishing Company, 1993.
This practical reference provides strategies that promote successful transitions for infants, toddlers, and young children with special needs. It is a useful resource for administrators, service providers, parents, and students.

Rosin, Peggy, Amy Whitehead, Linda Tuchman, George Jesien, Audrey Begun & Liz Irwin. *Partnerships in Family-Centered Care: A Guide to Collaborative Early Intervention.* Baltimore, MD: Brookes Publishing Company, 1996.
This comprehensive text was prepared with the assistance of parents of children with special needs. It features a straightforward approach to team-based, family-centered early intervention.

Schwartz, Sue & Joan E. Heller Miller. *The New Language of Toys: Teaching Communication Skills to Children with Special Needs.* Bethesda, MD: Woodbine House, 1996.
This book is designed for parents of children with developmental ages between birth and six who are experiencing language delays. It describes ways parents can use specific toys and games to improve their children's communication skills while keeping playtime fun.

Swan, William W. & Janet L. Morgan. *Collaborating for Comprehensive Services for Young Children and Their Families: The Local Interagency Coordinating Council.* Baltimore, MD: Brookes Publishing Company, 1993.
This useful book shows agency and school leaders how to coordinate their efforts to stretch human services dollars while providing quality programs. The building blocks needed to establish a successful local interagency coordinating council are provided, including practical guidelines for staff development and parent involvement.

# SPECIAL EDUCATION AND LEGAL RIGHTS

Cutler, Barbara Coyne. *You, Your Child and "Special" Education: A Guide to Making the System Work.* Baltimore, MD: Brookes Publishing Company, 1993.
This handbook shows parents of children with disabilities how to obtain appropriate educational services for their child with disabilities. It includes explanations of relevant legislation, directions for filing a complaint, and a resource list.

Goldman, Charles D. *Disability Rights Guide: Practical Solutions to Problems Affecting People with Disabilities, Second Edition.* Lincoln, NE: Media Publishing, 1991. This book is intended for people with disabilities and those who work with them. Chapters cover a variety of issues confronting people with disabilities, such as attitudinal barriers, employment, accessibility, housing, education, and transportation. The laws governing these areas are explained and discussed in clear language. A glossary of terms and a list of state contacts are included.

Guernsey, Thomas F. & Kathe Klare. *Special Education Law.* Durham, NC: Carolina Academic Press, 1993. This book is designed to take lawyers, educators, and other professionals through the process of providing special education services to children. It assumes no knowledge on the part of the reader and provides a solid background in special education law. Accompanying footnotes will be helpful to professionals wishing to do more detailed legal research.

Henderson, Anne T., Carl L. Marburger & Theodora Ooms. *Beyond the Bake Sale: An Educator's Guide to Working with Parents.* Columbia, MD: The National Committee for Citizens in Education, 1986. The authors address ways of developing positive home/school relations. They demonstrate that parents can and do make a big difference in promoting the positive characteristics of effective schools. Parents are challenged to be involved in what happens to their children in school and school staff is challenged to nurture positive relationships with parents.

Martin, Reed. *Extraordinary Children—Ordinary Lives: Stories Behind Special Education Case Law.* Champaign, IL: Research Press, 1991. Many court cases have shaped and defined key issues associated with special education law. This book tells the stories of the families behind these cases and how the decisions made affected all children with special needs. Among issues examined are: related services, least restrictive environment, extended school year, and attorney fee awards.

Mendelsohn, Steven B. *Tax Options and Strategies for People with Disabilities.* New York, NY: Demos Publications, 1993. This book provides a straightforward and practical guide to current tax provisions that will assist people with disabilities and their families to take maximum advantage of the current tax law.

Ordover, Eileen L. & Kathleen B. Boundy. *Educational Rights of Children with Disabilities: A Primer for Advocates.* Cambridge, MA: Center for Law and Education, 1991. This is a basic legal reference designed to assist parents, students, and their advocates in securing their rights to preschool, elementary, and secondary education guaranteed by the Individuals with Disabilities Education Act and Section 504 of the Rehabilitation Act of 1973. It discusses substantive and procedural rights, along with administrative and judicial remedies for their violation.

Orlove, Fred P. & Dick Sobsey, Ed. *Educating Children with Multiple Disabilities: A Transdisciplinary Approach, Third Edition.* Baltimore, MD: Brookes Publishing Company, 1996.

This text provides up-to-date strategies for working with children with mental retardation and motor or sensory impairments. Included is information on using assistive technology, planning transitions, and addressing families' needs and concerns.

Putnam, JoAnne W. *Cooperative Learning and Strategies for Inclusion: Celebrating Diversity in the Classroom.* Baltimore, MD: Brookes Publishing Company, 1993. This book provides strategies for tailoring curricula and instructional approaches to improve the academic achievement, social skills, and self-esteem of a diverse population of students, regardless of their individual abilities, backgrounds, and learning styles. It is an excellent resource for all educators, classroom support personnel, administrators, social workers, service providers, and parents.

Stainback, Susan & William Stainback, Ed. *Inclusion: A Guide for Educators.* Baltimore, MD: Brookes Publishing Company, 1996. This practical resource explains how to make inclusion work, providing educators with techniques needed to transform classrooms into places where all students succeed.

Strickland, B. & A.P. Turnbull. *Developing and Implementing Individualized Education Programs.* Columbus, OH: Merrill Publishing Company, 1990. This book describes legal requirements for developing IEPs and suggests best practices for implementation. It includes sample forms, checklists, and recordkeeping systems.

Turnbull, Ann P., H. Rutherford Turnbull III, Marilyn Shank & Dorothy Leal. *Exceptional Lives: Special Education in Today's Schools.* Englewood Cliffs, NJ: Prentice-Hall, Inc., 1995. These respected authors paint a picture of special education and their vision for its future. Using vignettes of real people, they examine exceptionalities, evaluation procedures, issues for professionals, and program options.

III Turnbull, H. Rutherford, David Bateman & Ann Turnbull. *ADA, IDEA and Families.* Lawrence, KS: Beach Center on Families and Disabilities, 1991. This publication analyzes the Americans with Disabilities Act and the Individuals with Disabilities Education Act and their implications for families, especially with respect to transition.

# Transition, Employment, Community Life & Future Planning

Bishop, Barb, Martha Blue-Banning, Frances Holt, Janie Irvin & Theresa Martel. *Planning for Life after High School: A Handbook of Information and Resources for Families and Young Adults with Disabilities.* Lawrence, KS: Full Citizenship, Inc., 1992. This book describes what questions to ask about transition and where to go for the answers.

Condeluci, Al. *Interdependence: The Route to Community*. Orlando, FL: Paul M. Deutsch Press, Inc., 1991.
*Interdependence* is a call for action to the human services—a prescription for a renewed sense of partnership. It explores the goals of human services, how and why the medical/expert paradigm has not done the job, and then introduces the interdependent paradigm as an alternative approach to human service.

Hagner, David and Dale Dileo. *Working Together: Workplace Culture, Supported Employment, and Persons with Disabilities*. Cambridge, MA: Brookline Books, 1993.
Aimed at employers and program personnel, this book presents a new approach to assisting individuals with disabilities achieve meaningful careers.

Nisbet, Jan. *Natural Supports in School, at Work, and in the Community for People with Severe Disabilities*. Baltimore, MD: Brookes Publishing Company, 1992.
This book acknowledges that assistance for people with severe disabilities must be shaped by the needs of individuals rather than by the requirements of service systems. Chapters on family supports, school inclusion strategies, and supported employment combine fresh insights and practical guidance.

Racino, Julie Ann, Pamela Walker, Susan O'Connor & Steven J. Taylor. *Housing, Support, and Community: Choices and Strategies for Adults with Disabilities*. Baltimore, MD: Brookes Publishing Company, 1993.
This book records new directions and creative strategies that are emerging today to support adults with disabilities in the homes and communities of their choice. In a time of consumer-directed decision making, students, parents and service providers will find help in these pages to make systems responsive to the needs of all adults.

Rusch, Frank R., Lizanne Destefano, Janis Chadsey-Rusch, L. Allen Phelps & Edna Szymanski. *Transition from School to Adult Life: Models, Linkages and Policy*. Sycamore, IL: Sycamore Publishing Company, 1992.
This book takes a comprehensive look at transition through the eyes of educators and researchers from many professional areas. It includes a wealth of models by which transition can be offered to students in different instructional settings.

Russell, L. Mark & Arnold E. Grant. *The Life Planning Workbook*. Evanston, IL: American Publishing Company, 1995.
This workbook is intended to help parents assure continuity of care for their child with a disability after their death through planning in four areas: personal needs; financial needs; estate plans; and critical records.

Russell, L. Mark, Arnold E. Grant, Suzanne M. Joseph & Richard W. Fee. *Planning for the Future: Providing a Meaningful Life for a Child with a Disability after Your Death*. Evanston, IL: American Publishing Company, 1993.
This authoritative resource on estate planning is full of practical ideas and important information on how a family can protect their loved one's future. It explains how to prepare a life plan, a letter of intent, a will, and a special needs trust. It discusses how to maximize government benefits, avoid probate, and reduce estate taxes.

Stengle, Linda. *Laying Community Foundations for Your Child with a Disability: How to Establish Relationships That Will Support Your Child After You're Gone.* Bethesda, MD: Woodbine House, 1996.
This book looks at the human side of providing for a child's future. It encourages parents to develop a network of people within their community who will provide support and continuity for their son or daughter after the parent dies.

Wehman, Paul. *The ADA Mandate for Social Change.* Baltimore, MD: Brookes Publishing Company, 1993.
This book focuses on the changes the Americans with Disabilities Act is generating for persons with disabilities in employment, transportation, independent living, and more.

Wehman, Paul. *Life Beyond the Classroom: Transition Strategies for Young People with Disabilities, Second Edition.* Baltimore, MD: Brookes Publishing Company, 1996.
This textbook is an essential guide to planning, designing, and implementing successful transition programs for students with disabilities. It is a must for practitioners, special education instructors, community service providers, students, vocational rehabilitation counselors, and disability advocates.

Witt, Melanie Astaire. *Job Strategies for People with Disabilities: Enable Yourself for Today's Job Market.* Princeton, NJ: Peterson's Guides, 1992.
The Americans with Disabilities Act opens the door for employment opportunities never before available to millions of people with disabilities. This book rings with sensitive and practical advice for getting that first job, being promoted, and making career changes. It answers questions about the law, career decision making, and job finding through the stories of real people.

# APPENDIX E
# 1997 CHANGES TO THE INDIVIDUALS WITH DISABILITIES EDUCATION ACT

**p. xiv, 32.** IDEA 97 changed Part H to Part C.

**pp. 33, 34.** IDEA 97 now requires parent notification and consent for *all* evaluations, not just the initial one.

**p. 38.** IDEA 97 adds that a variety of tools and strategies must be used to gather relevant functional and developmental information about your child. This includes information provided by you, the parents, and information about how your child will be involved in, and progress in, the general education curriculum. For preschool children, the information must include how the preschooler will participate in appropriate activities.

**p. 39.** Your written consent is required for all evaluations. Parent information must be included and a variety of strategies and techniques must be used.

**p. 46.** IDEA 97 has changed the process for re-evaluations. Parents must give their consent. If parents refuse to consent to re-evaluation, schools must use due process procedures to challenge the parents' decision. A full assessment is not required. The IEP team, which includes parents, determines what new information is needed and what tests and other means will be used to gather the data. If the team determines no additional testing is necessary, parents must be notified of their right to request further testing. If the parents request testing, the school must provide it.

**p. 60.** During re-evaluations, IDEA 97 gives parents the right to request and receive additional evaluations conducted by school personnel.

**pp. 67, 70, 72, 73.** IDEA 97 *requires* that parents be included as a member of the team in the eligibility process and decision making.

**p. 76.** The present level of functioning must also address how the child's disability affects his or her involvement and progress in the general education curriculum.

**p. 78.** IDEA 97 requires IEPs to include a statement of annual goals, including benchmarks or short-term objectives. These goals and objectives are designed to enable your child to participate in the general education curriculum and to meet each of your child's other educational needs resulting from his or her disability.

**p. 81.** At least one regular education teacher is now a required member of the IEP team if your child is being considered for, or is participating in, the general education classroom. The regular education teacher participates in the development of the IEP, including the determination of appropriate positive behavioral interventions and strategies, supplemental aids and services, program modifications, and support for school personnel.

**p. 82.** Related services and supplementary aids and services must be provided to: assist the child to advance toward annual goals, be involved and progress in the general curriculum, and participate in extracurricular and nonacademic activities with non-disabled children.

**p. 84.** Orientation and mobility services have been added to the list of specifically named related services. These services include assistance not only for children with visual impairments, but also for any child who needs to be taught to travel to, from, and around the school.

**p. 89.** IDEA 97 changes the least restrictive environment statement and requires an explanation of the extent, if any, to which the child will *not* participate with non-disabled children in the regular classroom. This underscores a basic principle of IDEA that placement in the general education setting is to be the first consideration.

**p. 93.** If parents want the school system to pay for a private placement, IDEA 97 adds new requirements. You, as a parent, must have notified the school of your intentions to withdraw your child at the most recent IEP meeting, or you must provide the school system with a notification letter at least 10 business days in advance of removing your child. The notice must include a statement that you are rejecting the placement proposed by the school; your specific concerns and why you believe your child can't receive an appropriate education in the program offered by the school; your intent to enroll your child in a private school; and your expectation the public school will pay for the private placement. The school system may refuse payment if they believe they can provide a free appropriate education for your child.

**p. 94.** IEP—Part 5: Time, Duration and Location of Services. IDEA 97 requires that the location where services are to be delivered must also be stated in the IEP.

**p. 95.** As you evaluate your child's IEP, look for the following new requirements under IDEA 97.
1. State and District-wide Assessments
   a. how your child will participate in standardized testing given to all children.
   b. modifications that may be needed.

   If the IEP team determines your child will not participate in standardized testing, the team must document the reasons why and state how your child's progress will be measured.

2. Beginning at least one year before reaching the age of majority, the student must be informed of the rights that will transfer to him or her.

3. The IEP team must consider special factors in developing each child's IEP:
   a. Positive behavioral supports and interventions for students whose behaviors disrupt their learning, or that of others;
   b. Students' language needs, for students with limited English proficiency;
   c. Instruction in Braille and the use of Braille for students who are visually impaired, unless the IEP team determines it is not necessary;
   d. The child's communication needs;
   e. The child's need for assistive technology devices and services.

**p. 96.** IDEA 97 requires the IEP to contain a statement of how your child's progress will be measured and how you, as parents, will be regularly informed of your child's progress. You should receive reports as often as parents of children who are not in special education.

**p. 106.** See note for page 81. In addition, at least one special education teacher or, where appropriate, at least one special education provider must be a part of the team.

**p. 107.** See note for page 89.

**p. 108.** IDEA 97 requires the following to be included in each student's IEP:
  a. Present Level of Performance (see note p. 76)
  b. Annual Goals and Short Term Objectives/Benchmarks (see note p. 78)
  c. A statement of Special Education and Related Services
   (see notes pp. 82, 84)
  d. A statement of the extent to which your child will not participate in the general education environment.
  e. A statement of needed transition services (see note p.146)
  f. Statement of time, location, and duration (see note p. 94)
  g. Reporting of progress
  h. Participation in state/district-wide assessments (see note p. 95)
  i. Consideration of special factors (see note p. 95)
  j. Informing student of rights at age of majority (see note p. 95)

**p. 115.** IDEA 97 changed Part H to Part C.

**p. 141.** IDEA 97 *requires* all states to offer mediation as a method to resolve disputes.

**p. 146.** IDEA 97 includes new provisions for students when they turn 14. The IEP must address transition services that focus on the course of study, such as participation in advanced placement courses or a vocational education program. At 16 or younger, a statement of needed transition services, including a statement of interagency linkages and services, must be included.

**p. 154.** See note page 146.

**p. 166.** IDEA 97 requires each state to establish mediation as a means for resolving disputes. Parents cannot be required to go to mediation. They can bypass mediation and go directly to due process.

**p. 166.** IDEA 97 requires parents to notify the school system that they intend to file for a due process hearing. The notice must contain the name and address of the child and where the child attends school, a description of the problem, and a proposed resolution. Schools must inform you of this notification requirement and provide you with forms and assistance.

**p. 167.** IDEA 97 now specifically includes children with disabilities suspended or expelled from school among those required to receive a free, appropriate public education.

**p. 167.** See note page 39.

**p. 178.** See note page 93. Written agreement is not required as long as you have fulfilled the notice requirements described in the note for page 93.

**pp. 193-194.** IDEA 97 has provided further clarification and protections.

When a child breaks the school's Code of Conduct, school personnel may order a change of special education placement to an appropriate interim alternative program or may order a suspension for not more than 10 days. In addition, they may order a change of placement for up to a maximum of 45 days when a child carries a weapon to school or a school function; if the student knowingly possesses, uses, or sells illegal drugs; or if a student solicits the sale of a controlled substance at school or a school function.

A more stringent requirement is placed upon the school system before school personnel are allowed to remove a student with disabilities if they feel that the student is apt to harm himself or herself, or harm other students or teachers. In order to pursue a change of placement based upon a student's likelihood to harm self or others, the school must request a hearing before a hearing officer. The hearing officer must determine that the school can demonstrate that the current placement is likely to result in injury to the child or to others, must consider the appropriateness of the child's current placement, and must consider whether or not the school made reasonable efforts to minimize the risk of harm in the current placement, including the use of supplementary aids and services. In other words, except for cases involving weapons or drugs, the school bears the burden to demonstrate that there is reason to suspend or expel a student. If there is no existing behavioral assessment, it must be conducted and a behavior management plan implemented immediately to address the inappropriate behavior.

A special review must be conducted by the IEP team to determine if there is a relationship between the child's disability and the behavior subject to disciplinary action. Such a review is called a "Manifestation of Determination Review." In deciding whether the behavior is due to the child's disability, the IEP team, including the child's parents, considers all relevant information. Information includes evaluation and diagnostic results, information supplied by the parents, observations of the child, and the child's IEP and placement. In essence, the IEP team is asking itself, "Did we properly plan for this child?"

The IEP team determines:

- In relationship to the behavior subject to disciplinary action, were the child's IEP and placement appropriate and were the special education services, supplementary aids and services, and behavior intervention strategies provided consistent with the child's IEP and placement?
- Did the child's disability impair his or her ability to understand the impact and consequences of the behavior subject to disciplinary action?
- Did the child's disability impair his or her ability to control the behavior subject to disciplinary action?

If the IEP team determines the behavior subject to review is **not** due to the child's disability, the child will be disciplined in the same manner as a child without a disability. IDEA provides, however, that a free, appropriate, public education is available to all children with disabilities including those who have been suspended or expelled from school. This means that the child must continue to receive special education services in an alternative setting. The alternative setting must enable the child to:

- continue to participate in the general education curriculum, although in another setting, and to receive the "service modifications" needed to meet current IEP goals; and
- receive the "service modifications" required to address the child's behavior that resulted in the disciplinary action so that it does not recur.

As with all special education programming, if the parents of the child disagree with the outcome of the Manifestation of Determination decision or with the decision regarding placement, they have a right to appeal.

# INDEX

4·12/05

# About the Authors

**Winifred G. Anderson** is a special education professional whose work has been devoted to the development of the relationships between families, children, and schools. She, along with Steve Chitwood, founded the Parent Educational Advocacy Training Center (PEATC), a training and information center for families and professionals who work with children and youth with disabilities located in Alexandria, Virginia. Prior to her work at PEATC, she was a founder and director of Resurrection Children's Center, an inclusive early childhood school also in Alexandria. Ms. Anderson is now working as a writer and consultant in the fields of special and adult education.

**Stephen R. Chitwood** is a Professor of Public Administration at The George Washington University in Washington, D.C., and the Director of the University's Center for Law Practice Strategy and Management. For fifteen years he served as a legal consultant for PEATC specializing in the educational rights of children with disabilities. As the parents of a child with special needs, he and his wife, Janet, worked for over twenty years to ensure their son received a free appropriate public education in the least restrictive environment.

**Deidre Hayden** is an experienced advocate for families of children with disabilities. She is the former Executive Director of PEATC. Ms. Hayden is currently the Executive Director of the Matrix Parent Network and Resource Center in San Rafael, California, a model center providing parent-to-parent support, training, and information to families of children with disabilities from birth through young adulthood. In addition, she is the family support consultant for a Maternal and Child Health Project which provides training to physicians who treat children with special needs.